CADOGAN
guides

THE BAY OF NAPLES & THE AMALFI COAST

D0367518

Cadogan Books plc
London House, Parkgate Road, London SW11 4NQ, UK

Distributed in North America by The Globe Pequot Press
6 Business Park Road, PO Box 833, Old Saybrook,
Connecticut 06475–0833

Copyright © Dana Facaros and Michael Pauls 1994
Illustrations © Horatio Monteverde 1994

Book and cover design by Animage
Cover illustrations by Povl Webb
Maps © Cadogan Guides, drawn by Thames Cartographic Ltd

Editing: Dominique Shead
Series Editors: Rachel Fielding and Vicki Ingle

Indexing: Dorothy Frame
Production: Rupert Wheeler Book Production Services

A catalogue record for this book is available from the British Library
ISBN 0–94–7754–814

The author and publishers have made every effort to ensure the accuracy of the information in this book at the time of going to press. However, they cannot accept any
responsibility for any loss, injury or inconvenience resulting from the use of information contained in this guide.

Output to bromide by Cooling Brown Ltd. Printed and bound in Great Britain by
Redwood Books on Jordan Opaque supplied by McNaughton Publishing Papers Ltd.

About the Authors

Michael Pauls and Dana Facaros, their two kids, three cats and a fierce bad rabbit live in a leaky old farmhouse in southwest France. They have written 15 guides for Cadogan.

Acknowledgements

The publishers would like to thank Horatio Monteverde for the illustrations, Horatio Monteverde and Kicca Tommasi at Animage for the design, Lindsay Hunt for her work on the practical information sections, the Italian State Tourist Board in London, Dorothy Frame for the index and Donald Paton, Paul Hopgood and Mike Adams at Thames Cartographic for the maps.

Please help us to keep this guide up to date

We have done our best to ensure that the information in this guide is correct at the time of going to press. But places and facilities are constantly changing, and standards and prices in hotels and restaurants fluctuate. We would be delighted to receive any comments concerning existing entries or omissions.

All contributors will be acknowledged in the next edition, and will receive a copy of the Cadogan Guide of their choice.

Contents

The Best of the Bay of Naples and the Amalfi Coast

Greek antiquities: Paestum, Naples Museum, Cumae, Velia.

Roman antiquities: Pompeii, Herculaneum, Naples Museum, Arch of Trajan, Benevento.

Curiosities: Sansevero Chapel, Naples; Egyptian relics in Benevento; San Martino monastery, Naples.

Festivals: *Sagra dei Gigli*, Nola; *Festa di Santa Anna*, Ischia.

Gardens: Royal Palace, Caserta; Villa Rufolo, Ravello; Cloister of the Clarisse, Naples; Gardens of Augustus, Capri.

Volcanic wonders: Vesuvius, Phlegraean Fields, Monte Nuovo.

Hotels: Luna and Cappucini Convento, Amalfi.

Picturesque villages: Ravello, Amalfi, Forio (Ischia), Procida, Positano.

Restaurants: La Cartinella, Naples; Don Alfonso, Sorrento; La Cambusa, Positano.

See map on inside front cover.

In Roman times, the land around the bay of Naples was *Campania Felix*—fortunate Campania. And a happy land it was, the richest and most beautiful province of Italy, its seaside villas the chosen abodes of the Roman elite. Campania had everything: a rich gloss of Greek and Etruscan culture, beautiful cities like Capua, Puteoli, Neapolis and Pompeii, a perfect climate and gorgeous landscapes,

Introduction

along with the peninsula's most fertile farmland and its most prosperous manufactures.

History (not to mention the earthquakes and volcanoes) has given it plenty of hard knocks in all the centuries since; nature does have a way of balancing out her favours, however long it takes. Shelley called Naples 'the metropolis of a ruined paradise'. That was back in the 1800s, a time when the soul of any poet would have been struck by the contrast between the colour and frivolity of this liveliest of all cities, set amidst the ruins of Roman grandeur that lay all around the shore. The contrast is even greater today; a city like Naples suffers more than anywhere from the troubles of a grey age like ours, an age of too much smoke and complexity and too little joy.

But the hints and fragments of paradise are still present on every side: the sweet, fading visions of heaven painted on the ceilings of Naples's churches, or the garden fantasy frescoes from the villas of Pompeii. Or the view down the bay from Posillipo, looking towards Vesuvius (at least when the air is clear enough to see that far). For paradise just a bit compromised, there's the voluptuous if overbuilt isle of Capri; and for paradise perfect, the most unforgettable settings anywhere on Italy's long coasts, we still have Ravello and Amalfi, and the miraculously unspoiled island of Procida.

Naples, still, is a bit of a problem. It is certainly possible to have a properly escapist holiday around the bay without ever spending much time in the metropolis; thousands do it every year. But that would be missing half the fun. For all its troubles Naples is still one of the most beautiful of Italian cities, and certainly the most entertaining. No city has a greater ability to pull at the heartstrings; you may well find it your favourite Italian city, and at the same time your least favourite. Such ambivalence could even affect a native like Enrico Caruso. Put out over a bad reception one night at the San Carlo opera, he swore he'd never return to Naples 'except for a plate of spaghetti'. Caruso kept his vow, coming back only once for a well-publicized dinner—which proves, if anything, that a simple plate of pasta in Naples can be a memorable experience.

Campania

Travel

By Air

From the UK

Flying is obviously the quickest and easiest way of getting to Naples, and not ruinously expensive if you avoid the scheduled flights in favour of a charter flying out of London (you can also fly from Manchester or Glasgow in the summer). Scheduled APEX fares to Naples on British Airways or Alitalia are currently around £250. Booking restrictions apply; you must book at least 7 days ahead, and stay a Saturday night abroad. Ticket changes involve high penalties.

London is a great centre for discounted flights, and you should be able to find a good deal if you allow enough time. Seat-only charters to Naples cost about £150 off-peak; contact a reputable agent (i.e. ABTA-registered, who won't bunk off with your cash and leave you stranded).

Alternatively you can book directly through some charter or holiday operators. The Italian specialist Air Travel Group, at 227 Shepherd's Bush Road, London W6 7AS, ℂ (081) 748 7575, incorporates Pilgrim Air, Magic of Italy and Italian Escapades. Classified sections of the weekend newspapers also advertise discounted fares (if you live in London, get *Time Out* or other listings magazines, and the *Evening Standard* or the free newspapers like *TNT* or *Trailfinder* you can pick up near tube stations). Peak season is Easter and summer, when there are generally at least a couple of flights a day from London (book well ahead). The major charter agencies are Italy Sky Shuttle (operated by Pilgrim Air), ℂ (081) 748 1333, and LAI, ℂ (071) 837 8492. Rock-bottom fares are generally subject to a number of restrictions, and departure or arrival times may be inconvenient. STA and Campus Travel offer particularly good deals for students.

Useful Addresses

Campus Travel, 52 Grosvenor Gardens, SW1, ℂ (071) 730 3402

Italiatours Ltd, 205 Holland Park Avenue, London W11 4XB, ℂ (071) 371 1114

Pilgrim Air, 227 Shepherd's Bush Road, London W6 7NL, ℂ (071) 748 1333

STA, 86 Old Brompton Road, London SW7, or 117 Euston Road, London NW1, ℂ (071) 937 9921

Trailfinders, 194 Kensington High St, London W8, ℂ (071) 938 3232; 42/48 Earls Court Road, London W8 6EJ, ℂ (071) 937 5400.

From Ireland

There are no direct flights from Ireland to Italy. The best bet is to travel to London and catch a flight from there. Cheapest flights from Dublin to London are operated by Ryanair (landing at Stansted or Luton), though Aer Lingus and British Midland take you directly into Heathrow which is more convenient and will probably save time and money in the end. From Belfast, both British Airways and British Midland operate to Heathrow. If you're a student, substantial discounts may be available: contact USIT at 12-21 Aston Quay, O'Connell Bridge, Dublin 2, ✆ (01) 679 8833 or Fountain Centre, College St, Belfast, ✆ (0232) 324073.

From the USA and Canada

Transatlantic airlines Delta, TWA, United Airlines and Air Canada all have direct flights to Rome or Milan from a number of cities, including New York, Boston, Miami, Chicago, Los Angeles, Toronto or Montreal, but Alitalia has the most options. Summer round-trip fares from New York to Rome cost around $1000, from Montreal or Toronto about $1300 Canadian. You could travel on southwards from these cities via an internal flight, or train of course. Alternatively, take a flight to London and change there for Naples, a reasonably economical option. Apex or SuperApex deals are better value than scheduled fares, though you may prefer to pay extra for security, flexibility and convenience on such a long journey (9–15 hours flying time). Beware the restrictions imposed on special fares, and plan well in advance. Obviously, low season flights (between November and March) tend to be a great deal cheaper than peak season ones, and mid-week fares are generally lower than at weekends.

As in Britain, a host of cheap deals are advertised in the travel sections of major newspapers like the *New York Times*, *LA Times*, *Toronto Star*, etc. If you are prepared to take pot luck, try for a stand-by or consolidated fare, or consider a courier flight (remember you can only take hand luggage with you on these deals). Now Voyager, ✆ (212) 431 1616, is one of the main US courier flight companies (annual membership fee), based at Suite 307, 74 Varrick St New York NY 10013. Board Courier Services operates in Canada, ✆ (514) 633 0740, in Toronto or Montreal; ✆ (604) 338 1366 in Vancouver. Both STA and Council Travel are well worth contacting for cheaper charter flights and budget student travel. Both agencies have branches in several major US cities. In Canada, TravelCuts specializes in discounted student fares. Numerous travel clubs and agencies also specialize in discount fares (you may have to pay a membership fee).

By Train

From London the journey time to Naples takes over 24 hours (two rail routes lead to Rome, via Paris, Turin and Genoa or Lille, Basel, Milan and Florence—services run daily in summer). You have to change stations in Paris, from Gare du Nord to Gare de Lyon. At around £204 return (plus £12 for a couchette), rail travel is scarcely cheaper than flying unless you are able to take advantage of student or youth fares, and isn't really a sensible option unless you have an insurmountable fear of flying, or want to see places on the way. **Interail** (UK) or **Eurail** passes (US/Canada) give unlimited travel for under-26s throughout Europe for one or two months. Buy them before leaving home, from **Eurotrain**, 52 Grosvenor Gardens, London SW1, ✆ (071) 730 3402, or **Wasteels Travel** 121 Wilton Rd, London SW1, ✆ (071) 834 7066. In the USA or Canada, contact **Rail Europe**, central office at 226-230 Westchester Ave, White Plains, NY 10604,

© (914) 682 2999 or (800) 438 7245. If you are just planning to see Italy, however, these passes may not be worthwhile. A month's full Interail pass costs £249, though you can now buy cheaper zonal passes covering three or four countries only. Check with your agent before you purchase.

Fares on FS (*Ferrovie dello Stato*), the Italian State railway, are among the lowest (kilometre for kilometre) in Europe. If you intend travelling extensively by train, one of the special Italian tourist passes may be a better bet, e.g. the **BTLC** (*Biglietto Turistico Libera Circolazione*), which allows periods of 8, 15, 21, or 30 days unlimited travel on Italy's trains, including all supplements and reservation fees. Prices range from £88 for 8 days to £152 (second class) for 30 days. To make significant savings, you must do a lot of travelling. **Flexi-Cards** allow a certain number of days' first-class travel within a given period. The **Chilometrico** is valid for up to five people for 20 trips or 3000km, whichever comes first (about £90 second class). Children under 12 travel half-price (under 4 free). The Cartaverde is available for young people (26 and under), and entitles you to a 20 per cent discount on all rail travel (L40,000 for one year). Obtain these passes from **Wasteels** (*see* address above) or **CIT** offices (the Italian state-run travel agency) before you leave home. CIT addresses are as follows:

UK: Marco Polo House, 3–5 Lansdowne Rd, Croydon, Surrey, © (081) 686 0677

USA: 666 5th Avenue, 6th Floor, New York NY 10113, © (212) 697 2100

Canada: 1450 City Councillors St. Suite 750, Montreal H3A 2E6, © (514) 954 8608.

Naples is a major rail hub and many services from the northern cities terminate here, rather than in Rome. There are hourly trains from Rome to Naples (journey time is about two and a half hours, and you can get a train straight from the airport without going into the city). A one-way ticket costs about L18,000. A convenient pocket-sized timetable detailing all the main and secondary Italian railway lines, is now available in the UK, costing £6 (plus 50p postage). Contact Accommodation Line Ltd, 11–12 Hanover Square, London W1; Y Knot Travel, Morley House, 1st Floor, 314/320 Regent St, London W1; or Italwings, Travel & Accommodation, 87 Brewer St, London W1. If you wait until you arrive in Italy, however, you can pick up the *Sud e Centro Italia* (southern Italy) timetable at any station for about L4,500.

By Coach

Eurolines is the main international bus operator in Europe, with representatives in Italy and many other countries. In the UK, they can be found at 52 Grosvenor Gardens, London SW1, © (071) 730 8235, and are booked through National Express. Regular services run to many northern Italian cities but terminate at Rome, so you will have to change to another bus or train there. Needless to say, the journey is long and excruciatingly uncomfortable over this distance, and the small savings on price (a return ticket from London to Rome costs about £140) make it a masochistic choice in comparison with a discounted air fare, or even rail travel. However, if it isn't pitch-dark, you'll get a fleeting glimpse of Mont Blanc, Turin, Milan, Venice, Bologna, Florence and Rome on the way.

By Ferry

Besides the whirl of ferries and hydrofoils connecting Naples with resorts further down the coast, and the islands in the Bay, regular boat services also link Naples with Palermo (daily), and less frequently with Cagliari, Syracuse, Reggio di Calabria, Catania, Milazzo, and the Aeolian Islands. International services also run to Tunisia and Malta about once a week. Siremar and Tirrenia are the main long-distance ferry companies operating from Naples.

By Car

To bring a GB-registered car into Italy, you need a vehicle registration document, full driving licence, and insurance papers. Non-EU citizens should preferably have an international driving licence which has an Italian translation incorporated. Your vehicle should display a nationality plate indicating its country of registration.

Distance by road from London to Naples is about 1750km (1050 miles), the best part of 24 hours' driving time even if you stick to fast toll roads. The most scenic and hassle-free route is via the Alps, avoiding crowded Riviera roads in summer, but if you take a route through Switzerland, expect to pay for the privilege. In winter the passes may be closed and you will have to stick to the tunnels. A car is certainly the best and most convenient way to get to the more remote parts of Campania, but sheer hell in Naples. If you must bring a car into the city, make sure you leave it securely in a guarded parking lot, with nothing valuable inside.

For more information on driving in Italy, contact the motoring organizations: AA, ✆ (0256) 20123, or RAC, ✆ (081) 686 0088 in the UK.

Entry Formalities

Passports and Visas

EU nationals with a valid passport can enter and stay in Italy as long as they like, or they may stay a year with a British Visitor's Passport, available from the post office. Citizens of the US, Canada, Australia and New Zealand need only a valid passport to stay up to three months in Italy, unless they get a special visa in advance from an Italian embassy or consulate:

UK: 38 Eaton Place, London SW1, ✆ (071) 235 9371; 32 Melville Street, Edinburgh 3, ✆ (031) 226 3631; 2111 Piccadilly, Manchester, ✆ (061) 236 3024.

Ireland: 63-65 Northumberland Road, Dublin, ✆ (01) 601 744; 7 Richmond Park, Belfast, ✆ (0232) 668 854.

USA: 690 Park Avenue, New York, NY, ✆ (212) 737 9100; 12400 Wilshire Blvd, Suite 300, Los Angeles CA, ✆ (213) 820 0622, fax (213) 820 0727.

Canada: 136 Beverley St., Toronto, ✆ (416) 977 1566.

Australia: 61-69 Macquarie St, Sydney 2000, NSW, ✆ (02) 2478 442; 509 St Kilda Rd, Melbourne, ✆ (03) 867 5744, fax (03) 866 3932.

New Zealand: 34 Grant Rd, Thorndon, Wellington, ✆ (04) 7473 5339.

Special-interest Holidays

Abercrombie & Kent (art and architectural tours, gardens and villas of Campania), Sloane Square House, Holbein Place, London SW1W 8NS, ✆ (071) 730 9600.

Andante Travels (Pompeii, Herculaneum—archaeology and volcanoes), Grange Cottage, Winterborne Dauntsey, Salisbury SP4 6ER, ✆ (0980) 61055.

Brompton Travel (Naples opera), Brompton House, 64 Richmond Road, Kingston-upon-Thames, Surrey KT2 5EH, ✆ (081) 549 3334.

Camper & Nicholsons (specialist yacht charters for motor and sailing boats), 25 Bruton Street, London W1X 7DB, ✆ (071) 491 2950.

Citalia (tailor-made holidays along the coast), Marco Polo House, 3–5 Lansdowne Road, Croydon, CR9 1LL, ✆ (081) 688 9989.

Cosmos (Grand Tour, including Vesuvius, Capri, Sorrento), Tourama House, 17 Holmesdale Road, Bromley, Kent BR2 9LX, ✆ (081) 464 3444.

Crystal Premier (Neapolitan Magic), Crystal House, The Courtyard, Arlington Road, Surbiton, Surrey KT6 6BW, ✆ (081) 399 5144.

Italian Escapades (Bay of Naples), 227 Shepherds Bush Road, London W6 7AS, ✆ (081) 748 2661.

Magic of Italy (Bay of Naples, escorted tour), 227 Shepherds Bush Road, London W6 7AS, ✆ (081) 748 7575.

Mark Warner (holiday villages, Campania), 20 Kensington Church Street, London W8 4EP, ✆ (071) 938 1851.

Martin Randall Travel (archaeology tours to Pompeii, Herculaneum, Amalfi coast, Naples, Campania—guest lecturers), 10 Barley Mow Passage, Chiswick, London W4 4PH, ✆ (081) 742 3355.

Page & Moy (Pompeii, Paestum and Herculaneum—archaeology), 136–140 London Road, Leicester LE2 1EN, ✆ (0533) 524433.

Prospect Music & Art (Pompeii, Paestum and Herculaneum—archaeology tours), 454/458 Chiswick High Road, London W4 5TT, ✆ (081) 995 2151.

Saga (Southern Italy for senior citizens), The Saga Building, Middelburg Square, Folkestone, Kent CT20 1AZ, ✆ (0303) 857000.

Solo's (singles holidays in Campania), 41 Watford Way, London NW4 3JH, ℂ (081) 202 0855.

Travel for the Arts (A journey along the Amalfi coast), 117 Regents Park Road, London NW1 8UR, ℂ (071) 483 4466.

Voyages Jules Verne, (tours down the Amalfi Coast based in Positano), 21 Dorset Square, London NW1 6QG, ℂ (071) 486 8080.

Getting Around

Itineraries

Campania and the three other southern regions have almost half of Italy's coastline, though most of it is flat and not too exciting. If you are looking for **classic Mediterranean scenery** and a spot on the beach, the first really obvious place to send you is the spectacular Amalfi coast and the islands around the Bay of Naples. If these long-established fleshpots are too overripe for your tastes, or simply too crowded, you'll need to press on further into the region. Try the small resorts of the Cilento (*see* p.160), south of Naples.

Those interested in the **ancient Greeks and Romans** must first visit Pompeii, Herculaneum, the splendid temples at Paestum and then Capua, though the best relics from all these sites are in the great museum in Naples. From the Middle Ages, there is exotic Arab-Norman architecture in Amalfi, Salerno and Ravello. Inland, queer old Benevento is another fascinating place to visit.

A tour of less than two weeks should get you through the major sights of Naples and the surrounding region (known as Campania)—almost all of them are along the coast. Begin with Naples (days 1–4), and if you like it enough, you can make the city a base for day-trips to Pompeii and Herculaneum (day 5), the Phlegraean Fields or Vesuvius (day 6), and the islands (days 7–8). Otherwise, Sorrento or any of the islands can provide a more pleasant base. The Amalfi drive along the coast is certainly worth two days (9 and 10; seeing Positano, Amalfi, Ravello, and a look at old Salerno when you finish) though you may never want to leave. Paestum and its Greek temples come next (day 11), and, if you're heading further south, you can continue from here along the Cilento coast (day 12), or else return to Naples through inland Campania, stopping at Benevento (alternative day 12), then visiting Capua and Caserta (day 13).

A seven-day excursion through classical antiquity: for ancient sites and museums, Campania is the equal of Sicily and even Rome itself. Again, start with Naples and its great Archaeological Museum, and a walk through the Spaccanapoli district (day 1). Pompeii and Herculaneum will each require a day if you wish to see them in detail (days 2 and 3), and another day can be spent exploring the sites west of Naples: Cumae, Baiae, Cape Misenum, Pozzuoli, and so on (day 4). Be sure to make at least a day-trip to Benevento to see the Arch of Trajan and the odd Egyptian relics around town (day 5). Capua, with its unique *mithraeum* and amphitheatre, comes next (day 6). Depending on what direction your travels are taking you, you may either begin or end this itinerary with mainland Italy's best-preserved Greek temples, plus an interesting museum, at Paestum (day 7).

By Sea

A complex network of ferries and hydrofoils run by half a dozen different companies links Naples with the islands in the Bay and several further afield (Sardinia, Malta, Corsica, Sicily), and other resorts down the coast. In summer, up to six ferries and 20 hydrofoils ply to Capri, and as many to Ischia. There are also regular departures to Procida. In addition, there are a few ferries and hydrofoils daily from Sorrento to Capri, from Pozzuoli to Procida, and between the islands of Ischia and Procida. All are very short rides, and in most cases day trips are quite viable ways of exploring the local islands. You can usually buy tickets when you turn up at the port; return tickets don't generally offer any savings over two separate single tickets. Services for Capri, Sorrento, Ischia, Procida, Forio and Casamicciola depart from the Molo Beverello in front of the Castel Nuovo in Naples. Boats for Palermo, Cagliari, Reggio di Calabria, Catania, Syracuse, Milazzo and the Aeolian Islands leave from the Stazione Marittima. Hydrofoils also serve the bay islands from Mergellina, another important terminal in the western suburb of Naples. Sample costs: Naples–Sorrento return L12,000; Naples–Capri return from L6800; Naples–Ischia from L7800 (ferries are predictably cheaper than the faster hydrofoil services, and less affected by rough weather). The daily newspaper *Il Mattino* gives a full list of current timetables.

By Train

Naples, the main rail hub for southern Italy, is served by a full range of *regionale*, *diretto*, *espresso*, intercity, EuroCity and ETR 450 fast trains. From the centre (the main station is Stazione Centrale at Piazza Garibaldi), a cat's cradle of funiculars, national and local lines straggles out through the disparate suburbs and down the coast to Sorrento and beyond, via Pompeii and Herculaneum. The state-run (FS) line offers a fast crow's flight service between Naples and Salerno; for other coastal destinations, you will probably rely on local rail systems. Inland, erratically scheduled and complicated train services head for Caserta, Capua and Benevento from Naples' Stazione Centrale. South of Salerno, Paestum and most destinations on the Cilento coast are served by the main rail route from Naples to Reggio di Calabria.

For coastal journeys, the **Circumvesuviana** is the most useful service, trundling right round the Bay of Naples every half hour or so from dawn till quite late at night, stopping just about everywhere. This is the best way to reach Pompeii, Herculaneum and Sorrento. The Neapolitan terminus is a modern station on Corso Garibaldi, but trains stop at Stazione Centrale too (on underground platforms). Main lines run east via Ercolano (the Herculaneum station), then diverge, passing Pompeii on opposite sides. One line takes you to Sorrento, the other to Sarno, east of Vesuvius. The journey to Sorrento takes about an hour. You can also get to Nola and Baiano on a separate line. To get beyond Sorrento to Positano, Amalfi, Ravello, etc. it's best to take a bus.

If you're heading westwards from Naples, you have a choice of the Naples underground or **Metropolitana**, which crosses the city centre and ends up at Pozzuoli-Solfatara, a half-hour run. Both the **Ferrovia Cumana** (running along the coast) and the **Circumflegrea** (via Cumae) take you as far as Torregaveta. For information on Italian rail passes, *see* Getting There (above).

By Bus

The main bus station in Naples is just in front of the central railway station. From here, a mass of routes heads for all the main towns and places of interest in Campania, and threads through the maze of suburbs and dormitory towns to outlying villages. Many are run by the Naples Public Transport Board (✆ 7005091) which has information offices in Piazza Garibaldi. Other services are operated by SITA (✆ 5522176, Via Pisanelli 3–7) and Curreri (✆ 8798524).

Italian buses are not the easiest system to crack; indications of destination and departure point are often mystifying and it's best to ask before you get on. Buy tickets in advance from tobacconists, news-stands or ticket booths at the bus stations, and validate them on the bus by punching them in the machine (many people don't bother buying tickets, but you can be heavily fined if you are caught travelling without one, or with an unvalidated ticket).

There are regular services to Sorrento, Salerno (SITA), Benevento, Caserta and Avellino (Naples Public Transport Board). Curreri runs a useful service from Capodichino Airport to Sorrento. Buses are also the best way to get around the islands in the Bay. The Circumvesuviana railway is generally more obvious to use for east bay destinations like Pompeii, but you can take buses too. Buses really come into their own on the Amalfi coast, which is not served by rail, and are far the most enjoyable way to hop from place to place. SITA services ply regularly between Sorrento and Salerno about every 50 minutes. Buy tickets in advance in local bars or shops bearing the SITA sign, or from the terminus depots. Paestum is an easy bus-ride from Salerno, about every half-hour. ATAC buses serve the Cilento coast, from Salerno to Sapri.

By Car

A car is certainly the best and most convenient way to get to the more remote parts of Campania, but sheer hell in Naples, whether moving or stationary. If you must bring a car into the city, make sure you leave it securely in a guarded parking lot, with nothing valuable inside. On the streets, if the thieves don't get it, a tow-truck may well offer a similar service—take care not to leave it in a *Zona Rimozione* area.

Third-party insurance is a minimum requirement in Italy (and you should be a lot more than minimally insured, as many of the locals have none whatever!). Obtain a Green Card from your insurer, which gives automatic proof that you are fully covered. Also get hold of a European Accident Statement form, which may simplify things if you are unlucky enough to have an accident. Always insist on a full translation of any statement you are asked to sign. Breakdown assistance insurance is obviously a sensible investment (e.g. AA's Five Star or RAC's Eurocover Motoring Assistance).

Don't give the local police any excuse to fine you on the spot for minor infringements like worn tyres or burnt-out sidelights. A red triangular hazard sign is obligatory; also recommended are a spare set of bulbs, a first-aid kit and a fire extinguisher. Spare parts may be tricky to find for non-Italian cars. Petrol (*benzina*, unleaded is *benzina senza piombo*, and diesel *gasolio*) is still very expensive in Italy despite price changes in 1992 (around L1500 per litre; fill up before you cross the border). Motorway (*autostrada*) tolls are quite high.

Italians are famously anarchic behind a wheel, and nowhere more so than within the city of Naples, where all warnings, signals and generally recognized rules of the road are ignored. The only way to beat the locals is to join them by adopting an assertive and constantly alert driving style. Bear in mind the ancient maxim that he/she who hesitates is lost (especially at traffic lights, where the danger is less great of crashing into someone at the front than being rammed from behind). All drivers from boy racers to elderly nuns seem to tempt Providence by overtaking at the most dangerous bend, and no matter how fast you are hammering along the *autostrada* (toll motorway), plenty will whizz past at apparently supersonic rates. North Americans used to leisurely speed limits and gentler road manners will find the Italian interpretation of the highway code especially stressful. Speed limits (generally ignored) are officially 130kph on motorways (110kph for cars under 1100cc or motorcycles), 110kph on main highways, 90kph on secondary roads, and 50kph in built-up areas. Speeding fines may be as much as L500,000, or L100,000 for jumping a red light (a popular Italian sport).

If you are undeterred by these caveats, you may actually enjoy driving in Italy, at least away from the congested tourist centres. Signposting is generally good, and roads are usually excellently maintained. Some of the roads (e.g. the Amalfi corniche) are feats of engineering that the Romans themselves would have admired: bravura projects suspended on cliffs, crossing valleys on vast stilts, winding up hairpins. Buy a good road map (the Italian Touring Club series is excellent).

The **Automobile Club of Italy (ACI)** is a good friend to the foreign motorist. Besides having bushels of useful information and tips, they offer a free breakdown service, and can be reached from anywhere by dialling 116—also use this number if you have to find the nearest service station. If you need major repairs, the ACI can make sure the prices charged are according to their guidelines. In Naples they can be found at Piazzale Tecchio 49/d, © (081) 614 511; in Salerno at Via G Vicinanza 11, © (089) 226 677; Caserta, Via N Sauro 10, © (0823) 321 442; and Benevento, Via S Rosa 24–26, © (0824) 21582.

car hire

Hiring a car or camper van is simple but not particularly cheap. In Italian it's called *autonoleggio*. There are both large international firms through which you can reserve a car in advance, and local agencies, which often have lower prices. Air or train travellers should check out possible discount packages. Most companies will require a deposit amounting to the estimated cost of the hire. Most companies have a minimum age limit of 21 (23 in some cases). A credit card makes life easier. You will need to produce your licence and a passport when you hire. Current 1994 rates are around L90,000 per day for a small car (Fiat Panda, for instance) with unlimited mileage and collision damage waiver, including tax (hire for three days or longer is somewhat less pro rata).

Several major companies have offices in Naples; mainly on Via Partenope (near the port), and at the airport or main station: **Avis**, ✆ 7645600; **Europcar**, ✆ 7645859; **Hertz**, ✆ 7645533; **InterRent**, ✆ 76436364. A hefty surcharge is levied because of the local theft problem, and if you hire elsewhere, check you are allowed to drive within Naples without penalty. You can take a car to Capri or Ischia, but rental facilities are available only on Ischia.

By Taxi

Try not to take taxis if you're on a budget. They are invariably expensive at the best of times, and foreign tourists are unfortunately sitting ducks for overcharging. In Naples, corruption is rife, and even a short trip may clock up an alarming bill because of the traffic jams. Minimum fares are L5000. Try to negotiate the fare in advance if you have to take one. Don't try to flag them down on the street; head for a taxi rank on a main square, or dial through the Radiotaxi system (✆ 5564444). In other resorts taxis aren't such bad news, but they are still expensive, especially on Capri, where a ride may cost up to L20,000.

By Motorcycle or Bicycle

You may have trouble hiring a *motorino* (moped) or Vespa (scooter) in Naples because of theft, but they are available in all the major resorts such as Sorrento, and on the islands. You must be at least 14 for a *motorino* and 16 for anything more powerful. Helmets are compulsory. Costs for a *motorino* range from about L20,000–L35,000 per day, scooters somewhat more (up to L50,000).

You can hire a bike in most Italian towns. Prices range from about L10,000–L20,000 per day, which may make buying one interesting if you plan to spend much time in the saddle (L190,000–L300,000). You can usually take your bike quite cheaply on slower trains.

Disabled Travellers

Italy has been relatively slow off the mark in its provision for disabled visitors. Uneven or non-existent pavements, the appalling traffic conditions, crowded public transport, and endless flights of steps in many public places are all disincentives. Progress is gradually being made, however. A national support organization in your own country may well have specific information on facilities in Italy, or will at least be able to provide general advice. The Italian tourist office, or CIT (travel agency) can also advise on hotels, museums with ramps, etc. If you book rail travel through CIT, you can request assistance if you are wheelchair-bound.

In the UK, contact the **Royal Association for Disability & Rehabilitation** (RADAR), and ask for their guide *Holidays & Travel Abroad: A Guide for Disabled People*. They are based at 250 City Road, London EC1V 8AS, ✆ (071) 250 3222. Another useful organization is **Mobility International**, at 228 Borough High Street, London SE1, ✆ (071) 403 5688 or PO Box 3551, Eugene, Oregon 97403, USA, ✆ (503) 343 1284.

If you need help while you are in Naples or the resorts of Campania, contact the local tourist office. Provincial tourist boards provide lists of hotels with specialized facilities, museums with wheelchair access, etc.

Practical A–Z

Climate

Southern Italy can be diabolically hot in summer, with daytime temperatures soaring to an enervating 35°C, but the drought that scorches every scrap of inland vegetation to a crisp by July is relieved by occasional bouts of violent, torrential rain. On the coast, temperatures are more moderate, refreshed by breezes, while annual rainfall is considerably higher in Amalfi than Rome or London. You can probably manage without an umbrella in summer, but take a light jacket for cool evenings. August is the most unforgiving month to stump through southern Italy. Transport facilities are jammed to capacity, prices are at their highest, Naples and the main sights like Pompeii are abandoned to hordes of tourists, while the locals sensibly remain indoors for most of the afternoon, or take to the beach.

Spring and early **autumn** are much more appealing seasons: spring for the infinity of wild flowers in the countryside, autumn for the colour of trees in the hills. Milder temperatures and fewer crowds make for much pleasanter touring, and you shouldn't need raingear until October. From December to March you can enjoy blissful solitude at reasonable temperatures anywhere close to the coasts, though it will probably be too cold for swimming. Anywhere in the mountains it can rain and rain, with valleys shrouded for days on end beneath banks of mist.

average monthly temperatures in °C

	Jan	Feb	Mar	Apr	May	June	July	Aug	Sept	Oct	Nov	Dec
Naples	9	9	11	14	18	22	25	25	22	18	15	10
Capri	11	11	12	13	17	22	24	26	21	17	14	12

Consulates

UK: Via Francesco Crispi 122, Naples, © (081) 663511
US: Piazza della Repubblica 2, Naples, © (081) 7614303

Crime and the Police

Southern Italy has more than its fair share of opportunist criminals. Naples, in particular, is notorious for street crime; here kindly waiters will tuck your necklace out of sight, and remind you as regularly as bus conductors to hang on tight to your camera. The local brand of *mafiosi* are known as *Camorra* in Naples (crime syndicates who keep a toehold in most walks of life, largely financed by protection rackets, drug-dealing and the proceeds of the *toto nero*, or illegal football pools). Purse snatchings, pickpocketing, minor thievery of the white collar kind (always check your change, and the taxi-meter), car break-ins and theft are rife. Violent crime is fortunately fairly rare, though injuries are sometimes caused by scooter-born bag-snatchers (stay on the inside of the pavement and keep a firm grip on your property). Pickpockets generally strike in crowded buses and gatherings: don't carry more cash than you need, and split it up so you won't lose the lot at once. Be vigilant in train stations, and don't leave valuables in hotel rooms. If at all possible, avoid taking a car anywhere near Naples. Theft is so tediously common that some car hire firms refuse to rent certain models for use in the city. If your car is stolen, ring the police on 794 14 35 but don't expect much sympathy. Always park cars in garages, guarded lots or well-lit streets with anything remotely portable or valuable removed or well out of sight. Outside Naples, organized crime is much less evident. For police emergencies, dial 113, or 112 outside city areas. The *Vigili Urbani* take care of minor everyday problems in towns. They are generally more easy-going and courteous than the quasi-military *Carabinieri*, who along with the *Polizia Statale* watch over the rural areas. Traffic offences are dealt with by the *Polizia Stradale*, who patrol the highways. Possession of any questionable substances could subject you to a very hard time in drug-ridden southern Italy, despite the theoretical legal limit of a few grams of soft stuff for personal use.

Festivals

In Campania, any excuse will do for throwing a party, especially if it can be combined with having a day off work, and the region plays host to some of Italy's most spectacular and colourful traditional *feste* (festivals). Most of the festivities are linked to religious events and feast days, and the Madonna features prominently, often decked out garishly with bright fairy-lights and gaudy flowers and hauled through the streets atop tiny Fiats hastily covered with red velvet (with peepholes for the driver), or on platforms stoically borne by the village's fittest and strongest young men. But many of the celebrations also have a strong pagan flavour, especially those linked to the land and the harvest, and some of the feast-day paraphernalia is unmistakably phallic (towers and obelisks are an obvious give-away).

Whatever the occasion, a village *festa* is a chance to see local traditions and ancient rites in full swing. They are jolly affairs, and outsiders are nearly always welcome. This being Campania, where eating is in itself a second religion, a visit to a *festa* will invariably involve consuming vast quantities of food, often superbly cooked in makeshift kitchens organized by the local women, and served at knock-down prices. The following are some of the best *feste* to look out for, but keep a watch for others by checking billboards in the piazzas of towns and villages.

January

1	Lively New Year's celebration, **Capri**, with musicians playing the *putipu*, a local folk instrument

17	Festa d'o' Cippo di Sant'Antonio (procession for St Anthony, protector of animals), **Naples**
Jan-April	Chamber music at the Teatro delle Palme, **Naples**
Jan-mid-July	Opera at the San Carlo, **Naples**

February

First week	Food and liquor show, **Naples**

April

Holy Week	Tableaux and processions at **Sorrento**

May

Last half	International music festival in **Naples**
3rd week	Comic strip and illustration show, **Naples**

June

27	Sant'Andrea, with fireworks, costumes and processions in **Amalfi**
4th Sun	Festa dei Gigli, in **Nola**, near Naples—procession of enormous 'lilies' (wooden tower floats), recalling the homecoming of Bishop Paolino after his imprisonment in Africa in 394; Challenge of the Trombonieri, arquebus shooting contest in period costume, recalling a defeat over the Angevins, at **Cava de'Tirreni** (Salerno)
Last week	*Panatenee Pompeiane*, opera, dance and symphonies in the ruins of **Pompeii**

July

26	Feast of St Anne, **Ischia**—a torchlight procession of hundreds of boats, transformed into floats, to honour the island's patron saint

August

15	Feast of the straw obelisk, **Fontanarosa**, near Avellino—a harvest thanksgiving ritual
15	Wheat festival, **Foglianise** (Benevento), procession of decorated tractors, with a light pageant in the evening
15	Feast of the Assumption, **Positano**, an ancient celebration in honour of the Virgin, which also recreates the landing—and the defeat—of the hated Saracens

September

First 10 days	Neapolitan song contest, fireworks, etc. at **Piedigrotta** (Naples)
19	Feast of San Gennaro, **Naples**, where the faithful gather to watch the liquefaction of the saint's blood

December

Food and Drink

There are those who eat to live and those who live to eat, and then there are the Italians, for whom food has an almost religious significance, unfathomably linked with love, La Mamma, and tradition. In this singular country, where millions of otherwise sane people spend much of their waking hours worrying about their digestion, standards both at home and in the restaurants are understandably high. Few Italians are gluttons, but all are experts on what is what in the kitchen; to serve a meal that is not properly prepared and more than a little complex is tantamount to an insult.

For the visitor this national culinary obsession comes as an extra bonus to the senses— along with Italy's remarkable sights, music, and the warm sun on your back, you can enjoy some of the best tastes and smells the world can offer, prepared daily in Italy's kitchens and fermented in its countless wine cellars.

Breakfast (*colazione*) in Italy is no lingering affair, but an early morning wake-up shot to the brain: a *cappuccino* (*espresso* with hot foamy milk, often sprinkled with chocolate— incidentally first thing in the morning is the only time of day at which any self-respecting Italian will touch the stuff), a *caffè latte* (white coffee) or a *caffè lungo* (a generous portion of *espresso*), accompanied by a croissant-type roll, called a *cornetto* or *briosce*, or one of the other fancy pastries that are a special talent of Naples. This can be consumed in any bar and repeated during the morning as often as necessary. Breakfast in most Italian hotels seldom represents great value.

Lunch (*pranzo*), generally served around 1pm, is the most important meal of the day for the Italians, with a minimum of a first course (*primo piatto*—any kind of pasta dish, broth or soup, or rice dish or pizza), a second course (*secondo piatto*—a meat dish, accompanied by a *contorno* or side dish—a vegetable, salad, or potatoes usually), followed by fruit or dessert and coffee. You can, however, begin with a platter of *antipasti*—the appetizers Italians do so brilliantly, ranging from warm seafood delicacies, to raw ham (*prosciutto crudo*), salami in a hundred varieties, lovely vegetables, savoury toasts, olives, pâté and many many more. There are restaurants that specialize in antipasti, and they usually don't take it amiss if you decide to forget the pasta and meat and just nibble on these scrumptious hors d'oeuvres (though in the end it will probably cost more than a full meal). Most Italians accompany their meal with wine and mineral water—*acqua minerale*, with or without bubbles (*con* or *senza gas*), which supposedly aids digestion—concluding their meals with a *digestivo* liqueur.

Cena, the **evening meal**, is usually eaten around 8pm. This is much the same as *pranzo* although lighter, without the pasta; a pizza and beer, eggs or a fish dish. In restaurants, however, they offer all the courses, so if you have only a sandwich for lunch you have a full meal in the evening.

In Italy the various terms for types of **restaurants**—*ristorante*, *trattoria*, or *osteria*—have been confused. A *trattoria* or *osteria* can be just as elaborate as a restaurant, though rarely is a *ristorante* as informal as a traditional *trattoria*. Unfortunately the old habit of posting menus and prices in the windows has fallen from fashion, so it's often difficult to judge variety or prices. Invariably the least expensive restaurant-type place is the *vino e cucina*, simple places serving simple cuisine for simple everyday prices. It is essential to remember that the fancier the fittings, the fancier the bill, though neither of these points has anything at all to do with the quality of the food. If you're uncertain, do as you would at home— look for lots of locals. When you eat out, mentally add to the bill (*conto*) the bread and cover charge (*pane e coperto*, between L2000–3000), and a 15 per cent service charge. This is often included in the bill (*servizio compreso*); if not, it will say *servizio non compreso*, and you'll have to do your own arithmetic. Additional tipping is at your own discretion, but never do it in family-owned and -run places.

People who haven't visited Italy for years and have fond memories of eating full meals for under a pound will be amazed at how much prices have risen; though in some respects eating out in Italy is still a bargain, especially when you figure out how much all that wine would have cost you at home. In many places you'll often find restaurants offering a **menu turistico**—full, set meals of usually meagre inspiration for L18,000–25,000. More imaginative chefs often offer a **menu degustazione**—a set-price gourmet meal that allows you to taste their daily specialities and seasonal dishes. Both of these are cheaper than if you had ordered the same food à la carte. When you leave a restaurant you will be given a receipt (*scontrino* or *ricevuto fiscale*) which according to Italian law you must take with you out of the door and carry for at least 60m. If you aren't given one, it means the restaurant is probably fudging on its taxes and thus offering you lower prices. There is a slim chance the tax police (Guardia di Fianza) may have their eye on you and the restaurant, and if you don't have a receipt they could slap you with a heavy fine (L30,000).

There are several alternatives to sit-down meals. The 'hot table' (*tavola calda*) is a stand-up buffet, where you can choose a simple prepared dish or a whole meal, depending on your appetite. The food in these can be truly impressive (especially in the centre of Naples, where the sign out front may read *Degustazione*; some of these offer the best gourmet delights to be had in the south, and are always crowded). Many offer only a few hot dishes, pizza and sandwishes, though in every fair-sized town there will be at least one *tavola calda* with seats where you can contrive a complete dinner outside the usual hours. Little shops that sell pizza by the slice are common in city centres.

At any grocer's (*alimentari*) or market (*mercato*) you can buy the materials for countryside or hotel-room picnics; some places in the smaller towns will make the sandwiches for you. For really elegant picnics, have a *tavola calda* pack up something nice for you. And if everywhere else is closed, there's always the railway station—bars will at least have sandwiches and drinks, and perhaps (usually in unlikely locations in the south) some surprisingly good snacks you've never heard of before. Some of the station bars also prepare *cestini di viaggio*, full-course meals in a basket to help you through long train trips. Common snacks you'll encounter include *panini* of prosciutto, cheese and tomatoes, or other meats; *tramezzini*, little sandwiches on plain, square white bread that are always much better than they look; and pizza, of course.

Many Italian dishes need no introduction—pizza, spaghetti, lasagne and minestrone are familiar to all. What is perhaps less well known is the tremendous regional diversity at the table. Naples, of course, invented both pizza and spaghetti, the classic staples of Italian cuisine. A genuine Neapolitan pizza cooked in a wood-fired brick oven is the archetypal local eating experience, and watching it being made, whirled and slapped high in the air with lightning speed, is just as much of an entertainment as consuming it. The popular *marinara* is anointed with tomato, garlic and basil. *Calzoni* are half-moon envelopes of pizza dough, often filled with ham and cheese and sold as street snacks. Pasta often appears with engaging simplicity, smothered in oil and garlic, or tomato and basil. In the south, factory spaghetti gives way to the real monarch of pasta—nothing more than thick homemade spaghetti, but unmistakably different from the mass-produced commodity. Mozzarella, rather than parmesan, appears most often in pasta sauces. *Mozzarella in carrozza* is a fried sandwich of cheese, often sold as a street snack.

Campania tends to be overly modest about its cuisine. Its biggest favourites are simple enough: *pasta e fagioli* (pasta and beans), *spaghetti alle vongole* (with baby clams); the seafood, as everywhere else along the southern coasts, is exceptional. Besides the ubiquitous clams, squid, octopus and mussels (*zuppe di cozze*, mussels in a hot pepper sauce) appear frequently, along with oily fish like mackerel and sardines. Vegetables (often served as *contorni*, an appetising assortment) are excellent too. Aubergines and courgettes make their way into many local dishes, especially *melanzane parmigiana* (eggplant/aubergine baked with tomato and mozzarella), *misto di frittura* (deep-fried potato, aubergine and courgette flowers), or *zucchini a scapace* (courgettes in tomato sauce). In Campania, as elsewhere around the south, specialities tend to be hotter and spicier than in the north, and are often seasoned with condiments like capers, garlic, anchovies, lemon juice, oregano, olives and fennel. Dishes described as *alla napoletana* usually contain tomato, capers, black olives and garlic.

Puddings and cakes are rich and sweet in the south. *Pasteria* is one of the most celebrated local sweets, a ricotta pie full of wheat berries, candied fruit and spices, traditionally eaten at Easter. Another irresistible speciality of Naples is *sfogliatella* (flaky pastry, sometimes stuffed with ricotta and candied peel), which is sometimes eaten at breakfast time. If this sounds too much of a good thing, the best deal of all (in season) is a fresh peach, naked and unadorned.

Wine

Italy is a country where everyday wine is cheaper than Coca-Cola or milk, and where nearly every rural family owns some vineyards or has some relatives who supply most of their daily needs—which are not great. Even though they live in one of the world's largest wine-growing countries, Italians imbibe relatively little, and only at meals.

If Italy has an infinite variety of regional dishes, there is an equally bewildering array of regional wines, many of which are rarely exported because they are best drunk young. Unless you're dining at a restaurant with an exceptional cellar, do as the Italians do and order a carafe of the local wine (*vino locale* or *vino della casa*). You won't often be wrong. Most Italian wines are named after the grape and the district they come from. If the label says DOC (*Denominazione di Origine Controllata*) it means that the wine comes from a specially defined area and was produced according to a certain traditional method. DOCG (*Denominazione di Origine Controllata e Garantia*) is allegedly a more rigorous classification, indicating that the wines not only conform to DOC standards, but are tested by government-appointed inspectors. At present few wines have been granted this status, and those mainly from Italy's more prestigious Tuscan vineyards, but the number is planned to increase steadily.

Italians are fond of postprandial brandies (to aid digestion)—the famous Stock or Vecchia Romagna labels are always good. Grappa (acquavitae) is usually tougher, and often drunk in black coffee after a meal (a *caffè corretto*). Other members of any Italian bar include Campari, the famous red bitter, drunk on its own or in cocktails; Vermouth, Fernet Branca, Cynar and Averno, popular aperitifs/digestives; and liqueurs like Strega, the witch potion from Benevento, apricot-flavoured Amaretto, cherry Maraschino, aniseed Sambuca, as well as any number of locally brewed elixirs, often made by monks.

Campania was known for wine in Roman times. The legendary full-bodied Falerno was highly regarded by the ancients, and praised by Horace and Pliny. Today, the region produces surprisingly little, and not much of any note. The most famous is Lacrima Cristi, grown on the slopes of Vesuvius and only recently granted DOC status. Others to look out for include the white Greco di Tufo or Fiano di Avellino, or the deep, heavy red, Taurasi.

Health and Emergencies

Citizens of EU countries are entitled to reciprocal health care in Italy's National Health Service and a 90 per cent discount on prescriptions (bring Form E111 with you). The E111 does not cover all medical expenses (no repatriation costs, for example, and no private treatment), and it is advisable to take out separate travel insurance for full cover. Citizens of non-EU countries should check carefully that they have adequate insurance for any medical expenses, and the cost of returning home. Australia has a reciprocal health care scheme with Italy, but New Zealand, Canada and the USA do not. If you already have health insurance, a student card, or a credit card, you may be entitled to some medical cover abroad.

In an **emergency**, dial 113 for an ambulance in Italy (*ambulanza*); in Naples, ℰ 7520696 (24 hours), daytime only 7520850. The hospital (*ospedale*) in Naples is Policlinico, Via Sergio Pansini, ℰ 7461111—though this is a regular subject of horror stories in the local newspapers. Less serious problems can be treated at a *Pronto Soccorso* (casualty/first aid department) at any hospital, or at a local health unit (*Unità Sanitariale Locale*—USL). Airports and main railway stations also have first-aid posts. If you have to pay for any health treatment, make sure you get a receipt.

Pharmacies are generally open 8.30am–1pm and 4–8pm. Pharmacists are trained to give advice for minor ills. Any large town has a pharmacy that stays open 24 hours; others take turns to stay open (the address rota is posted in the windows of pharmacies and in the newspaper *Il Mattino*). The 24-hour pharmacy in Naples is Carducci, Via Carducci 21–23, ✆ 417283. There is also a public health service doctor in Naples on call 24 hours on ✆ 7513177.

No specific vaccinations are required or advised for citizens of most countries before visiting Italy; the main **health risks** are the usual travellers' woes of upset stomachs or the effects of too much sun. Occasional, much-publicized outbreaks of more serious disease have occurred in Naples in recent years (cholera, for example), but these are rarely likely to affect travellers. Take a supply of useful medicaments with you (e.g. insect repellent, anti-diarrhoeal medicine, sun lotion and antiseptic cream), and any drugs you need regularly. Stick to bottled water (dehydration is a serious risk in those southern climes) and avoid uncooked shellfish around the polluted Bay of Naples.

Money and Banks

It's a good idea to order a wad of *lire* from your home bank to have on hand when you arrive in Italy, the land of strikes, unforeseen delays and quirky banking hours. Take great care how you carry it, however (don't keep it all in one place). **Banking hours** vary, but core times are usually Monday to Friday 8.30am–1.20pm and 3–4pm, closed weekends and on local and national holidays (*see* below).

Obtaining money is often a frustrating business involving much queueing and form-filling. The major banks and exchange bureaux licensed by the Bank of Italy give the best exchange rates for currency or traveller's cheques. Hotels, private exchanges in resorts and FS-run exchanges at railway stations usually have less advantageous rates, but are open outside normal banking hours. Remember that Italians indicate decimals with commas and thousands with full points.

In **Naples**, you can change money outside normal banking hours at the post office (*see* p.23), in most good hotels, and at travel agents such as Ashiba, Piazza Municipio 1, ✆ 5512366; CIT, Piazza Municipio 70, ✆ 5525426; and Partenotour, Piazza dei Martiri 23, ✆ 7643415.

Besides traveller's cheques, most banks will give you cash on a recognized **credit card** or **Eurocheque** with a Eurocheque card (taking little or no commission), and in big cities such as Naples you can find automatic tellers (ATMs) to spout cash on a Visa, American Express or Eurocheque card. You need a PIN number to use these. Make sure you read the instructions carefully, or your card may be retained by the machine. MasterCard (Access) is much less widely acceptable in Italy. Large hotels, resort area restaurants, shops and car hire firms will accept plastic as well; many smaller places will not. From sad experience, Italians are wary of plastic—you can't even use it at motorway petrol stops.

You can have money transferred to you through an Italian bank but this process may take over a week, even if it's sent urgent *espressissimo*. You will need your passport as identification when you collect it. Sending cheques by post is inadvisable.

National Holidays

Most museums, as well as banks and shops, are closed on the following national holidays:

1 January (New Year's Day)

6 January (Epiphany)

Easter Monday

25 April (Liberation Day)

1 May (Labour Day)

15 August (Assumption, also known as *Ferragosto*, the official start of the Italian holiday season)

1 November (All Saints' Day)

8 December (Immaculate Conception)

25 December (Christmas Day)

26 December (*Santo Stefano*, St Stephen's Day)

In Naples, the feast of San Gennaro (19 September) is also a holiday.

Opening Hours, Museums and Churches

Although it varies from region to region most of Italy closes down at 1pm until 3 or 4pm to eat and properly digest the main meal of the day. Afternoon hours are from 4–7, sometimes from 5–8 in the hot summer months. Bars are often the only places open during the early afternoon. Shops of all kinds are usually closed on Saturday afternoons, Sundays, and Monday mornings as well—although grocery stores and supermarkets do open on Monday mornings.

Italy's **churches** have always been a prime target for art thieves and as a consequence are usually locked when there isn't a sacristan or caretaker to keep an eye on things. All churches, except for the really important cathedrals and basilicas, close in the afternoon at the same hours as the shops, and the little ones tend to stay closed. Always have a pocketful of coins for the light machines in churches, or whatever work of art you came to inspect will remain shrouded in ecclesiastical gloom. Don't do your visiting during services, and don't come to see paintings and statutes in churches the week preceding Easter—you will probably find them covered with mourning shrouds.

Many of Italy's **museums** are magnificent, many are run with shameful neglect, and many have been closed for years for 'restoration' with slim prospects of reopening in the foreseeable future. With two works of art per inhabitant, Italy has a hard time financing the preservation of its national heritage; it's as well to inquire at the tourist office to find out what is open and what is 'temporarily' closed before setting off on a wild goose chase.

In general, Sunday afternoons and Mondays are dead periods for the sightseer—you may want to make them your travelling days. Places without specified opening hours can usually be visited on request—but it is best to go before 1pm. We have listed the hours of important sights and museums, and specified which ones charge admission. Expect to pay between L2000 and L6000 to get in. The more important sites such as Pompeii may cost up to L10,000. EU citizens under 18 and over 65 get free admission to state museums, at least in theory.

Post Offices and Telephones

Dealing with *la posta italiana* has always been a risky, frustrating, time-consuming affair. One of the scandals that has mesmerized Italy in the past few years was the one involving the minister of the post office, who disposed of literally tons of backlog mail by tossing it in the Tiber. When the news broke, he was replaced—the new minister, having learned his lesson, burned all the mail the post office was incapable of delivering. Not surprisingly, fed-up Italians view the invention of the fax machine as a gift from the Madonna.

If you want to take your chances, post offices are usually open from 9am until 1pm (Mon–Sat), or until 6 or 7pm in a large city. To have your mail sent poste restante (general delivery), have it addressed to the central post office (*Fermo Posta*) and expect three to four weeks for it to arrive. Make sure your surname is very clearly written in block capitals. To pick up your mail you must present your passport and pay a nominal charge. Stamps (*francobolli*) may be purchased in post offices or at tobacconists (*tabacchi*, identified by their black or blue signs with a white T). Prices fluctuate. The rates for letters and postcards (depending how many words you write!) vary according to the whim of the tobacconist or postal clerk.

You can also have money telegraphed to you through the post office; if all goes well, this can happen in a mere three days, but expect a fair proportion of it to go into commission.

In **Naples** the main **post office** is in Piazza Matteotti, © 5511456, near Via Toledo, and is open 8am–8pm Mon–Fri, 8am–12 noon Sat. You can also send faxes and telegrams from here.

Public telephones for **international calls** may be found in the offices of SIP (Società Italiana Telefoni, Italy's telephone company). They are the only places where you can make reverse-charge calls (*a erre*, collect calls) but be prepared for a wait, as all these calls go through the operator in Rome. Rates for long-distance calls are among the highest in Europe. Calls within Italy are cheapest after 10pm; international calls after 11pm. Most phone booths now take either coins, *gettoni* (L200 tokens often given to you in place of change) or phone cards (*schede telefoniche*) available in L5000 or L10,000 amounts at tobacconists and news-stands. In smaller villages and islands, you can usually find *telefoni a scatti*, with a meter on them, in at least one bar (a small commission is generally charged). Try to avoid telephoning from hotels, which often add 25 per cent to the bill. Telephone numbers in Italy currently change with alarming regularity as the antiquated system is updated.

Phone centres in Naples are at the Stazione Centrale, at Via Depretis 40, and in the Galleria Umberto I. The code for Naples is 081.

Direct calls may be made by dialling the international prefix (for the UK 0044, Ireland 00353, USA and Canada 001, Australia 0061, New Zealand 0064). If you're calling Italy from abroad, dial 39 and then drop the first 0 from the telephone prefix.

Shopping

You'll find some of the lowest shopping prices in **Naples**, especially in its various markets (*see* p.80). **Amalfi**'s specialities are fine stationery (paper-making was already an art and an important industry here in the Middle Ages) and ceramics—mostly tourist bric-à-brac, but some of it very well done. Every conceivable luxury item Italy makes is sold in the shops of **Sorrento**—but make sure you come in the off-season (December and January are best) when you'll find some outstanding bargains in fashions, Murano glass and other trinkets. Sorrento's own speciality is *intarsia*, inlaid wood scenes on tables or trays, or simply framed for hanging. They are exquisite things, and prices are often reasonable.

Prices for clothes in Italy are generally very high, and sizes are tailored for slim Italian builds. Shoes, in particular, tend to be narrower than in most Western countries.

Sports and Activities

Football

Soccer (*il calcio*) is a national obsession. For many Italians its importance far outweighs tedious issues like the state of the nation, the government of the day, or any momentous international event—not least because of the weekly chance (slim but real) of becoming an instant lira billionaire in the Lotteria Sportiva. The sport was actually introduced by the English, but a Renaissance game, something like a cross between football and rugby, has existed in Italy for centuries. Modern Italian teams are known for their grace, precision, and teamwork; rivalries are intense, scandals, especially bribery and cheating, are rife. The tempting rewards offered by such big-time entertainment attract all manner of corrupt practices, yet crowd violence is minimal compared with the havoc wreaked by other countries' lamentable fans. Serie A is the equivalent of the first division, comprising 18 teams. The big southern Serie A team is, of course, Napoli, whose most charismatic player's name still trips off the tongue of the least *sportif* foreigner. The legendary Maradona no longer plays for Naples after his fall from grace. But almost any weekend (matches are generally played on Sunday afternoons) you should find a good game somewhere in the region. Tickets aren't cheap for the top matches (L25,000–100,000). In Naples, the main ground is the Stadio di San Paolo in Fuorigrotta (a western suburb—take Ferrovia Cumana as far as Mostra and the stadium is directly outside), ✆ 61 56 23.

Fishing

Many freshwater lakes and streams are stocked, and if you're more interested in fresh fish than the sport of it, there are innumerable trout farms where you can practically pick the fish up out of the water with your hands. Sea fishing, from the shore, from boats, or underwater (though not much with an aqualung) is possible almost everywhere without a permit; to fish in fresh water you need to purchase a year's membership card (currently L189,000) from the Federazione Italiana della Pesca Sportiva, which has an office in every province. In Naples it's in Piazza Santa Maria degli Angeli, ✆ (081) 417579; they will inform you about local conditions and restrictions.

Watersports and Beaches

At most resorts it is possible to hire boats and equipment, and go windsurfing, waterskiing, or diving (in Naples contact the Subacquei Napoletani, Piazza Santa Maria degli Angeli 11, ✆ 764 49 21). Capri is one of the best choices for such activities, with some of the cleanest waters in the Bay of Naples. You can also take submarine trips around the island. For scuba diving, waterskiing, canoeing and boat hire, contact the Sea Service Centre, Marina Piccola, Via Mulo 63 (✆ 837 02 21). Sorrento, Positano, Amalfi and Salerno also offer a range of watersports, and lots of cruises.

Many southern Italian beaches are disappointingly flat, and scarcely improved by regimented lines of parasols and sunbeds. Those around the Bay of Naples tend to be of grey volcanic sand and the free public ones are small, crowded and neglected with few facilities. Accept the fact, then, that to enjoy Italian beaches you will have to pay: most of the best stretches of sand (some of them artificial) are operated by private concessionaires. For the most attractive resort beaches, head for Positano, Minori or Maiori. Despite the appalling pollution immediately around Naples, the water is generally cleaner than in the northern resorts, and there's no denying that the Amalfi coast is scenically the most dazzling stretch of shoreline in the whole of Italy. Below the Gulf of Salerno, the Cilento coast is less spectacular, and generally rocky rather than sandy, more popular for scuba diving than swimming.

Sailing

Almost all the islands have some facilities for **yachts**, though they may not be equipped for a long stay. You can bring your own boat to Italy for six months without any paperwork if you bring it by car; if you arrive by sea you must report to the Port Authority. The harbour-master (*capitaneria di porto*) at your first Italian port of call will give you a document called a *costituto*, which you will have to produce for subsequent harbour-masters;

this permits the purchase of tax-free fuel. For further information, contact the Italian State Tourist Office or write to either of these organizations:

Federazione Italiana Vela (Italian Sailing Federation), Via Brigata Bisagno 2/17, Genoa, ✆ (010) 565723.

Federazione Italiana Motonautica (Italian Motorboat Federation), Via Piranesi 44/B, Milan, ✆ (02) 7610502, fax (02) 718581.

One of the main local sailing clubs is Nantic Coop, Piazza Amedo 15, Naples ✆ (081) 415 5371. The main Bay of Naples yacht harbours are Capri; Procida; Ischia (Porto, Casamicciola, Lacco Ameno and Forio d'Ischia).

Rowing

Once every four years Amalfi hosts the annual race between the four Old Maritime Republics (Genoa, Pisa, Amalfi and Venice), on the first Sunday in June. Amalfi's next turn is in 1997.

Golf

Despite the popularity of golf in Italy as a whole, there are very few courses in and around Naples. The most important is the Naples-Afsouth club (9 holes only), Via Campiglione 11, 80072 Arco Felice, ✆ (081) 526 296. Minigolf Kennedy, in the Chiaiano suburb to the west of Naples, is in Via Camillo Guerra 60 ✆ (081) 587 1386.

Tennis

Many of the more expensive hotels have courts, and non-residents may be able to use them by arrangement with the hotel or local tourist office. There are public courts in **Naples**, Via Giochi del Mediterraneo ✆ (081) 760 3912; **Benevento**, Viale Atlantici, ✆ (0824) 29920; and **Ischia Porto**, Lungomare Colombo, ✆ (081) 991013.

Time

Italy is one hour ahead of Greenwich Mean Time. From the last weekend of March to the end of September, Italian Summer Time (daylight saving time) is in effect.

Tourist Offices Abroad

UK: 1 Princes Street, London W1R 8AY, ✆ (071) 408 1254

US: 630 Fifth Avenue, Suite 1565, New York, NY 10111, ✆ (212) 245 4961; 12400 Wilshire Blvd, Suite 550, Los Angeles, CA 90025, ✆ (310) 820 2977; 500 North Michigan Ave, Suite 1046, Chicago, IL 60611, ✆ (644) 0996

Canadian: 1 Place Ville Marie, Suite 1914, Montreal, Quebec H3B 3M9, ✆ (514) 866 7667 or 866 7669

Japanese: 2–7–14 Minimi, Aoyama, Minato-ku, Tokyo 107, © 347 82 051—also responsible for Australia and New Zealand.

Tourist and travel information may also be available from Alitalia (Italy's national airline) or CIT (Italy's state-run travel agency) offices in some countries.

Where to Stay

All accommodation in Italy is classified by the Provincial Tourist Boards. Price control, however, has been deregulated since 1992. Hotels now set their own tariffs, which means that in some places prices have rocketed, even in the poorer south. After a period of rapid and erratic price fluctuation, tariffs are at last settling down again to more predictable levels under the influence of market forces. The quality of furnishings and facilities has generally improved in all categories in recent years. But you can still find plenty of older style hotels and *pensioni*, whose eccentricities of character and architecture (in some cases undeniably charming) may frequently be at odds with modern standards of comfort or even safety. In Naples, particularly, good accommodation is scarce and should be booked ahead. Campania's tariffs are generally lower than in the Grand Tour towns and cities further north, but Capri's ritziest establishments vie with any in Italy on price.

Hotels and Guesthouses

Italian *alberghi* come in all shapes and sizes. They are rated from one to five stars, depending what facilities they offer (not their character, style or charm). The star ratings are some indication of price levels, but for tax reasons not all hotels choose to advertise themselves at the rating to which they are entitled, so you may find a modestly rated hotel just as comfortable (or more so) than a higher rated one. Conversely, you may find a hotel offers few stars in hopes of attracting budget-conscious travellers, but charges just as much as a higher-rated neighbour. *Pensioni* are generally more modest establishments, though nowadays the distinction between these and ordinary hotels is becoming blurred. *Locande* are traditionally an even more basic form of hostelry, but these days the term may denote somewhere fairly chic. Other inexpensive accommodation is sometimes known as *alloggi* or *affittacamere*. There are usually plenty of cheap dives around railway stations; for somewhere more salubrious, head for the historic quarters. Whatever the shortcomings of the decor, furnishings and fittings, you can usually rely at least on having clean sheets.

Price lists, by law, must be posted on the door of every room, along with meal prices and any extra charges (such as air conditioning, or even a shower in cheap places). Many hotels display two or three different rates, depending on the season. Low-season rates may be about a third lower than peak season tariffs. Some resort hotels close down altogether for several months a year. During high season you should always book ahead to be sure of a room (a fax reservation may be less frustating to organize than one by post). If you have paid a deposit, your booking is valid under Italian law, but don't expect it to be refunded if you have to cancel. Tourist offices publish annual regional lists of hotels and pensions with current rates, but do not make reservations for visitors. Major railway stations generally have accommodation booking desks; inevitably, a fee is charged. Chain hotels or motels are generally the easiest hotels to book. but are often less interesting to stay in. If you arrive without a reservation, begin looking or phoning round for accommodation early in the day. If possible, inspect the room (and bathroom facilities) before you book, and check the tariff carefully. Italian hoteliers may legally alter their rates twice during the year, so printed tariffs or tourist board lists (and prices quoted in this book!) may be out of date. Hoteliers who wilfully overcharge should be reported to the local tourist office. You will be asked for your passport for registration purposes.

Prices listed in this guide are for double rooms; you can expect to pay about two-thirds the rate for single occupancy, though in high season you may be charged the full double rate in a popular beach resort. Extra beds are usually charged at about a third more of the room rate. Rooms without private bathrooms generally charge 20–30 per cent less, and most offer discounts for children sharing parent's rooms, or children's meals. A *camera singola* (single room) may cost anything from about L25,000 upwards. Double rooms (*camera doppia*) go from about L40,000 to L250,000 or more. If you want a double bed, specify a *camera matrimoniale.*

Breakfast is usually optional in hotels, though obligatory in *pensioni.* You can usually get better value by eating breakfast in a bar or café if you have any choice. In high season you may be expected to take half board in resorts if the hotel has a restaurant, and one-night stays may be refused.

Youth Hostels

There aren't many of these in Italy (where they are known as *alberghi* or *ostelli per la gioventù*), but they are generally pleasant and sometimes located in historic buildings. The Associazione Italiana Alberghi per la Gioventù (Italian Youth Hostel Association, or AIG) is affiliated to the International Youth Hostel Federation. For a full list of hostels, contact AIG at Via Cavour 44, 00184 Roma, © (06) 487 1152, fax (06) 488 0492. An international membership card will enable you to stay in any of them (cards can be purchased on the spot in many hostels if you don't already have one). Hostels around Naples include: Agerola-S. Lazzaro or Mergellina (Naples), Irno (Salerno), Surriento (Sorrento). Rates are usually somewhere between L12,000 and L18,000, including breakfast. Discounts are available for senior citizens, and some family rooms are available. You generally have to check in after 5pm, and pay for your room before 9am. Hostels usually close for most of the daytime, and many operate a curfew. During the spring, noisy school parties cram hostels for field trips. In the summer, it's advisable to book ahead. Contact the hostels directly.

Camping

Most of the official sites are near beach resorts, though there are a few inland in scenic areas or near major tourist centres such as Pompeii or Paestum. Camping is not the fanatical holiday activity it is in France, for example, nor necessarily any great bargain, but it is popular with many holidaymaking families in August, when you can expect to find many sites at bursting point. Unofficial camping is generally frowned on and may attract a stern rebuke from the local police. Camper vans (and facilities for them) are increasingly popular. You can obtain a list of local sites from any regional tourist office. Campsite charges generally range from about L7000 per adult; tents and vehicles additionally cost about L7000 each. Small extra charges may also be levied for hot showers and electricity. A car-borne couple could therefore spend practically as much for a night at a well equipped campsite as in a cheap hotel.

To obtain a camping carnet and book ahead, write to the **Centro Internazionale Prenotazioni Campeggio**, Casella Postale 23, 50041, Calenzano, Firenze, ✆ (055) 882381, fax (055) 8825918 (ask for their list of campsites as well as the booking form). The **Touring Club Italiano** (TCI) publishes a comprehensive annual guide to campsites and tourist villages throughout Italy. Write to: TCI, Corso Italia 10, Milan, ✆ (02) 85261/8526245. Note that camping is strictly forbidden on Capri (though there are several sites on Ischia and Procida). The closest site to Naples is near the bubbling, sulphurous, rotten-egg-smelling volcanic crater of Solfatara, in the Pozzuoli district west of the city. It's usually crowded.

Agriturismo

For a breath of rural seclusion, the normally gregarious Italians head for a spell on a working farm, in accommodation (usually self-catering) that often approximates to the French *gîte*. Often, however, the real pull of the place is a restaurant in which you can sample some home-grown produce (olives, wine, etc.). Outdoor activities may also be on tap (riding, fishing, and so forth). This branch of the Italian tourist industry has burgeoned in recent years, and every region now has several Agriturist offices. Prices of farmhouse accommodation, compared with the over-hyped 'Tuscan villa', are still reasonable (expect to pay around L40,000–60,000 for a cottage or double room). Agriturismo isn't as well established in Campania as in Tuscany or Umbria, but possibilities certainly exist. To make the most of your rural hosts, it's as well to have a little Italian under your belt before you bury yourself in an olive grove. Local tourist offices will have information on this type of accommodation in their areas; otherwise you can obtain complete listings compiled by the national organization Agriturist, Corso Vittorio Emanuele 101, 00186 Rome, ✆ (06) 65 12342, or Turismo Verde, Via Mariano Fortuny 20, 00196 Rome, ✆ (06) 366 9931. Both publications are available in Italian bookshops. The local office in Naples is at Via S. Lucia 90, 80132 Napoli, ✆ (081) 425 238.

Self-catering Tour Operators

One of the most enjoyable, and best-value, ways of visiting Italy is to opt for self-catering accommodation, with the family or friends. Centralized booking agencies exist in many countries as well as Italy, and can organize holidays on the coast or in genuinely rural settings, sometimes offering discounted air or ferry fares and fly-drive schemes to egg you on. Watch for the small ads, or see the list below.

Citalia, Marco Polo House, 3–5 Lansdowne Road, Croydon, CR9 1LL, ✆ (081) 688 9989: tailor-made holidays and self-catering along the coast.

CV Travel, 43 Cadogan Street, London SW3 2PR, ✆ (071) 581 0851: villa holidays.

Interhome, 383 Richmond Road, Twickenham, Middx, ✆ (081) 891 1294.

Italian Chapters, 102 St John's Wood Terrace, London NW8 6PL, ✆ ✆ (071) 722 9560: villa holidays.

Italian Escapades, 227 Shepherd's Bush Road, London W6 7AS, ✆ (071) 748 7575.

Magic of Italy (same address as Italian Escapades): villa-appartments along the coast.

Sovereign Italia, Astral Towers, 2nd Floor, Betts Way, Crawley, W. Sussex RH10 2GX, ✆ (0293) 560777: villa-appartments in Ravello.

Vacanze in Italia, Bignor, Nr Pulborough, W. Sussex, RH20 1QD, ✆ (0987) 426: individual villa holidays specialists.

History and Art

Masaniello

History

800–358 BC: in which young Campania gets a heavy dose of Hellenic culture

How do places and nations get their names? Sometimes it's better not to ask. *Italy*, originally *Vitellia*, seems to mean 'cow pasture' in one of the old languages of the peninsula. The name was bestowed by the Greeks, and we can painfully imagine some old Greek explorer, long before Homer's time, landing somewhere on the Tyrrhenian coast, strolling up to some simple cowherds and asking as best he could in gestures, 'What place is this?'

It is with the Greeks that written history begins here. When they arrived in force, in the 8th century, they found Campania inhabited by a number of powerful, distinct tribes with related languages. Chief among them were the Samnites, who occupied much of inland Campania and the south, while the area around the bay was inhabited by the Ausones, or Oscans, and the Opici. The Greeks, whose trading routes had long covered Italy's southern coasts, looked upon that 'underdeveloped' country as a New World for exploration and colonization. All over the south, there are tantalizing archaeological clues that the Greeks had begun settlements even earlier, in the Mycenaean age before the fall of Troy, but about these little is known.

In 775, Greeks founded a trading settlement at Pithecusa, on the island of Ischia, squarely in the middle of the important trade route that carried Tuscany's iron to the east. The first planned urban colony in Campania was Cumae, in 750, and not long after that another band of Greeks founded a city called Parthenope, on the hill called Pizzofalcone that now divides the old and new quarters of Naples, and on the nearby island where the Castel dell'Ovo is now. Centuries later, the poet Virgil, who loved this coast and spent much of his life on it, dressed up the city's origins with the story of a siren named Parthenope; according to Virgil, Odysseus visited here, and when he resisted all her attempts to seduce him into remaining with her, Parthenope threw herself off the cliff and drowned.

The city Parthenope didn't fare too well either. Throughout Greek Italy, neighbouring cities tended to fight like Kilkenny cats, and Cumae and Parthenope slugged it out until the latter succumbed. The Cumaeans may have destroyed their rival; in any case they founded a new city—*Neapolis*—right next to it. Like most Greek foundations, Neapolis was laid out in a rigid rectangular grid, like Manhattan or Chicago, a pattern that has survived with almost no changes in the Spacca district today.

The Greeks could never hope to have such a desirable land entirely to themselves. In the 6th century, the Etruscans arrived from the north. This powerful and talented nation, then at the height of its culture and expanding in all directions, colonized much of Campania's interior, founding the cities of Capua, Nola and Acerra (modern historians trace Etruscan expansion by their manic habit of surveying land into 700m squares; besides gladiatorial combats, portrait busts, rampant religious superstition and many other contributions, the Etruscans also taught their Roman neighbours how to make straight roads). Conflict with the Greeks, their greatest trade rivals, was inevitable, and serious. Serious warfare began in 524 with an unsuccessful Etruscan siege of Cumae. The Greeks got the better of it from then on, and finally defeated the Etruscans at sea in the decisive Battle of Cumae (474). Their southern colonies straggled on for a while, but the taking of Capua by the Samnites in 432 put an end to Etruscan pretensions in the south forever.

Greek Campania by this time was only the northernmost province of a genuine New World—*Magna Graecia*, a land of rich culture and wealthy cities that included all of southern Italy's coasts and Sicily. Greek Italy's painters and sculptors took their places among the greatest of Greece's golden age, but its most memorable contributions were in philosophy. The famous Elean School (from the city of Elea, in the Cilento) included some of the most important pre-Socratics: Parmenides, who invented the concept of atoms, and Zeno, with his pesky paradoxes. Down in Calabria and Sicily, the Greeks also distinguished themselves by a consistent bestiality towards each other—constant wars between cities and civil wars within them, with the losers usually massacred or sold off as slaves. Somehow the Campanian towns managed to avoid most of the unpleasantness, while playing an important role in teaching art and culture to their Italian neighbours. The Ausones, Samnites and other nations became more or less Hellenized, while a bellicose and rapidly growing little republic up north was proving a less gifted student—Rome.

358 BC–AD 406 : a ride on the Roman rollercoaster

In the 6th century, Rome had chased out its Etruscan rulers and began terrorizing all the towns and tribes of central Italy. By the 4th century, she had gobbled up the lot, and the borders of the Roman state extended into Campania. About 358 the senators were able to turn their attention to the only power in Italy capable of competing with Rome on an equal basis: the Samnites. These rugged highlanders of the southern Apennines, with their capital at Benevento, had begun to seize parts of coastal Campania from the Greeks. The Romans drove them out in 341, but in the Second Samnite War the Samnites dealt them a severe defeat (Battle of the Caudine Forks, in 321). In the third war, feeling themselves surrounded by Roman allies, the Samnites formed an alliance with the Northern Etruscans and Celts, leading to a general Italian commotion where the Romans beat everybody, annexing almost all of Italy by 283.

After the Samnites, it was the turn of the Greeks. The frightened cities of Magna Graecia sent off for Pyrrhus of Epirus, a brilliant adventurer with a big army, to help keep the barbarians out. Pyrrhus won a string of inconclusive 'Pyrrhic' victories, but after losing a battle in 275, at Benevento, he quit and returned home, allowing the Romans leisurely to snatch up the deserted Greek cities one by one. Now the conquest was complete. All along the Romans had been diabolically clever in managing their new demesne, maintaining most of the tribes and cities as nominally independent states, while planting Latin colonies everywhere in the ruins of cities they had destroyed (Paestum, Puteoli [Pozzuoli], and Benevento were such colonies).

Rome went on to fatten on even bigger prey—the Carthaginians in the 3rd century, the rest of the Mediterranean in the 2nd—while Campania became thoroughly integrated into the Roman system. Wealthy Romans lined the Bay of Naples with their villas, while Puteoli grew up as the leading port of Italy, the terminus for the grain ships that fed the capital. Campania was booming, largely from the manufacture of ceramics and luxury goods; its metropolis, Capua, a city renowned for perfume and fair ladies, was in population and wealth the second city of Italy.

But even in favoured Campania, Roman rule had its darker side. The conquerors appropriated most of the good land and divided it among themselves, creating vast estates called *latifundiae* and a new society where a small class of fantastically wealthy landowners lorded it over an increasingly impoverished peasantry and middle class. Debt and Roman law pushed large numbers of the poor into slavery. In other parts of Italy the situation was much worse; the 1st century BC witnessed a continuous political and social crisis, breaking out into a series of civil wars and rebellions that did not end until the accession of Augustus and the end of the Roman Republic. In the year 91, a coordinated revolt broke out among the southern peoples called the Social Wars, a genuine threat to Rome that was finally defeated by the campaigns of Marius and Sulla, and by an offer to extend Roman citizenship to all Italians. Both generals, the former a populist and the latter an arch-reactionary, later ruled as dictators in Rome. Under the tyrannous Sulla, an effective autocracy was created and all opponents either murdered or exiled. Italy careered into anarchy, with many rural districts reverting to bandit-ridden wastelands, a setting for the remarkable revolt in 73 of Spartacus, an escaped gladiator of Capua who led a motley army of dispossessed farmers and runaway slaves—some 70,000 of them—back and forth across the south until the legions finally defeated him in 71.

The later civil wars—Pompey vs. Caesar and Augustus vs. Antony—largely spared Campania, though many of the plots were hatched in villas around the bay. Under Augustus and his imperial successors, things settled down considerably, while the bay continued its career as the favoured resort of the emperors and the rich. In the economic decline of the late empire, troubles returned. The rural south sank deeper into decline, while even the commerce of wealthy Campania gradually began to fail, ruined by foreign competition, high taxes and bureaucracy. The great eruption of Vesuvius in 79 AD must have increased the economic disarray; three sizeable towns, Pompeii, Herculaneum and Stabiae, completely disappeared, and vast tracts of fertile land withered under volcanic ash. In northern Italy, meanwhile, a sounder, more stable economy led to the growth of new centres—Milan, Padua, Verona, Florence and others. The economic north–south divide, a problem for which no solution is in sight even today, was already beginning.

406–1139: Goths, Greeks, Lombards and Normans try on the Roman boot, and none find a good fit

The 5th-century barbarian invaders of Italy, Goths and Vandals, passed through Campania without any notable outrages, and after they passed the region and the rest of the peninsula got a half-century's breathing space under Theodoric's tolerant, well-run Gothic Kingdom of Italy. The real disaster began in 536, with the invasion of Italy by the Eastern Empire, part of the relentlessly expansionist policy of the great Justinian. Campania, still largely Greek by race and sentiment, welcomed the largely Greek army from Constantinople, but much of the worst fighting of the Greek–Gothic War took place in the region; Neapolis, or Naples, by now the largest city on the coast, was captured and sacked in turn by both sides. Justinian's brilliant generals, Belisarius and Narses, ultimately prevailed over the Goths in 563, but the damage to an already stricken society and economy was incalculable. Italy's total exhaustion was exposed only five years later, when the Lombards, a Germanic tribe who worked hard to earn the title of barbarians, overran northern Italy and parts of the south, establishing a kingdom at Pavia in the north and a separate duchy at Benevento (571). A new pattern of power appeared, with semi-independent Byzantine dukes defending much of the coastal areas, and Lombard chiefs ruling most of the interior. Byzantine control was always tenuous at best, and cities like Naples and Salerno gradually achieved a *de facto* independence.

No one usually bothered to write down what was going on in Campania during the Dark Ages, but enough records have come down to suggest that some of the coastal cities, at least, weren't doing too badly for themselves. Naples, which proclaimed its complete independence in 763 under its dukes, along with Sorrento and Salerno, all seemed to have been keeping themselves afloat and carrying on at least a little trade. And in this unpromising time a new city rose up to join them, and cut a surprising career for itself as a merchant republic: Amalfi. As early as the 7th century, Amalfi had its fleet. In the 900s, the city established its independence from Naples and elected a doge, like Venice's. Its trading stations extended across the eastern Mediterranean, and there was a large colony of Amalfitan merchants in Constantinople.

The year 1000, the dawning of the millennium, makes a convenient date for the dawning of the Middle Ages, and the great economic and cultural upsurge that came with it. In southern Italy, the major event of this time was the arrival of the Normans. The first of these arrived in the 9th century, as mercenaries or pilgrims to Monte Sant'Angelo in the Gargano. They liked the opportunities they saw for booty and conquest, and from about 1020 younger sons of Norman feudal families were moving into the south, first as mercenaries but gradually gaining large tracts of land for themselves in exchange for their services. Often allied with the popes, they soon controlled most of Apulia and Calabria. One of their greatest chiefs, Robert Guiscard came to control much of the south as Duke of Apulia. In 1084, he descended on Rome for a grisly sack that put the best efforts of the Goths and Vandals to shame. His less destructive brother, Roger de Hauteville, began the conquest of Sicily from the Arabs in 1060, six years before William the Conqueror sailed for England. Naples fell to Roger's armies in 1139.

1139–1494: in which, thanks to a despised Frenchman, Naples becomes a Kingdom

Roger de Hauteville eventually united all of the south into the 'Kingdom of Sicily', and by the 1140s, under Roger II, this strange Norman-Arab-Jewish-Italian-Greek state, with its glittering, half-oriental capital of Palermo, had become the cultural centre of the Mediterranean, a refuge of religious tolerance and serious scholarship. Under Roger and his successors (William the Bad, who wasn't bad at all, and William the Good, who was something of a weakling), it remained one of the strongest and best-organized states in

Europe. In 1194, the line of the Hautevilles became extinct and the Kingdom of Sicily fell to Holy Roman Emperor Henry IV of Hohenstaufen, who brought down an army from Germany to claim it. His son, the legendary Frederick II (1194–50), the 'Wonder of the World', was at once Emperor and King of Sicily, though he preferred to spend most of his time in southern Italy, presiding over a court even more brilliant than that of Roger II, one in which some of the first Italian poetry was written. Frederick gave his lands a constitution, the *Constitutio Melfitani*, and founded Naples's University, the third in Italy and first in the south.

Frederick did not have an easy reign, largely thanks to his most dangerous political enemies, the popes; during his reign they excommunicated him twice. After his death, Pope Urban IV began an ultimately disastrous precedent by inviting in Charles of Anjou, a powerful, ambitious leader and brother of the King of France, to seize the southern kingdom. Charles defeated Frederick's son Manfred (Battle of Benevento, 1266) and murdered the last of the Hohenstaufens, Conradin, in 1268. He held unchallenged sway over southern Italy until 1282, when the famous revolt of the Sicilian Vespers chased the hated French from Sicily and inaugurated a period of wars and anarchy.

The South, despite its unity under the Normans and Hohenstaufens, was falling behind both politically and economically. The Normans may have ruled their domains fairly and intelligently, but they also deserve the blame for introducing feudalism into a country that had never known it—just as the mercantile states of the north were breaking loose from the feudal arrangements brought down by the Goths and Lombards. Now the 'Kingdom of Naples', as the southern state had become known, to distinguish it from the now separate Kingdom of Sicily, was a tapestry of battling barons, each busily building or improving his castle and increasingly less inclined to listen to kings or popes or anyone. The trading cities, especially Naples and Amalfi, saw their woes increase with strong competition from the Venetians and Genoese. With little encouragement from king or barons, they could only continue to decline.

Robert the Wise (1309–43) was a good king, and patron of Giotto, Petrarch and Bocaccio. For a successor, he left only a granddaughter, Giovanna I, and under her unsteady hand the barons mightily increased both their power and their contentiousness. Her reign witnessed the Black Death (1347–48), in which Italy lost one third of its population, and also the beginnings of civil war between Angevin factions, something that would continue fitfully through a century of confusing intrigues and insurrections. It ended in the hands of yet another foreigner, Alfonso the Magnanimous, King of Aragon, who conquered Naples and tossed out the last Angevins in 1442 (Alfonso, a student of the classics, had been reading an account of how Belisarius took Naples in the Greek–Gothic Wars by sending men through the channel of a Roman aqueduct that breached the walls; he located the exact spot, with the ruined aqueduct still present, and sent his soldiers in the same way). Once more the Kingdom was reunited with Sicily, part of the Aragonese crown since the Sicilian Vespers. Alfonso and his successor, the cruel King Ferrante, ruled Naples with harshness and skill; both were typical Renaissance princes who, as leaders of the only kingdom in Italy, played major roles in the Byzantine political manoeuverings of the age.

1494–1713: the kingdom falls to the Spaniards, who make a mess of it

The Wars of Italy, that terrible series of conflicts that eventually rang down the curtain on the Renaissance and on Italian liberty, began in 1494 with a quarrel over Naples. Charles VIII, King of France, took advantage of Italian disunity to invade the peninsula, seeking to make good the claim to the kingdom he had inherited from the Angevins. The last Aragonese king, the ineffectual Alfonso II, fled the city rather than face him. Spain, at this time, was at the height of its powers after the union of Aragon and Castile in 1492, under Ferdinand and Isabella. The Spaniards sent a strong army under *El Gran Capitan*, Gonsalvo di Córdoba, and he restored Naples to its Spanish king the following year. Some more fighting between Aragonese factions followed, and when the dust settled, in 1502, Naples and its kingdom were directly under the Spanish crown, and ruled by a viceroy.

In the decades to come, nearly all Italy would be beaten or bullied into the Spanish system, either through puppet rulers, alliances or outright control, but nowhere more than in Naples was the Spanish influence stronger. The Inquisition snuffed out the city's intellectual life, while the nobles of the realm learned to forsake their wonted gay colours and dress all in black; they came to affect the haughty manners from the grandees, and started calling each other *Don*, and they carried rapiers and poignards in the streets—in the atmosphere of the Wars of Italy, it had become an extremely violent age. The greatest of the viceroys, Don Pedro de Toledo, was a benefactor to Naples, and rebuilt much of it; he also built Castel Sant'Elmo on the highest hill to keep watch over the Neapolitans.

Spanish rule lasted over two centuries, and as Spain decayed into senile decadence its government in southern Italy grew ever more oppressive and useless. Times would have been bad enough, in the general Italian economic collapse of the 17th century, but Spanish misrule gradually turned the already-poor rural south into a nightmare of anarchic depravity, haunted by legions of bandits and beggars, and controlled more tightly than ever by its violent feudal barons. Peasants by the thousand gave up their lands and villages for a marginally safer life in Naples, and the city ballooned in population—an estimated half million by 1700—to become the largest in Europe. To everyone's surprise, the south rose up and staged an epic rebellion. Beginning in Naples (Masaniello's Revolt, 1647), the disturbances soon spread all over the south and Sicily. For over a year peasant militias ruled some areas, and makeshift revolutionary councils defended the cities. But when the Spanish finally defeated them, they massacred some 18,000, and tightened the screws more then ever.

1713–1860: a mild case of Bourbonic Plague

In 1713, after the War of the Spanish Succession, the Habsburgs of Austria came into control of most of the Spanish possessions, including Naples. The Austrians made no impression on anyone, and Naples' hard luck continued when the Austrians were forced to transfer it to a branch of the House of Bourbon (1734); under them the kingdom was again independent, but just as poorly governed as before. For the next century and a quarter, the southern *Regno* enjoyed a colourful era of poverty, backwardness, bad art and intellectual torpor, in which the city of Naples perfected the peculiar charms and vices it displays today. An exception was the reign of Charles III (1734–59) who introduced many long overdue reforms. Charles built the San Carlo Opera, the Archaeological Museum, and the palaces at Capodimonte and Caserta. His son, Ferdinand I, has gone down in history as the 'Lazzarone King' (*lazzarone*, a key Neapolitan word, refers to the crowds of gainfully unemployed men that lounged on every streetcorner of old Naples; it does not literally mean 'good-for-nothing', but that would be an accurate translation). The perfect king for the time, Ferdinand ruled with a light hand and spoke only Neapolitan dialect; state visitors found him generally surrounded by noise, food and children.

The French invasion of 1799, during the Napoleonic Wars, woke Naples up with a start from its Baroque slumbers; local patriots gaily joined the French cause—even the monks of San Martino, who sewed tricolour flags for the new 'Parthenopean Republic, invited all the French officers up to the monastery for a banquet. In 1799, however, while Napoleon was off in Egypt, the advance through Italy by an Austro-Russian army, aided by Nelson's fleet, restored the status quo. This was often accompanied by bloody reprisals, as peasant mobs led by clerics, the 'Army of the Holy Faith' or *Sanfedisti*, marched across the south massacring liberals and French sympathizers.

In 1800, after Marengo, Napoleon returned, and crowned himself King of Italy; Joseph Bonaparte, and later Joachim Murat, ruled at Naples. For the second time, Admiral Nelson and his fleet had to remove the king and his family to Sicily for safety. Napoleonic rule lasted only until 1814, but in that time important public works were begun and laws, education and everything else reformed on the French model; immense church properties were expropriated, and medieval relics everywhere put to rest.

The 1815 Congress of Vienna put the clock back to 1798; indeed the Bourbons seemed to think they could pretend the Napoleonic upheavals had never happened, and the political reaction in their territories was fierce (from this time on, incidentally, the *Regno* was officially called the 'Kingdom of the Two Sicilies'). But the experience had given Italians a taste of the opportunities offered by the modern world, as well as a sense of national feeling that had been suppressed for centuries. Almost immediately, revolutionary agitators and secret societies like the famous *Carbonari* kept Italy convulsed in plots and intrigues. A big revolt in Naples forced King Ferdinand, now a bitter old reactionary after his experiences with the French, to grant a constitution (1821), but when Austrian troops came down to crush the rebels he took it back.

The next king, Ferdinand II (1830–59), gets a bad press; his subjects gave him the nickname *Re Bomba* (King Bomb) after his army shelled Messina during the next popular revolt, in 1848–9. On the credit side, Ferdinand exerted himself mightily to bring his kingdom into the modern world, building the first railroads, and laying the foundations for a modern industry and merchant fleet (he also built the Amalfi drive, a great feat of engineering). His autocratic, paternalistic rule was entirely out of step with the atmosphere of the Italian *Risorgimento*, however, and when the climactic events of national reunification took place in 1859–60, few were even left in Naples to support the Bourbon monarchy.

In 1860, when the entire north was in revolt, and ready to unite under the Piedmontese King Vittorio Emanuele, Giuseppe Garibaldi and his red-shirted 'Thousand' sailed from

Genoa to Sicily, electrifying Europe by repeatedly beating the Bourbon forces in a quick march across the island. The Thousand had become 20,000, and they soon crossed the straits and marched towards the capital, meeting little resistance. Garibaldi entered Naples on 7 September (on Ferdinand's new railroad), and though a few bitter-enders still held out in the Abruzzo, the Bourbon kingdom was finished.

1860–1944: in which the cure proves worse than the disease

The new Italy established a constitutional monarchy under Vittorio Emanuele, one in which the radical aspirations of Garibaldi and his followers were given little hearing. The new parliament almost immediately decomposed into cliques and political cartels representing various interests. Finances started in disorder and stayed that way, and corruption became widespread. There were other problems too. Naples's loss of capital status was a heavy blow to the city, both politically and culturally, and the new state's tariff policies, dictated by northern interests, caused a sharp decline first in the south's small industrial base, and then in its agriculture. So was the new Italy born with the 'problem of the south' as the biggest item on its agenda—and with a regime doing little or nothing about it.

In the disappointed south, agents of the displaced Bourbons and of the pope contributed to the continuing unrest, though conditions were such that most of the troubles began spontaneously. Through the 1860s over a hundred thousand troops were tied down pursuing the 'bandits' of the south. The guerrilla bands concentrated on killing landowners and officials of the new government, raiding town halls to burn the tax and property records; the army responded in kind, with the brutality of an occupying power, and the woes of the south found scant sympathy in the more developed regions of Italy. Ironically, southerners came to hold a disproportionate share of power and positions in the new regime. The *galantuomini*, the ignorant, parasitical class of local bosses and landlords, soon learned the possibilities offered them by Italy's limited democracy, and found it as easy to manipulate as the Bourbon kingdom had been. Their influence contributed much to Italy's political troubles in all the years since. Meanwhile, southerners were solving the problem in their own way, by packing their suitcases. Some two and a half million Italians emigrated for the Americas and elsewhere between 1880 and 1914, many of them from Naples and Campania.

For all the south's discontent, Fascism made very little headway in the region in the years after World War I. Mussolini choreographed his march on Rome in 1922, but even a year after that, his power in the south was negligible. The Fascist takeover here only occurred when it became clear that the Duce was dismantling the parliamentary state; Neapolitans realized that they were to have a new master, and adjusted accordingly. While the most powerful party, the Socialists, dithered and fiddled incomprehendingly, suddenly the local authorities began turning a blind eye to the terror tactics of the Fascist *squadri* (as their more willing northern counterparts had already been doing for three years). Fascist Party groups around Campania, usually bankrupt and squabbling among themselves, just as suddenly found themselves swamped with new members and contributions; when the dust settled everyone who was anyone was in the party, and Naples went on as before, run by the same faces only in new uniforms.

Mussolini did well by Naples, contributing plenty of public works, as elsewhere, and waging a constant and relatively successful war against the Camorra—a rival gang, after all, was the last thing the Fascists would tolerate. It isn't commonly realized how much the city suffered in '43 and '44. First came intensive Allied bombings, after the landings in Sicily; with the port area so close to the centre, many monuments were severely damaged, such as the church of Santa Chiara. After the Salerno landings, the successful short-cut that put the Allies on Naples' doorstep, the city surprised everyone, perhaps surprised itself, by staging a tremendous and entirely spontaneous popular revolt, the 'Four Days in Naples' that drove the Germans from the city. Before they left, though, the Germans had a chance to blow up the docks, the railroads, the water and electric supplies, and whatever else there was time for, like the Filangieri Museum.

1944–Present: once again, Naples illustrates its talent for making the present look very much like the past

Neapolitans found liberation a sad disappointment, a nightmare of destitution and corruption brilliantly chronicled in Norman Lewis's book *Naples '44*. The Allied government tried, but the problems of a city with no services and an economy in total collapse proved overwhelming. Cholera and malaria became widespread. Possibly a third of the female population was forced into prostitution to survive, and a third of all the supplies unloaded by the Allies in Naples disappeared, fuelling a gigantic black market in everything from flour to armoured vehicles. Robber bands appeared once more in the countryside, and the Camorra resurfaced and tightened its grip over Naples and its suburbs.

In the 1946 referendum that established the Italian Republic, the south was the only region that said no; in Naples, 80 per cent voted to keep the monarchy. Still, change came quickly in the postwar decades: a wave of building, most of it *abusivo* or illegal, on the hill-sides around the city, and new industry, like the Alfa-Sud plant and Bagnoli steel works, both financed by the government's southern reconstruction fund, the *Cassa per il Mezzogiorno*. Postwar politics were turbulent, and the era was dominated by 1950s mayor Achille Lauro, a shipping magnate who had been well-connected with the Fascists under Mussolini, though he opposed the war. When the Christian Democrats didn't meet his terms, he founded his own rightist-populist movement, *Uomo Qualunque* ('everyman'). Amidst the usual claims of graft, most of them justified, this eventually fizzled out, to be replaced by a close Christian Democrat–Camorra machine that ran the city until 1993 under 'modern bosses' such as Antonio Gava.

So far this history has said little about one of the most prominent features of life in this region, the disasters—there would have been little room for anything else. But we could mention the Black Death of 1347–8, the plague of 1529 that carried off 50,000, the plague of 1656 that took 200,000 more, a dozen or so volcanic eruptions and as many earthquakes, especially the terrible one of 1688 that wrecked much of Naples, or the severe cholera epidemics of 1884, 1944 and 1973; finally the earthquake of 1980, largely ignored in the press, that caused tremendous damage and suffering in rural Campania. More than anything else, these are the events that have made Naples and its region what they are. They help to explain the sombre, fatalistic side of the Neapolitan character, its philosophical seriousness—and the other side too, the frivolous, laugh-in-the-face-of-Vesuvius manner that animated the old Bourbon *Regno*, as well as the strong, often underestimated resilience of a city that has already recovered and rebuilt so many times.

Lately most of the catastrophes have been man-made: a deep, lasting recession, wide-spread political corruption, the vampirism of the Camorra and an ever-increasing degradation of public services. Currently, the new leftist city administration has to deal with an urban crisis of the first order: hospitals, public transport and sanitation in scandalous condition, reports of contamination in the city's water and municipally-run dairies, chronic traffic gridlock; the list runs depressingly on and on. In the hinterlands, refugees from the 1980 earthquake still live in public buildings and hotels; in Benevento you can still see ruins and bomb damage left from the war. With Italy in the midst of its torturous political revolution—they're already calling it the 'Second Republic'—it's anybody's guess as to what will happen.

Art and Architecture

Greek and Roman

With the arrival of the Greeks and Etruscans in the mid-8th century BC, Italy finally joined the wider Mediterranean world, artistically as well as politically. The wealthy cities of Magna Graecia imported classical Greek art and artists wholesale, and even though many of the cities themselves have disappeared, the Museo Archaeologico in Naples has a huge store of ceramics, architectural decoration, figurines and lovely terracotta ex-votos. Native Campanian artists also made endless copies of painted Greek ceramics, many of them excellent. For Greek architecture, there is the great Doric temple at Paestum (which also has an extremely rare Greek fresco in a tomb), and ruins at Cumae and Velia.

In Campania, as everyone knows, all the art and architecture of the Roman world is out on display, in Naples' museum and at the matchless sites of Pompeii and Herculaneum. There are plenty of other ruins of Roman buildings to see: at Pozzuoli, Baia, and other sites around the western bay, including some grandiose survivals of Roman engineering, such as the reservoirs and canals of the great naval base at Cape Misenum and the Fuorigrotta road tunnel, the longest ever built in antiquity, in Naples. What's left of the second and third largest amphitheatres of the Roman world can be seen at Capua and Pozzuoli; Capua also has a remarkable, well-preserved underground Mithraic temple.

Most of these spectacular works came in the confident, self-assured age of the Flavian and Antonine emperors (late 1st–2nd centuries), a time that also saw important progress in sculpture. Until then, Roman work had been closely bound to Hellenistic styles, or was expressed in outright copies of classical Greek sculpture. The new departure, a vivid, arresting style which some scholars have called 'impressionism' can be seen on the reliefs of Trajan's arch in Benevento.

Painting and mosaic work were both present from at least the 1st century BC, though Romans always considered them as little more than decoration, and only rarely entrusted to them any serious subjects. Both are a legacy from the Greeks, and both found their way to Rome by way of talented, half-Greek Campania. Painting, in the days of Caesar and Augustus, usually meant wall frescoes in the homes of the wealthy (*see* p.102), with large scenes of gardens in the form of window views, making small Roman rooms look brighter and bigger; also mythological scenes, paintings of battles and, occasionally, portraits (the best, courtesy of Vesuvius, are at Pompeii and Herculaneum, also in the museum of Naples and in the Mithraeum in Capua).

Mosaics, another import that had its greatest centre at Antioch, in Hellenized Syria, only became a significant medium in Italy as painting was declining. As with the other arts, mosaics were done better in cultured Campania. If Rome too, had been buried under volcanic lava, at whatever period, it is unlikely that much would be found to surpass the 2nd- and 1st-century paintings and mosaics discovered at Pompeii.

Middle Ages

So much from every age has been lost due to earthquakes and neglect, it is not surprising that even the most rudimentary structure from the Dark Ages is a rarity. Two churches that survived are the small 5th-century S. Maria Maggiore, near Nocera Inferiore, and the 8th-century Santa Sofia, at Benevento, both central-plan temples more in keeping with the contemporary architecture of Byzantium than of Rome. Naples' cathedral retains its 5th-century baptistry.

In the 10th–12th centuries, cultural revival was made possible by a number of factors: the trade and overseas contacts of Amalfi and Naples, not only creating wealth but bringing in influences from Byzantium and the Muslim world; the ascent of the Normans, bringing the blessings of political stability and a sophisticated court; and, artistically, the work of Abbot Desiderius at the great Abbey of Montecassino, between Naples and Rome, importing artists and architects from Constantinople, and helping to spread their advanced styles and techniques across the south—one good example being finely incised bronze church doors, a Greek speciality. Nearly a score of southern towns have them, beginning with the set made for Amalfi (1066). The fashion spread to many other cities, and it was not long before Italian artists were producing their own, notably those of Barisano da Trani at Ravello. Reintroducing art into southern Italy, in this age, was indeed largely a matter of importing styles and artists from Greece, and Byzantine art, so unfairly disparaged by the Renaissance, would continue to influence all of Italy, not only the south, until the fall of Constantinople. Byzantium's own medieval 'renaissance' shows up clearly in the exceptional 11th-century frescoes at S. Angelo in Formis in Capua.

Because of religious and cultural prejudices, the role of Muslim influence in Italian medieval art has never been satisfactorily examined. In Campania it is often obvious, in the interlaced arches of **Amalfi** cathedral, and the exotic patterned decoration in its façade, and in the churches of **Salerno** and **Caserta Vecchia**. Another southern speciality to which Muslim art probably contributed is the decoration of pavements, pulpits, paschal candlesticks and tombs with geometric patterns in chips of coloured stone or glass, an art that reached a plateau of excellence at Amalfi, Ravello, and Salerno, spreading to many other towns and reaching as far north as Tuscany; this exotically precise work became the prime inspiration for the Roman decorative style called Cosmatesque.

Romanesque architecture, so important in northern Italy and the rest of Europe, does not seem to have made much of an impression in Campania (unlike neighbouring Apulia, which has scores of Romanesque works that rank among the finest anywhere). Interiors were always much more important to the region's architects than the outside, and almost all of these were completely remodelled in the Baroque era or later. One of the most ambitious buildings of the early Middle Ages was Salerno cathedral, begun by Robert Guiscard in 1085, an idiosyncratic work that shows a faithfulness to early Christian fashions (like the exterior *quadroporticus*). Gothic churches are more common than elsewhere in Italy; the style was brought down by the French under the rule of Charles of Anjou after 1266 (San Domenico Maggiore in Naples is one of the best examples). Survivals of painting and sculpture are also sadly few. Giotto came down to Naples to work for Robert the Wise, and he painted a series of frescoes for the Castel dell'Ovo, now completely lost.

An Imported Renaissance

In the 15th and 16th centuries, while the rest of Italy was making a revolution in western art and culture, the south unfortunately was not often able to take part. With the relative economic backwardness of the southern cities, there was little opportunity for artistic advance. Northern artists, especially Tuscans, still came to Naples in the 1400s, but like the Gothic masons and sculptors of 200 years before they must have found themselves acting as cultural missionaries. They left some fine works behind, but for reasons that are difficult to see clearly they never seemed to make a strong impression on the southern sensibility (notable visitors at Naples include Donatello and Michelozzo, tomb in S. Angelo a Nilo; Antonio Rossellino, tombs at Monteoliveto; Giuliano da Maiano, the Capua Gate; almost all the important early Renaissance painters are represented at the Capodimonte museum).

There are a few exceptions, unexpected little candles in the prevailing gloom. Giovanni da Nola, a first-rate sculptor though little known, decorated many churches in Naples. That city also contributed some fine and original work, such as Romolo Balsimelli's Santa Caterina a Formiello. The most important Renaissance achievement in Naples was the Castel Nuovo (1454–67), and especially its triumphal arch. Built for Alfonso I, this was a Renaissance landmark, a mythological rendering of statesmanlike virtue entirely equal to the arches and columns of antiquity. Local talent, such as Tommaso Malvito's Cappella Carafa at the Duomo, tried to carry the trend onwards, but in Naples the ideals of the Renaissance would never really take hold.

Baroque and Neoclassicism

If the Baroque began in Rome, it soon found a warm welcome throughout the south. With its escapism, emotionalism and excess, the new style proved an inspiration to a troubled and long somnolent region, and the concentration of wealth in the hands of the court and the Church ensured a lavish patronage. In Naples, the greatest exponent of the Baroque was a brilliant, tortured soul named Cosimo Fanzago (1591–1678), sculptor, architect and decorative artist who designed the great cloister of San Martino, the *guglia* in Piazza San Domenico and a little masterpiece of a church, Santa Maria Egiziaca at Pizzofalcone (a *guglia* is a tall, elaborately decorated religious monument for a piazza, a Neapolitan speciality). Fanzago is known for his love of *pietra dura* work, exquisite floral patterns in brightly coloured marble inlay (as in S. Domenico Maggiore), an art from late-Renaissance Florence; it set the trend for the lush interiors of Neapolitan churches over the next century. Another Neapolitan worthy of mention is Ferdinando Sanfelice, a light-hearted pastry chef of churches (the Nunziatella) and palaces, famous for his fascinating, geometrically complex grand staircases (Palazzi Sanfelice, Bartolomeo di Maio, Serra di Cassano).

In sculpture, the best Neapolitan works are the most eccentric—the spectacular virtuosity of Francesco Queirolo, Antonio Corradini and Giuseppe Sammartino in the Sansevero Chapel; art historians always damn these to the lowest circles of the inferno, but you might enjoy them. Almost all the Neapolitan sculptors devoted much effort to figures for *presepi*—Christmas cribs; the San Martino museum has a delightful collection. In painting, Naples and the south began the Baroque era under the spell of Caravaggio, who arrived in Naples in 1607 (paintings at Capodimonte). Among his followers, adapting the dark and dramatic realism of the master to different ends, were the Spaniard José Ribera (San Martino) and the Calabrian Mattia Preti, one of the most talented of all southern artists, who did much of his best work for the Knights of Malta (also Capodimonte, and at S. Pietro a Maiella). Another important painter, at his best in unusual, highly original landscapes, was the native Neapolitan Salvator Rosa (1615–73).

Later Neapolitan painting, frivolous and colourful, with little to challenge the intellect or the imagination, was just right for the times and enjoyed a widespread influence. Luca Giordano, the mercurial and speedy 'Luca fa presto'(1634–1705), painted all over Italy, spent ten years at the court in Madrid, and still found time to cover acres of Neapolitan ceilings with clouds and *putti*, tumbling horses and pastel-robed floating maidens (as at the Duomo and San Martino). His greatest follower, in his time perhaps the most popular painter in Italy, was Francesco Solimena (1657–1747; S. Paolo Maggiore, Gesù Nuovo).

A more modern, sober turn in Neapolitan art came with the reforming King Charles III, in 1750. That year saw the death of Fernando Sanfelice, and the arrival of two architects from the north who brought the neoclassical manner to Naples. Ferdinando Fuga was for a time court architect to the Bourbons (his work includes the *Albergo dei Poveri* on Via Foria, the biggest and fanciest poorhouse in the world). The 18th century, though, belonged to Luigi Vanvitelli (1700—73), son of the Italianized Dutch painter Gaspar van Wittel and favourite architect of King Charles, the most assiduous builder among the Bourbon kings. Most of Vanvitelli's energies were expended on the huge Royal Palace at Caserta, fully in line with the international neoclassicism of the time with its tastefully unimaginative façades, grand stairways and axis-planned gardens. Neoclassicism in Naples, a surprising reaction against the city's longstanding love affair with the Baroque and the bizarre, dominated the 1700s and indeed the remainder of the Bourbon period, as seen in such buildings as the Capodimonte palace and the San Carlo opera house (both by G. A. Medrano, in the 1730s) and the grandiose domed San Francesco di Paola (1817).

Topics

Some people like it straight, a short sharp shot of rich dark liquid, usually downed in one gulp while standing at the bar. Others temper their favourite brew with a dash of hot milk—a caffè macchiato, literally, a stained coffee. In Italy, there are almost as many ways of taking a caffè as there are of eating pasta, and Naples is generally regarded as the capital of the country's coffee culture.

There is also the latte macchiato—a long glass of hot milk with a dash of milk to give it colour and flavour, a wimp's drink by macho Neapolitan standards. The cappuccino, an espresso coffee topped with steam-whipped milk, is known to all, but it can be ordered in a myriad number of ways, con schiuma (with froth), senza schiuma (without froth), freddo, tiepido or bollente (cold, warm or piping hot). It may be scuro or chiaro, depending on the amount of milk desired. And it will always be restricted to the first coffee of the day. The foreign tourists' habit of ordering a milky cappuccino after lunch or dinner is enough to make any Neapolitan stomach heave.

In Naples, more than anywhere else, the all-important act of going out to the bar for a fix of caffeine is a ritual that is repeated every few hours. For Neapolitans, coffee is a sacred thing, its preparation an art form. At the best bars in town, barmen in starched white jackets with gleaming brass buttons serve the dark syrupy brew with a glass of water, to prepare the palate for the treat in store. In Naples your coffee will usually be served already sugared. If you want it without, you must ask the barman for a caffè amaro.

Every Neapolitan has his favourite bar—and his favourite barman—but the 150-year-old Caffè Gambrinus on Piazza Trieste e Trento is widely recognised as the most venerable temple of them all. Also favoured are the Verdi in Via Verdi, the Caflish, in Via Toledo, and La Caffettiera in Piazza dei Martiri, a popular spot with well-dressed Neapolitan ladies after a busy morning's shopping.

On summer evenings, outside the bars along the seafront at Mergellina, you'll see Neapolitans indulging in the ultimate bliss, a cup of coffee served to them in the comfort of their own car, on trays which slot conveniently over the window of the driver's seat.

As any Neapolitan barman worth his salt will tell you, the perfect espresso is made with a blend of arabica coffees, with water passed through at a temperature of 90° C, for precisely 30 seconds. Connoisseurs can tell whether the coffee will be good or not before they even taste it. The foam is the give-away. It should be a uniform light brown colour, dappled with darker brown. Very dark brown or greyish foam is a clear warning sign that the barman is an amateur, or the coffee second rate. Most self-respecting Neapolitans would rather leave such a brew untouched on the counter and head for another bar. A bad cup of coffee can cast a blight over the entire day.

If they had had postcards back in the Roman Empire, your Aunt Vulpecula would certainly have sent you one from Campania—*Having a Wonderful Time in Baiae on the Sinus Puteolanus*. The photo on the front would show gaily painted pleasure-boats in the bay, with silken canopies and slaves waving golden fans over the languorous occupants; in the background would be a row of delicious villas, each with two or three levels of gleaming marble porticos perched on the cliffs over the blue Tyrrhenian. This playground of the Roman world is the place where holidays as we know them were probably invented. The young world had never seen anything like it. Everyone in the Empire, from Londinium to Baalbek, had heard of the bay and its prodigies of beauty and luxury; no doubt everyone dreamed of actually going there.

The first mention of a villa on the bay comes from the early 2nd century AD. The Roman state, which had seized all the land in the area after conquering it, was now selling it off to help finance the Second Punic War, the bloody and expensive struggle against Hannibal and the Carthaginians. One of the first buyers was Scipio Africanus, the general who brought that war to a successful conclusion, and became the richest man in Rome in the process. He built himself a villa near Liternum, overlooking the sea, and other members of the Roman elite soon followed. In the two centuries that followed, as Rome spread its rule over the Mediterranean world and the booty rolled in, the dour senators and knights found something they had never had before—*otium*, or leisure. Thanks to contact with the cultured Greek world, in Campania and in Greece itself, Rome was growing up, even becoming a tiny bit civilized in its awkward and bumptious way.

If they hadn't yet acquired many of the accomplishments of culture, at least the Romans knew how to tack up a good façade: the villas housed copies of Greek statues, frescoes, Greek cooks, poets and musicians. The nabobs affected Greek dress, the elegant *chlamys* worn by the locals, instead of their impractical togas. Some of them even learned the language, and impressed their friends at dinner parties by extemporizing a few lines of verse. In the 1st century BC, everyone who was anyone in Rome had a villa, and the Campanian coast entered its golden age of opulence. The populist dictator Marius had one, and the reactionary dictator Sulla who followed him built an even bigger model, which he shared with his family, a few hundred of his picked slaves, kept ladies, whichever of his clients and hangers-on were lucky enough to be invited, and plenty of entertainment: among others, 'Roscius the comedian, Sorex the mime, and Metrobius the female impersonator', as a historian of the time solemnly recorded it. Julius Caesar owned a few villas, and his murderers plotted the deed at Cinna's place just up the coast.

These famous names of history, and the clique of politicians and speculators that went with them, had serious money; when Rome conquered the world a select few raked in the lion's share of the loot, amassing fortunes that make the greatest private hoards of our day seem pocket change in comparison. The honest Cicero often wrote disapprovingly of his fellows' ostentatious displays of wealth—but he had three villas on the bay himself, and a string of lodges all the way to Rome so he would always have some where cosy to sleep as he travelled back and forth; we can imagine how the folks in the fast lane must have been carrying on.

The holiday trip was called the *peregrinatio*, and everyone would come down in mid-April. In the heat of summer they would go back to Rome if there was money to be made or intrigues to be hatched, or else retire to a cooler villa up in the mountains. Most would be back on the bay in autumn, and stay as long as there was blessed *otium* left to enjoy. In whatever season, amusements were never lacking. There were the famous baths of Baiae, the most sumptuous such establishment in the ancient world, and above all the dinner parties, which would fill up nearly every evening. For the afternoon, lazy cruises on the bay were in favour, or rides in slave-born litters to Puteoli or Neapolis or the countryside. In Caesar's time pet fish were a craze among the bay set—bearded mullets decorated with jewels, trained to leap up and eat out of their masters' hands. Humbler citizens must have been as fascinated with the doings of the rich as they are today, and even if they had no patron to invite them to stay over, they must have come in great numbers to gawk and dream.

The bay, having invented holidays, can also probably take credit for the first secular souvenirs. Archaeologists have dug up plenty of examples: small items of Puteoli's famous glassware decorated with hand-painted scenes of the coastline and its villas. Almost incredibly, contemporaries describe the entire bay, from Misenum to Sorrentum, as being solidly lined with these palaces, giving the impression of a single, tremendous marble city. It must have been the grandest sight of the classical world, and it isn't certain that our own time has anything to match it.

The bay remained in fashion well into the Imperial age. Augustus bought Capri from the city of Neapolis, and covered it with pavilions and terraced gardens; his house was decorated with whale bones and other marvels of the sea, and with relics of classical heroes. All the other early emperors spent much of their time there, notably Tiberius (*see* p.115). Some of the glamour wore off in greyer times, under Vespasian and after, when the wealth and glory of the emperors shamed everyone else's into the shade; later emperors would build their own pleasure palaces in places closer to the necessities of power or military leadership; some of these were huge cities in themselves, such as Trajan's, near Tivoli, or Diocletian's, which survives today as the city of Split, Croatia.

By the late 5th century, there were no more pleasure boats in the bay—only prowling Vandal pirate craft from Africa. The last mention of any of the villas in antiquity was when Romulus Augustulus, the last pathetic emperor of the west, was sent off to live under close guard in the Villa of Lucullus (now Naples' Castel dell'Ovo) by his Gothic conqueror, Odoacer. Many of the villas must have been destroyed in this era; earthquakes, Vesuvius, time and stone quarriers have done for the rest. So often, in and around Naples, the most affecting and unforgettable sights are the ones no longer present. Constant reminders of the impermanence of all our glories may be a major contributor to the melancholy many visitors to Naples have always felt. But there's no need to be melancholy; the Neapolitans, true heirs of antiquity, hardly ever are. Or as Martial put it, gazing at Caesar's tomb through the window of his Roman flat :

> The great dead themselves, with jovial breath,
> Bid us be merry, and remember death.

The *Civitas Hippocratica*

As the industrial world struggles with its problems of health care—costs, ethical issues and disconcerting technology—it is refreshing to go back a thousand years to Salerno, where the first medical school of modern Europe was founded in the 11th century. Founded by the legendary 'Four Doctors'—an Italian, a Greek, a Jew and an Arab—it was for centuries the finest in Europe, the *Fons Medicinae* as Petrarch called it. Its doctors and teachers played an important role in the transmission of Greek and Arab science into Europe. Before the teachings of Salerno became widespread in Europe, what succour existed lay in the hands of monks and priests, who often blamed any illness on divine wrath. Salerno's school marked a definite improvement, by going back to Hippocrates and seeking natural causes. The school also marked the beginnings of medicine as a commercial enterprise, giving its students sound advice on collecting bills: 'When the patient is nearly well, address the head of the family, or the sick man's nearest relative, thus God Almighty having deigned by our aid to restore him whom you asked us to visit, we pray that He will maintain his health, and that you will now give us an honourable dismissal. Should any other member of your family desire our aid, we should, in grateful remembrance of our former dealings with you, leave all else and hurry to serve him.' At the same time, a natural sliding fee was the order of the day; a king was expected to pay a hundred times more for his cure than a small merchant.

Much of Salerno's teaching was based on numerology and astrology, following the science of the time, but there was a more practical side too. Medieval doctors sought to maintain a balance between the four humours of the body: phlegm (cold and moist), blood (hot and moist), bile (hot and dry) and black bile (cold and dry)—a poetic, metaphorical way of looking at things, but one that experience found instructive for centuries. To judge the soundness of this approach, consider the Health Rule of Salerno. Famous throughout the Middle Ages, the Rule was compiled by a certain Robert of Normandy, who was wounded during the First Crusade and convalesced in the city. Originally in Latin verse, its recommendations were translated into English by an Elizabethan, Sir John Harington:

> A king that cannot rule him his diet
> Will hardly rule his realm in peace and quiet.

> For healthy men may cheese be wholesome food,
> But for the weak and sickly 'tis not good.

> Use three doctors still, first Dr Quiet,
> Next Dr Merry-man and Dr Diet...

Wine, Women, Baths, by art of nature warme,
Us'd or abus'd do men much good or harme.
Some live to drinke new wine not fully fin'd.
But for your health we wish that you drink none,
For such to dangerous fluxes are inclin'd,
Besides the lees of wine doe breed the stone.
But such by our consent shall drink alone.
For water and small biere we make no question
Are enemies to health and good digestion;
And Horace in a verse of his rehearses,
That water-drinkers never make good verses.

Oil for the Madonna

Sotto questo cielo non nascono sciocchi
(Under these skies no fools are born)

Neapolitan proverb

Camorra means a short jacket, of the kind the street toughs of Naples used to wear in the days of the Bourbon kings. But as with Sicily's Mafia, the origin of the Neapolitan Camorra is lost in legend. Some accounts put it in the slums of the *Quartiere Spagnuole*, under the rule of the Spanish viceroys of the 16th century. Spanish soldiers of that time lived the life of picaresque novels—or at least tried to—and the fathers and brothers of the district did their best to defend their girls from such picaresqueness, which usually meant a knife in the back in some dark alley.

There may be some truth to that, or it could all be romantic bosh. Criminals in southern Italy seem to always have been well-organized, with a hierarchy, initiations, a set of rules, and a code of *omertà*. Foreign visitors to the city in the 1700s wrote that when something was stolen, they were able to get in touch with the 'King of Thieves' who would magically get it restored—stealing from guests, after all was a discourtesy. It's doubtful they were ever so polite to their fellow citizens, for as long as there has been a Camorra it has lived mainly by extortion, with a fat finger in whatever rackets of the age looked most profitable. For a long time, the gang's biggest takings came from the prisons, which they controlled. In the old days, prisoners in Naples, as anywhere else, had to pay for their upkeep, and each new arrival would be met by the Camorristi with a subtle request for 'money for oil for the Madonna': that is, to keep the light burning at the shrine in the Camorra's favoured church, the Madonna del Carmine in the Piazza del Mercato; you can imagine that the Madonna required a lot of fuel.

Relations between the Camorra and the authorities have always been rather complex. In the last days of the *Regno*, Ferdinand II made use of them as a kind of anti-liberal secret police. In 1860, it was claimed that Garibaldi had to make a deal with them, handing over control of the city government in return for nobody shooting at him and his army when they entered the city. The new Italian state, run by northerners, could not see the logic in this, and tried to wipe out the Camorra by vigorous police action. The mob trumped that ploy easily by going into politics, setting the pattern of close alliance between organized crime and centre-rightist parties that continues in Italy to this day. In a typical irony of parliamentary democracy, the titled gentry of the ruling class and the thugs found that their interests coincided perfectly, and by 1900 the theory and practice of southern machine politics had been refined to an art. As people used to say: 'the government candidate always wins'. In another place that might seem a cliché; in Naples it was a proverb, a piece of the deepest folk wisdom.

Like the Mafia in Sicily, the Camorra took some hard knocks under Mussolini. If there was any cream to be skimmed, the Fascists wanted it all for themselves, and the ambience of the dictatorship proved wonderfully convenient for getting around the legal niceties of arrest and conviction. And like the Mafia, the Camorra was able to easily manipulate the Allied Military Government after 1944 to get back on its feet. Perhaps the Americans were sincerely convinced that the mobsters would be a useful ally in an impossible situation, or maybe they had got a message that a little cooperation would save their army a lot of trouble (accidents can happen...). In any case it seems always to have been Allied policy on the Italian front to throw open the prisons in every town they captured.

In 1944, top American mobster Lucky Luciano went to Sicily to arrange things. He was swindled royally by his supposed brothers; there has always been less of a connection between the native and foreign Mafias than one might suppose. One of his New York lieutenants, Vito Genovese, was from around Naples; he went back there, and had better luck than Lucky, insinuating his way into the confidences of the Allied High Command. From the old Camorra stronghold of the 'Triangle of Death', in the villages north of the city, and from the *bancarelle* of the Forcella market, Genovese oversaw an incredible orgy of black market wheeling and dealing, largely over stolen army supplies, while the old Camorra hands revived the hallowed traditions of extortion.

Today, it is estimated that 60 per cent of all businesses in the Naples area pay protection money to the Camorra. The gang takes its cut from most sorts of common crime, and like the Mafia has become heavily involved in drugs—not so much exporting them as pushing them on their neighbours. If the old Camorra ever knew any bounds or limits, or had any sense of decency, the current model has forgotten it; even the youngest children are forced and tricked into crime. Unlike the Mafia, the Camorra has no recognized central authority; factions settle their differences with reciprocal assassinations, spectacles conducted out in the streets of the old quarters where all may enjoy them. The politicians in league with the Camorra have robbed and cheated Naples of fantastic amounts, enough to make the difference between the modern European metropolis it could be and the decomposing live body it is.

As late as 1992, your newspapers and Italy's newspapers managed to cover events in the south without ever daring to mention the obvious fact that government and organized crime were one and the same; it wasn't 'proved', and so even the most discreet insinuation might have been risky. Today, when Italy is in the midst of a revolution, things aren't so clear. The Camorra and the Mafia are undergoing a possibly serious crisis, thanks to the determined efforts of a few incorruptible policemen, prosecutors and judges. They are trying to make their arrangements with the new powers that be, wherever they can; meanwhile we all may wonder, as the Italians do, just what our newspapers aren't telling us now.

The New Science

> It is the driest, obscurest, metaphysicalest book I ever got hold
> of. Confucius is a more lucid writer. Mortgages and remainders
> are pleasanter to peruse.

John Fiske, a Harvard scholar (1858)

Probably only a Neapolitan, living in the shadow of Vesuvius, could have written *La Nuova Scienza*, and Giambattista Vico was a true son of the city. Born in a little room over his father's bookshop on Via San Biagio dei Librai, he spent most of his life among the mouldering alleys of the *Spacca* and the University. Vico tells his very Neapolitan story in his *Autobiography*, a classic of unintentional hilarity. The fun starts on the first page; after getting his own birth date wrong by two years, Vico continues (writing in the third person):

> He was a boy of high spirits and impatient of rest, but at the age
> of seven he fell head first from the top of a ladder to the floor
> below, and remained a good five hours without conscious-
> ness....The surgeon, indeed, observing the broken cranium and
> considering the period of unconsciousness, predicted that he
> would either die of it or grow up an idiot. However by God's
> grace neither part of his prediction came true, but as a result of
> this mischance he grew up with a melancholy and irritable
> temperament, such as belongs to men of ingenuity and depth,
> who thanks to the one, are quick as lightning in perception, and
> thanks to the other, take no pleasure in verbal cleverness or false-
> hood.

The rest of the autobiography is pretty much in the same tone, with lofty, pompous phrasings, befitting a man who held the chair of rhetoric at Naples University, and with a prickly defensiveness that came from a lifetime of being ignored or laughed at by his colleagues and nearly everyone else. Teaching rhetoric earned Vico a measly hundred ducats a year, and to get by he had to squander his talent writing fulsome eulogies and panegyrics for the king and the grandees of Naples. All the while, the poor philosopher was spending much of his time feeding and caring for his flock of children, a job his horrible, illiterate wife didn't much care for. A turning point in Vico's life came at the age of 55, when he tried to secure appointment to the much better-paying chair of law. For the occasion, he composed a brilliant treatise on the philosophical basis of law, and delivered it to the assembly blissfully unaware that almost all his fellows had been bribed to support one of the other candidates. The winner, best known as 'a notorious seducer of servant girls', eventually tried to publish a book and was found out as a plagiarist. The disgusted Vico gave up trying to get ahead, and devoted the rest of his life to his great work, the *New Science*. To get it printed, in 1726, he had to sell his diamond ring, and even then he could only afford to do it in type so small it could barely be read.

Nevertheless, the work brought him some fame and respect in his last years, and the position of Official Historiographer to the King. Vico died in 1744; at the funeral, a quarrel broke out between his fellow professors and his religious confraternity over who would carry the coffin to the church; somehow this degenerated into a general neighbourhood brawl, and Vico was abandoned in the middle of Via dei Tribunali. Finally someone carted him off to the Girolamini Church, and fifty years later his last surviving son got around to putting up a marker on the tomb, where it can be seen today.

As James Joyce put it (writing of Finnegan, and maybe Vico): 'A good clap, a fore marriage, a bad wake, tell hell's well'. But Vico has had the last laugh. In our troubled times, when the airy certainties of Voltaire and Locke begin to look a bit superficial, Vico may well be the only thinker of the 18th century still worth a serious reading; his strange and utterly subversive book has increased its renown and influence with every generation since his death. Vico called the *New Science* an essay on the 'principles of Humanity'; his system is expressed in the language of myth, partly from Vico's own imaginative turn of mind, and possibly also from a desire to not arouse the Inquisition, still in business in 18th-century Naples. Vico has been called an 'Orphic voice', an oracle. He explains the development of language, for example, as beginning in a 'mute speech' of gestures and signs, a 'divine poetry'. The next stage is symbols—heraldic arms; only then comes conventional speech. After a spin through the Wonderland of the *New Science*, this begins to make sense. The major theme of the book is an exploration of the origins of culture and society, and the circular 'course the nations run' through four stages: first a theocratic age, founded by giants out of barbarism; next comes the age of heroes, an aristocratic society, and then 'human' government, where equality is recognized, though this inevitably declines into monarchy (like Augustus's Rome). At last, man's egotism causes disintegration and fall, and the stage is cleared for the whole cycle to start afresh.

Scholars today emphasize Vico's contributions to social thinking—somewhat primitive ones, in their view—and he has been called the 'first political scientist'. They do not get the point. James Joyce did, and he turned the *New Science* inside out and tickled and teased it to make an even stranger book: *Finnegans Wake*. As Norman O. Brown put it, 'Joyce wore his eyes out staring at Europe and seeing nothing'. Western civilization, for him, was over, simply biding time until the barbarians come (who could argue?), and he arranged his murky masterpiece in four parts, following Vico's four stages of history. Joyce's 'farced epistol to the hibruws' is just that—a farce, appropriate to our time of disarray, something to instruct and entertain us while we all wait for the Word, the divine thunderclap of Jove to sound and start civilization, by ' a commodious vicus of recirculation', back on its circle again. Why not take Joyce and Vico along on your trip? (along with *A Skeleton Key to Finnegans Wake* by Joseph Campbell and H. M. Robinson)—a little light reading for the beach, a beach with a view of Vesuvius on the horizon.

Naples

Porto di Napoli

> *The most loathsome nest of human caterpillars I was ever forced to stay in—a hell with all the devils imbecile in it.*
>
> John Ruskin

> *...it reveals itself only to the* simpatici.
>
> Peter Gunn

For many, Naples is the true homeland of a particular Italian fantasy, the last bastion of singing waiters and red checked tablecloths, operatic passion and colourful poverty, balanced precariously between Love's own coastline and the menace of Vesuvius. But mention Naples or the Neapolitans to any modern, respectable north Italian, and as they gesticulate and roll their eyes to heaven you will get a first-hand lesson in the dynamics of Italy's 'Problem of the South'. Many Italians simply cannot accept that such an outlandish place can be in the same country with them, a sentiment that probably contains as much envy as contempt. Naples, the city that has given the world Enrico Caruso, Sophia Loren, pizza, and syphilis (the disease appeared here in 1495, and was immediately blamed on the French garrison) may also be the first city to make social disorder into an art form.

Degradation, Italian Style

On Naples' Piazza Garibaldi you can buy a boiled pigs' organ on a stick, served with a slice of lemon, and watch eight-year-old *scugnizzi*—street children—puff on contraband Marlboros while casually tossing firecrackers into traffic. Fireworks, along with slamming doors, impromptu arias, screams, ambulance sirens and howling cats, are an essential part of the Neapolitan ambience. This anarchic symphony is harder to catch these days, unfortunately, drowned as it is under the roar of Italy's worst traffic problem. In central Naples, three-quarters of a million rude drivers chase each other around a street plan that hasn't changed much since Roman times. Meanwhile, the nation's worst air pollution keeps the hospitals full, in spite of occasional half-hearted attempts to solve the problem by only allowing drivers to take their cars out on alternate days, and every few weeks some old lady on a back street burns to a crisp while the firemen, just down th e block, gamely push illegally parked cars out of their way.

Another chronic problem is housing, enough of a nightmare even before the earthquake of 1980; on the outskirts of the city, you may see Napoletani living in stolen ship cargo containers, with windows cut in the sides, in shacks made of sheet metal and old doors, or in abandoned buses. In the city centre, thousands of earthquake refugees are still camping in hotels. One bizarre side-effect of this housing shortage—found all over Italy, but particularly visible here—is the 'quivering car' phenomenon. You'll see them everywhere, especially up on Posillipo hill, cars parked nose to tail, their windows blacked out with newspaper, turned into temporary bedrooms by courting couples or even married couples who have no privacy at home. A cruel but popular prank with Neapolitan kids is to sneak up on the cars and set fire to the newspaper.

No hope for reform seems yet in sight. Even if Naples' notorious city government should some day miraculously turn competent and honest, it would still first have to deal with the spectre of the *Camorra*, a loose term for the crime syndicates that keep Naples as securely strung up as any mountain village in Sicily. Crime is so well organized here, to give one example, that seagoing smugglers have formed a trade union to protect their interests against the police.

In the 18th century, when the city and its spectacular setting were a highlight of the Grand Tour, the saying was 'See Naples and die. . . '. Nowadays you usually can't see much of anything through the smog, and you'll probably survive if you're careful crossing streets. Don't let Naples' current degradation spoil your visit, though; you haven't seen Italy—no, you haven't seen the Mediterranean—until you have spent some time in this fascinating metropolis. The only thing subtle about Naples is its charm, and the city will probably win your heart at the same time as it is deranging your senses.

On the Other Hand...

If Naples immediately repels you, however, it means you are probably a sticky sort, and will miss all the fun. The city has an incomparable setting, and much of it is still admittedly beautiful, but its real attraction is a priceless insight into humanity, at the hands of a population of 2.2 million dangerous anarchists. The Napoletani may be numbered among the few peoples of Europe who realize they are alive, and try to enjoy it as best they can. Their history being what it is, this manifests itself in diverse ways. The Napoletani do not stand in lines, or fill out forms, or stop for traffic signals; they will talk your ears off, run you over in their ancient Fiats, criticize the way you dress, whisper alarming propositions, give you sweets, try to pick your pockets with engaging artlessness, offer surprising kindnesses, and with a reassuring smile they will always, always give you the wrong directions. In an official capacity, they will either break the rules for you or invent new ones; in shops and restaurants, they will either charge you too much or too little. The former is much more common, though, whichever it is, they will do it with a flourish.

If the accounts of long-ago travellers are to be believed, Naples has always been like this. Too much sunshine, and living under such a large and ill-mannered volcano, must contribute much to the effect. It would be somewhat harder to explain some of Naples' ancient distinctions. First and foremost, Naples is Italy's city of philosophers. Her greatest, Giambattista Vico, was a Neapolitan, and others, such as St Thomas Aquinas and Benedetto Croce, spent much of their time here. Naples can also claim to be first in music.

Among native composers are Gesualdo, Scarlatti, and Leoncavallo, and the conservatory is claimed to be the oldest in Europe. Even today, members of the opera company at San Carlo look down on their colleagues at Milan's La Scala as a band of promising upstarts who could stand to take their jobs a little more seriously. Neapolitan popular song, expressive and intense, is an unchained Italian stereotype; the Napoletani maintain its traditions as jealously as they do their impenetrable dialect, one of the most widely-spoken and robust in modern Italy.

History

Naples' rise to become the metropolis of Campania was largely the result of the lucky elimination of her rivals over the centuries. Capua, Cumae, and Benevento rose and fell, and Pompeii and Herculaneum disappeared under volcanic ash, but fortune has always seemed to protect Naples from the really big disasters. As a Greek colony founded by Cumae in 750 BC, the city began with the name Neapolis, and prospered moderately throughout the periods of Greek, Samnite, and Roman rule. Belisarius, Justinian's famous general, seized the region for Byzantium in 536, after invasions of the Goths and Vandals, but a Duke of Naples declared the city independent in 763, acknowledging only the authority of the pope.

The chronicles are understandably slim for this period; early medieval Naples offers us more fairy-tales than facts. Many of its early legends deal with none other than the poet Virgil; somehow, folklore in the dark ages had transformed the greatest Latin poet into Master Virgil, a mighty magician who was given credit for many of the unexplainable engineering feats of the ancient Romans. Naples claimed him for its founder, and its legends told of how he built the Castel dell'Ovo, balancing it on an egg at the bottom of the harbour. Master Virgil also built a talking statue that warned the city of enemies, earthquakes, or plagues, and medieval chroniclers mention the bronze horses and bronze fly he built over two of the city's gates, still to be seen in those days, and said to be magical charms on which the fortune of the city depended.

Naples lost its independence to the Normans in 1139, later passing under the rule of the Hohenstaufen emperors along with the rest of southern Italy. Charles of Anjou took over in 1266, and lopped off the head of the last Hohenstaufen, Conradin, in what is now Naples' Piazza del Mercato. Under the Angevins, Naples for the first time assumed the status and architectural embellishments of a capital. The Angevin Kings of Naples, however, did little to develop their new realm, expending most of their energy in futile attempts to recapture Sicily, lost to them after the Sicilian Vespers revolution of 1282. After their line expired in 1435 with the death of Giovanni II, the kingdom fell to Alfonso V of Aragon—a fateful event, marking Spain's first foothold on the Italian mainland.

Habsburgs and Bourbons

Aragonese rule seemed promising at first, under the enlightened Alfonso. In later decades, though, it became clear that the Spaniards were mainly interested in milking Italy for taxes with which to finance further conquests. The city itself, as the seat of the viceregal court, prospered greatly; by 1600 its population of 280,000 made it perhaps the largest city on the Mediterranean. The long period of Spanish control did much to give Naples its distinct character, especially during the 17th and 18th centuries, when the city participated almost joyfully in the decadence and decay of the Spanish Empire. This period saw the construction of the scores of frilly, gloomy Baroque churches—now half-abandoned, with bushes growing out of the cornices—that add so much to the Neapolitan scene. In manners especially, the Imperial Spanish influence was felt; 'Nothing', in the words of one observer, 'is cheaper here than human life'.

In 1707, during the War of the Spanish Succession, Naples passed under the rule of Archduke Charles of Austria. Prince Charles of Bourbon, however, snatched it away from him in 1734, and mouldering, picturesque Naples for the next century and a half made the perfect backdrop for the rococo shenanigans of the new Bourbon kingdom. The new rulers were little improvement over the Spaniards, but immigrants from all over the South poured into the city, chasing the thousands of ducats dropped by a free-spending court. Naples became the most densely populated city in Europe, a distinction it still holds today, and crime and epidemics became widespread.

Nevertheless, this was the Naples that became a major attraction for thousands of northern aesthetes doing the Grand Tour in the 18th and 19th centuries. Goethe flirted with contessas here, while the English poets were flirting with dread diseases and Lord Nelson was making eyes at Lady Hamilton. The Neapolitans are frank about it; Naples owed its prominence on the Grand Tour less to Vesuvius and the ruins of Pompeii than to good old-fashioned sex. Naples at the time was incontestably the easiest place in Europe to find some, and everyone knew it—saving Goethe and the rest the trouble of ever mentioning the subject in their travel accounts and letters home.

Garibaldi's army entered Naples in February, 1861. As the new Italy's biggest basket case, the city has since received considerable assistance with its planning and social problems—though not nearly enough to make up for the centuries of neglect. World War II didn't help; for four days in late September 1944, the city staged a heroic though unsuccessful revolt against the Germans. Even more damage was done by Allied bombing, and the destruction of the city's port and utilities by the retreating Nazis.

While the post-War period saw considerable rebuilding, it also brought new calamities. Illegal and speculative building projects grabbed most of the already crowded city's open space (you'll notice the almost total absence of parks), and turned the fringe areas and much of the once-beautiful Bay of Naples shore into a nightmare of human detritus, one of the eeriest industrial wastelands of Europe. At the moment, there seems to be a common realization that Naples has reached a point of no return, and it will soon have either to clean itself up or perish; discussions of the city's problems in the press are often conducted in alarmingly apocalyptic tones. Leave some room for exaggeration—the Napoletani probably couldn't enjoy life properly without a permanent state of crisis.

In the political turmoil that has taken over Italy since the beginning of the nineties, with the collapse of the old parties, Naples has become one of the major bases of support for the neo-Fascist MSI party, in yet another twist to the city's history. It has, though, marked up one genuine accomplishment in the books in the last few years, though not one that will have much effect on the most serious problems—the *Centro Direzionale*, a huge modernistic development built over the wastelands around Corso Malta, north of the Central Station. In spite of a few hiccups, most notably when the new palace of justice was mysteriously burnt to the ground (no prizes for guessing by whom), the project is currently nearing completion, its aim being to provide a new centre for the regional economy.

Getting There

by air

Naples' **Capodichino airport** is on the north side of the city, relatively close to the centre. It has frequent direct services to and from all major Italian destinations and to many foreign cities, including London (several flights daily). For airport information, call © 7092815. From 6am to midnight there is a half-hourly bus service (city bus no. 14), between the airport and the Stazione Centrale in central Naples. The journey takes 20–45min, depending on the time of day. As on all city buses, tickets should be bought at a news-stand or ticket booth before boarding.

If you opt for a taxi, remember that on top of the fare on the meter you will offi- cially be charged extra supplements for the airport trip and for luggage—plus, very possibly, additional unexplained 'extras' as well (see below). If in doubt, ask to see the list of prices, which should be displayed in the cab, or try to agree on the fare to your destination before getting into the cab. If traffic is not too heavy—and this is a big if—the fare to the centre should not exceed L40,000.

by sea

Naples' port has more ship and hydrofoil connections than anywhere else in the Mediterranean, so you can choose to arrive by sea from—or flee to—a wide variety of places, among them the islands in the Bay of Naples, Sicily, Sardinia, Reggio Calabria, the Aeolian Islands or points further afield such as Corsica or Malta. Generally, ferries are cheaper than hydrofoils, but take approximately twice as long. One of the loveliest of the possible sea excursions is the night ferry to the Aeolian Islands, which arrives as the sun is rising over Vulcano.

Ferries and hydrofoils leave from three different points in Naples, but most longer- distance ferries operate from the **Stazione Marittima**, in the centre of the port near the Castel Nuovo. Consult the individual companies for timetables, or look in the daily newspaper *Il Mattino*. The main companies operating from the Stazione Marittima are **Tirrenia**, © 7613688, for Palermo, Cagliari, Reggio Calabria and Malta; **Siremar**, © 7613688, for the Aeolian Islands; and **Lauro**, © 5513352, for Corsica. In addition, one company, **SNAV**, © 7612348, operates a long-distance hydrofoil service from Mergellina quay to the Aeolian Islands.

For more information on all boat services from Naples and hydrofoil services to the islands and ports around the bay, *see* pp.8 and 110.

Most visitors arrive by train, at the modern **Stazione Centrale** (for information, call ✆ 5534188), on Piazza Garibaldi, which is convenient since this is also a junction for city buses and the local *Circumvesuviana* railway. Trains along the coast towards Rome or Reggio Calabria pass through every half hour on average. In addition, many trains also stop at **Napoli Mergellina** and **Napoli Campi Flegrei**, on the western side of the city, and at some other local stations. There are also good rail connections from Naples to Palermo (4–8 hours, depending on the train) via Messina.

As well as the state FS lines, there are three local railway lines serving the Bay of Naples area. One, the **Ferrovia Circumvesuviana** (information ✆ 7792444), runs trains to Herculaneum, Pompeii and Sorrento from the **Stazione Circumvesuviana** in Corso Garibaldi, and from the Stazione Centrale. Another separate line, the **Ferrovia Cumana**, ✆ 5513328, runs regular trains to the Campi Flegrei area, including Pozzuoli and Baia, from the station at Piazza Montesanto. A third line, the **Ferrovia Circumflegrea**, also ✆ 5513328, runs from the same station at Piazza Montesanto to points west, including Licola and Cuma. For more information on the regional rail lines *see* p.90.

by long-distance bus

Most services to destinations within the province and the Campania region operate from the Piazza Garibaldi, in front of the FS Stazione Centrale. An exception is the bus service to Salerno along the coast, which runs from Via Pisanelli, near Piazza Municipio (*see* p.92).

by road

The A2 *autostrada* from Rome approaches Naples from due north, via Caserta, and in the outskirts of the city, just east of Capodichino airport, meets up with a series of massive road junctions: the A16 turns off east for Avellino, Bari and the Adriatic, and then two roads head off to the west, the P1 for the coast and the Naples inner ring road, the *tangenziale*, which leads around the back of the city towards Pozzuoli and the Campi Flegrei. Using the *tangenziale* makes it possible to reach most areas of the city without going through the centre. Traffic going further south should stay on the A2 until it meets the A3, so avoiding the city entirely.

Once you arrive at wherever you are staying in Naples, you are categorically advised to park your car in a safe place (such as a hotel garage) and not attempt to use it anywhere within the city (*see* p.65).

The best place to go for information about Naples itself is the well-run and friendly information booth run by the city's **Azienda Autonoma di Soggiorno** on Piazza Gesù Nuovo, ✆ 5523328/5512701, in the old town *(open 9am–7pm Mon–Sat; 9am–3pm Sun)*. Their main office is in the Royal Palace, ✆ 418744, fax 418619. In summer they open offices in the Castel dell'Ovo, ✆ 764 5688, on the harbour at Mergellina, ✆ 7614585, and in a trailer in Piazza Garibaldi, in front of the Stazione Centrale. Information about excursions outside the city and so on is only available from the less helpful provincial **EPT**, Piazza dei Martiri 58, ✆ 405311. The EPT also has another, intermittently manned office at the Stazione Centrale, which, if anyone is around, may be some help in finding a hotel. Look out for the free monthly handbook *Qui Napoli*, available at tourist offices and some hotels, which carries a great deal of useful information, timetables, listings and calendars of events.

Naples

500 metres
500 yards

Getting Around

Travelling around the city is a fascinating subject. Such is the state of most public transport and so impenetrable is the traffic that walking is often by far the most practical way of getting anywhere, apart from up to the heights by the *funicolari*.

Orientation is a little difficult. If you arrive by sea—the only proper way to do it—you'll get a good idea of the layout. Naples' dominant landmarks, visible from almost anywhere in town, are Castel Sant'Elmo and the huge, fortress-like monastery of San Martino. They are neighbours on the steep hill that slopes down to the sea near the port, neatly dividing the city into its old and new quarters.

Modern Naples is on the western side, the busy, pleasant districts of Mergellina, Vomero and Fuorigrotta, to which middle-class Napoletani escape from the city centre each night on their creaking old funicular railways. To the east, towards Vesuvius, lies the centre, along Via Toledo, and beyond it the oldest neighbourhoods, tall tenements jammed into a grid of narrow streets, reaching a climax in the oriental bazaar atmosphere of the Piazza Mercato and the Piazza Garibaldi.

For more on travel by train or bus to destinations outside the city, around the Bay of Naples or further into Campania, *see* pp.8–9, 90, 92, 148 and 158.

by bus

Given the problems involved in using their own cars and even taxis in Naples, visitors often find themselves left with the local buses, which is small cheer, since the city indisputably has the worst bus system in Italy. Buses will be slow and usually indecently crowded. There are no schedules, no maps, and nowhere you can get accurate information; even the drivers usually do not have the faintest idea what is happening. The ultimate Neapolitan experience is waiting an hour for a bus after being misinformed by line employees, and then finding out the right bus is the one marked 'out of service'. Most lines start at either Piazza Garibaldi or Piazza del Plebiscito. Some that might be useful are:

1 and **4** trolleys, from Piazza Garibaldi to Corso Umberto, Piazza Plebiscito, Riviera di Chiaia, and Mergellina.

24, from Piazza Plebiscito up Via Toledo to Capodimonte.

120, **127**, from Piazza Garibaldi to Piazza Cavour and Capodimonte.

150, **152**, to Pozzuoli.

by Metro and funicolare

Naples also has a sort of underground. The **Metropolitana**, a single line from Piazza Garibaldi (basement of the Stazione Centrale) to Fuorigrotta, is really a part of the state railway, and uses the same underground tracks as the long-distance trains. The FS runs it as anarchically as the buses, but it will be helpful for reaching the station, the archaeological museum, and points in Vomero and Fuorigrotta. As on the buses, few people ever buy tickets.

A much more agreeable way to travel, though you can't go very far, is on the three **funicolari**, or inclined railways, up to Vomero. The longest—one of the longest in the world, in fact—is the **Funicolare Centrale**, from Via Toledo, just behind the Galleria, up to Via Cimarosa. The **Funicolare di Chiaia** also ends nearby in the same street, having started from Piazza Amedeo in Chiaia. Finally, the **Funicolare di Montesanto** travels up to Via Morghen from Montesanto Station, the start of the suburban Circumflegrea and Cumana rail lines. All three funicolari bring you out near the San Martino Museum and the Castel Sant'Elmo. All run until about 7pm daily.

by taxi

Neapolitan taxi drivers are uniformly dishonest, and try out any number of scams involving fixed meters, turning the meter on before you get in the car, imaginary 'surcharges' and so on. Also, the traffic is frequently so thick that relatively short journeys can take so long (and cost so much) that they're really not worth it. If you want to take a taxi to a specific destination, always try to agree on the fare in advance, whether there is a meter or not.

by car

The first thing to get straight is simply—*leave your car elsewhere*. Cars disappear in Naples with alarming frequency, and foreign number plates are especially prized. Even if you get to keep your wheels, you'll be sorry. Driving in Naples is a unique experience. Motorists studiously disregard all traffic signals and warnings, and the city has given up trying to coerce them. There are no rules, except to get there first, and fatalities are common. Even if this sounds exciting, note that the novelty soon wears off, even for the most boorish motorhead. For scant sympathy about stolen cars, call the city police on © 313131.

Several **car hire** firms have offices in Naples, mainly on Via Partenope (near the port), at the airport, and/or at the Stazione Centrale: **Avis**, © 7645600; **Europcar**, © 7645859; **Hertz**, © 7645533; **InterRent**, © 7646364. Be warned though that as car theft is so rife in Naples some companies will not rent certain models in the city, so you may find your choice restricted.

Piazza del Plebiscito—the Parking Lot of Naples

It's a shame this immense and elegant square, the centre of modern Naples, should suffer such a fate, but for the present there seems to be little hope of improvement. The huge domed church, embracing the piazza in its curving colonnades as does St Peter's in Rome, is **San Francesco di Paola**. King Ferdinand IV, after the British restored him to power in

1815, made a vow to construct it; the great dome and classical portico were modelled after the Pantheon in Rome. There's little to see in the austere interior, and anyone with a little understanding of Naples will not be surprised to find the colonnades given over to light manufacturing and warehouse space.

Across the square rises the equally imposing bulk of the **Royal Palace** (*Palazzo Reale*), begun by the Spanish viceroys in 1600, expanded by the Bourbons and finished by the kings of Italy *(open 9–1.30, 4.30–7.30, daily; adm)*. Umberto I, a good friend of the Neapolitans, added the eight giant figures on the façade, representing the eight houses that have ruled at Naples. It seems the 19th-century sculptors had trouble taking some of them seriously; note the preposterous figures of Charles of Anjou, whom the Neapolitans never liked, and Vittorio Emanuele II, the latter probably an accurate portrayal. There are Ruritanian stone sentry boxes and stone peacocks in the courtyard to recall the Bourbons, and a number of rooms inside that can be visited—the ones that escaped t! ɔ bombings in World War II, including a suitably grand staircase, a theatre, and several chambers in 18th-century style. The palace's theatre saw the premières of many of the works of Alessandro Scarlatti. The rear of the palace, now the home of Naples' important **Biblioteca Nazionale**, faces a pretty, little-visited garden across from the Castel Nuovo.

The Bourbons were great opera buffs, and they built Italy's largest opera house, the **San Carlo**, right next to their palace. Begun in 1737, making it older than La Scala, the theatre was sumptuously restored after a fire in 1816, during the period when Naples was the unquestioned capital of opera; so important was the theatre to the people of Naples that King Ferdinand made sure the the workmen got the job done in record time—300 days. Today the San Carlo is still among the most prestigious in the world (the Neapolitans of course would place it first), and its productions are certainly among the most polished and professional, and occasionally among the most adventurous. Also, each season at least one lesser-known Neapolitan opera is performed. Tickets are as expensive as anywhere (up to L400,000 on an opening night), but you can take a brief tour of the theatre for consider-ably less *(© 7972111; tours 9am–2pm Mon–Fri; 9am–1pm Sun; adm)*.

Opposite the San Carlo is the grandest interior of Southern Italy, the **Galleria Umberto I**. This great glass-roofed arcade, perhaps the largest in the world, was begun in 1887, nine years after the Galleria Vittorio Emanuele in Milan. The arcade is cross-shaped, with a mosaic of the zodiac on the floor at the centre, and its dome is 56m tall; surprisingly, the Neapolitans do not seem to like it as much as much as they once did; even at high noon, you are likely to find its vast spaces deserted but for a few small clouds of grey-suited men arguing politics around the entrances.

Castel Nuovo

The port of Naples has been protected by this odd, beautiful castle, looming over the harbour behind the Royal Palace and San Carlo, for some 700 years now. Charles of Anjou built it in 1279; many Napoletani still call it by the curious name of *Maschio* (male) *Angioino*. Most of what you see today, however, including the eccentric, ponderous

Castel Nuovo

round towers, is the work of Guillermo Sagrera, the great Catalan architect who built the famous Exchange in Palma de Mallorca. Between two of these towers at the entrance, the conquering Aragonese hired the finest sculptors from all over Italy to build Alfonso's **Triumphal Arch**, a unique masterpiece of Renaissance sculpture and design inspired by the triumphal arches of the ancient Romans. The symbolism, as in the Roman arches, may be a little confusing. The figure at the top is Saint Michael; below him are a matched pair of sea gods, and further down, allegorical virtues and relief panels portraying Alfonso's victories and wise governance.

Inside, the castle currently houses parts of the Naples city administration and some cultural societies. If you come during office hours *(8am–1pm Mon–Fri)*, someone will probably be around to show you the **Sala dei Baroni**, where the city council meets; it has a cupola with an unusual Moorish vaulting, an eight-pointed star made of interlocking arches. King Ferrante used this as his dining hall, and it takes its name from the evening when he invited a score of the kingdom's leading barons to a ball, and then arrested the lot. There are also two museums *(open 9am–2pm Mon–Fri; 9am–1.30pm Sat; adm)*. One, housed in the Gothic **Cappella Palatina**, next to the council hall, contains 14th and 15th-century frescoes; the other, in the south wing, has paintings, and a good collection of silver and bronzes, from the 15th century to the present day.

King Ferrante's Dungeons

Guillermo Sagrera was the Frank Lloyd Wright of the Renaissance, a brilliant, iconoclastic architect who dreamt up shapes and forms never seen before. In his rebuilding of the Castel Nuovo, with its arch and massive and eccentric towers, he and his intelligent patron, King Alfonso, must have been fully aware of the revolutionary design statement (as we might call it today) they were making—a castle meant to be not only a royal residence and stronghold, but a landmark and symbol for Naples.

Even before the arrival of the Spaniards and the rebuilding, the Castel Nuovo had witnessed a good deal of history. Here, when the castle was brand new, Charles of Anjou had received the news of the Sicilian Vespers, and reportedly cried out: 'Lord God, since it has pleased you to ruin me, let me only go down by small steps!' 1294 saw the visit of Pope Celestine V, who had been a simple and slow-witted hermit in the Abruzzo before his surprise election. The church bosses, who wanted a stronger hand on the papal throne, meant to get rid of him as soon as possible, and in this castle they tricked him into abdicating by whispering into his room through a hidden tube, claiming to be the voice of God and commanding him to quit. King Robert the Wise kept his great library here, and graciously received Petrarch and Boccaccio in his royal apartments.

Poor Sagrera would be quite sad to hear that the Castel Nuovo seems somewhat dark and sinister to many visitors today. It isn't his fault; perhaps it isn't even a matter of changing architectural tastes. Most of the credit must surely go to the ruler who stamped his own personality on the castle more than anyone else, the monstrous King Ferrante. Illegitimate son of Alfonso the Magnanimous (or just as likely, people whispered, of a certain Moor of Valencia), Ferrante took the throne of Naples in 1458; he was a devious and capable ruler, just the sort of man the state needed among the dangerous intrigues and ever-shifting political fortunes of Renaissance Italy. He is better remembered for his calculated cruelty. On one occasion, he invited an enemy back to Naples, professing great affection, and treated him to a month of parties before suddenly arresting him and sending him off to the torture room. A surprise invitation to the King's table for dinner was often as good as a death warrant. Ferrante was known to keep a 'museum of mummies' of executed foes and rebellious barons at the castle, each dressed in his own clothes. And stories went round that he kept a crocodile in the castle's dungeons, which was fed only on live prisoners.

Via Toledo

From the landward side of Piazza del Plebiscito and the Palace, Naples' most imposing street, the Via Toledo, runs northwards past the Galleria. Its name commemorates its builder, Don Pedro de Toledo, the Spanish viceroy at the beginning of the 16th century, and a great benefactor of Naples. Stendhal, in 1817, rightly called this 'the most populous and gayest street in the world', and it is still the city's main business and shopping street, leading up to Capodimonte and the northern suburbs (many Neapolitans still call it by its Mussolini-era name, Via Roma). Don Pedro's elegant Renaissance tomb, among others, can be seen in the little church of **San Giacomo degli Spagnuoli**, now swallowed up by the 19th-century Palazzo Municipale complex, originally a home for the Bourbon royal bureaucracy.

Going north along Via Toledo, any street on your left can be the entrance to the dense, crumbling, slightly sinister inner sanctum of the Neapolitan soul, the vast slum called the *Quartieri Spagnuoli*. It can be a fascinating place to walk around, in daytime at least.

Lately though, thanks to battling factions of the Camorra, the *Quartieri* have achieved even more than their accustomed share of notoriety; for a while the hoods were bumping each other off at a rate of one per week. Though the *Quartieri* cover almost all the area sloping up to San Martino and Vomero, the most populous and colourful part is that immediately adjoining Via Toledo, a strict grid of narrow streets laid out by Don Pedro de Toledo and now called the *Tavoliere*, or chessboard.

Four Days in Naples

The contempt that many northern Italians often show for this city and its accomplishments can look a bit silly when compared with the facts. Just for the record, we note that in September 1944 Naples did more than its part in redeeming Italian honour by becoming the first city to liberate itself, and the only one to do so until the German collapse at the end of the war.

At the time of the Allied landings in Salerno, the city was in a bad way. Rations of everything were short, sometimes non-existant, and the Germans were preparing to dynamite all the important facilities in case the Allied advance should reach Naples.

Worst of all, SS units were combing every quarter for able-bodied males to ship off to forced labour in the north or in Germany. No one knows exactly what incident touched off the great revolt. In the excellent 1960s film account, *Quattro Giornate a Napoli*, a group of men who escaped from the Germans here in the *Quartiere Spagnuole* is recaptured and lined up against a building to be shot. A basket on a string suddenly appears among them, the kind old women would send down from their windows in the tall tenements to buy tomatoes or chestnuts from the street vendors; this time, though, the basket contained a gun—unexpected aid from heaven has always been a common theme in Neapolitan mythology.

However it started, the uprising spread like a prairie fire through the city. Pistols and old rifles came out from their hiding places, and the police arsenals were broken into for more. *Scugnizzi* (street children) waited in doorways with stolen grenades, ready to try and tip one into a passing Nazi truck or tank. The prisons were thrown open, and while many of their inmates scuttered off into the shadows, plenty of others took what arms they could find and joined in the fight. Not long after, the rebels surrounded the heavily defended football stadium in Vomero, full of captured Neapolitans waiting to be sent to Germany; they took it, despite heavy casualties, and freed the lot.

At the beginning the rebels carried on without any leadership whatsoever—except of course among the Communists. The totally anarchic, overwhelming, totally spontaneous movement of the city's people was something that few cities but Naples could ever produce. The Germans found it the ultimate Neapolitan experience; it was as if they had kicked over a beehive. They responded with customary brutality—massacres of prisoners and tanks firing point-blank into apartment blocks—but stung and pestered on every side, they could not endure long. A hastily-formed committee went to negotiate terms with the exasperated German commander, and a deal was cut: the troops would depart immediately, and attacks on them would cease. An eerie silence fell over the city and indifferent faces watched from their windows as the German columns filed out. And then Naples went back to being Naples.

To the right of Via Toledo, the confusion of Naples' half-crumbling, half-modern business centre conceals a few buildings worth a look. The **Palazzo Gravina**, on Via Monteoliveto, is a fine palace in the northern Renaissance style, built between 1513 and 1549. Almost directly across the street, the church of **Monteoliveto** is a little treasure house of late Renaissance sculpture and painting, with tombs and altars in the various chapels by southern artists like Giovanni da Nola and Antonio Rosellino, as well as some frescoes by Vasari.

Spaccanapoli

This street's familiar name means 'Split-Naples', and that is exactly what it has done for the last 2600 years. On the map, it changes its name with alarming frequency—Via Benedetto Croce and Via San Biagio dei Librai are two of the most prominent—but in Roman times you would have found it by asking for the *decumanus inferior*, the name for the second east–west street in any planned Roman city. No large city in all the lands conquered by Rome has maintained its ancient street plan as completely as Naples (the Greeks laid out these streets, of course, but the Romans learned their planning from them). It is easier here to imagine the atmosphere of a big ancient city than in Rome itself, or even in Pompeii. The narrow, straight streets and tall *insulae* cannot have changed much; only the forum and temples are missing.

This is the heart of old Naples—and what a street it is, lined with grocery barrows and scholarly bookshops, shops that sell old violins, plaster saints, pizza, or used clothes pegs. Drama is supplied by the arch-Neapolitan characters who live here, haunting the street-corners and entertaining wan hopes of dodging the manic motorists; the colour comes from the district's laundry—down any of the long alleys of impossibly tall tenements you may see as many as a hundred full clothes-lines, swelling bravely in the breeze and hoping for a glint of southern sun.

It has always been a poor neighbourhood, though even now it is not a desperate one. As always, its people live much of their life on the streets, carrying on whatever is their business from makeshift benches on the kerbs. The visitor will probably find that claustrophobia is right around the corner, but anyone born and raised here would never feel at home anywhere else.

Santa Chiara and the Gesù Nuovo

Your introduction to this world, just off Via Toledo, is the cramped, disorderly, most characteristic of Neapolitan squares: the **Piazza Gesù Nuovo**, decorated by the gaudiest and most random of Neapolitan decorations, the **Guglia della Immacolata**. A *guglia* (pinnacle), in Naples, is a kind of rococo obelisk, dripping with frills, saints and *putti*, of which there are three, all in this area. The unsightly, unfinished façade behind the Guglia, covered with pyramidal extrusions in dark basalt, belongs to the Church of **Gesù Nuovo**. As strange as it is, the façade, originally part of a late 15th-century palace, has become one of the landmarks of Naples. The interior is typically lavish Neapolitan Baroque, gloriously overdone in acres of coloured marbles and frescoes, some by the Spanish artist Ribera and some by Solimena.

Santa Chiara, just across the piazza, dates from the early 14th century, though it once had a Baroque interior as good as the Gesù; Allied bombers remodelled it to suit modern tastes in 1943, and only a few of the original Angevin tombs have survived. To get some idea of what the interior must have been like, stop in and see the adjacent **Cloister of the Clarisse**, nothing less than the loveliest and most peaceful spot in Naples—especially in contrast to the neighbourhood outside. So much in Naples shows the Spanish influence— like the use of the title 'Don', now largely limited to Camorra bosses—and here someone in the 1740s transplanted the Andalucian love of pictures done in painted *azulejo* tiles, turning a simple monkish cloister into a little fairyland of gaily coloured arbours, benches and columns, shaded by the only trees in the whole district.

Recently, during the restoration of a vestibule off the cloister, it was discovered that underneath the indifferent 18th-century frescoes there were some earlier, highly original paintings of the Last Judgement. They have since been uncovered and restored, revealing an inspired 16th-century vision of the event, in a style utterly unlike the slick virtuosity of the time, with plenty of novel tortures for the damned and angels welcoming some cute naked nuns among the elect.

The Sansevero Chapel

A few streets further down Via Benedetto Croce is tiny Piazza San Domenico, which has monuments from Naples' three most creative periods. **San Domenico Maggiore**, built in 1289, was the Dominican church in Naples. St Thomas Aquinas lived in the adjacent monastery. Later this became the favourite church of the Spanish, and it contains some interesting Renaissance funerary monuments; a better one, though, is across the Piazza in the church of **Sant'Angelo a Nilo**—the tomb of Cardinal Brancaccio, designed by Michelozzo, with a relief of the *Assumption of the Virgin* by Donatello. The second of the Baroque pinnacles decorates the Piazza, the **Guglia di San Domenico**, a work of Cosimo Fanzago, who also designed the church. Best of all, just around the corner on Via F. De Sanctis, you can inspect Neapolitan Rococo at its very queerest in the **Sansevero Chapel** *(open 10–1, 5–7, Mon, Wed–Sat; 10am–1pm Tues, Sun; adm)*.

Prince Raimondo di Sangro (b. 1701), who was responsible for the final form of this, his family's private chapel, was a strange bird, a sort of aristocratic dilettante mystic. Supposedly there is a grand allegorical scheme behind the arrangement of the sculptures and frescoes he commissioned, but a work like this, only 200 years old, seems as foreign to our sensibilities and understanding as some Mayan temple. The sculptures, by little-known Neapolitan artists like Giuseppe Sammartino and Antonio Corradini, are inscrutable allegories in themselves, often executed with a breathtakingly showy virtuosity. Francesco Queirolo's *Il Disinganno* (disillusion) is an extreme case; nobody else, perhaps, has ever tried to carve a fishing-net, or the turning pages of a book, out of marble. Others, such as Sammartino's *Cristo Velato*, display a remarkable illusion of figures under transparent veils. There are a dozen or so of these large sculptural groups, all under a crazy heavenly vortex in the ceiling fresco, by Francesco Mario Russo. Down in the crypt are two complete human cardiovascular systems, removed from the bodies and preserved by Prince Raimondo in the course of his alchemical experiments. Ask to see them (if you care to).

Near San Domenico, a block south of the Spacca, is Naples' **University**, one of Europe's oldest and most distinguished. The Emperor Frederick founded it in 1224, as a 'Ghibelline' university to counter the pope's 'Guelph' university at Bologna, as well as to provide scholars and trained officials for the new state he was trying to build. It still occupies its ancient, woefully overcrowded quarters around Via Mezzocannone.

Around the Piazza del Duomo

Continuing down the Spaccanapoli (now Via San Biagio ai Librai), just around the corner on Via San Gregorio is the **San Gregorio Armeno** church, with another gaudy Baroque interior. In December, this street and others around it become Naples' famous Christmas Market, where everyone comes to buy figurines of the Holy Family, the Three Kings and all the other accessories required for their Christmas *presepi*, or manger scenes, one of the most devotedly followed of local traditions. For several weeks, hundreds of stands fill up the neighbourhood's narrow streets.

The Presepi

It would not be easy to explain why the genius of Naples should have chosen Christmas cribs as a subject to elevate to an art form. After philosophy, pizza, and music, it's what this city does best. Churches and private homes have always had a little competitive edge on when they begin their displays (some time in November, if not earlier). The most extreme cases have been assembled inside the Museo Nazionale di San Martino. One is as big as a bus, and must have taken someone a lifetime; another is fitted inside an eggshell—still with over a hundred figures in it. The best parts are the large, finely carved individual wooden or ceramic figures. Most represent Neapolitans of two or three centuries ago, from every walk of life; with their painstakingly detailed and wonderfully expressive faces, each is a genuine portrait. To have them all here in one place is like old Bourbon Naples appearing before your eyes. For do-it-yourself, modern cribs, Via San Gregorio is the place to go. At Christmas time, the whole street is taken over by the stalls of artisans who make and sell figurines for the crib scene, as well as little trees, sheep, donkeys, amphorae, cooking pots, Turks, salamis, dogs, chickens, angels, cheese wheels, and all the other items without which no Neapolitan *presepe* would be complete.

Convention requires that, quite apart from the Holy Family, certain things be present in every crib. Besides the usual angels, shepherds, and animals, a *Roman ruin* is absolutely necessary, as are several *Turks* in Ottoman Empire dress (which come in handy if one of the Three Kings gets lost). A *band of musicians* is also expected, and all the better if they too are Turks. *Beggars and dwarfs* earn envy for the crib-maker—there is a whole display of figures called the 'deformities'—but above all there must be *tons of food* everywhere there is room for it. The best cribs have the busiest cooks and the most bulging pantries, with tiny wooden roast pigs, sausages, eggs, plates of macaroni, cheeses and fancy cakes—even a pizza or two. Look out for the giant *presepe* in the Galleria Umberto at Christmas time, and watch Neapolitans throw money at it to pay for its upkeep for another year.

A little further north up Via San Gregorio is **San Lorenzo Maggiore** (*c.* 1330), one of Naples' finest medieval churches; Petrarch lived for a while in the adjacent monastery. In addition, recent excavations have also uncovered some interesting Greek and Roman remains on the site. **San Paolo**, across the street, isn't much to see now, but before an earthquake wrecked it in the 17th century, its façade was the portico of an ancient Roman temple to Castor and Pollux. Andrea Palladio studied it closely, and it provided much of the inspiration for his classical palaces in the Veneto.

After Spaccanapoli, **Via dei Tribunali** (the *decumanus major*) is the busiest street of old Naples, and has been for a long time. The arcades that line the street in places, a sort of continuous covered market, are a thousand years old or more. Here, at the otherwise unremarkable **Girolamini Church**, you may see the modest tomb of Naples's greatest philosopher, Giambattista Vico (*see* 'Topics', p.52). Northwest of the Girolamini, around Via dell'Anticaglia, you'll find a few crooked streets, the only ones in old Naples that do not stick to the rectilinear Roman plan. These follow the outline of the **Roman Theatre**, much of which still survives, hidden among the tenements. A few arches are all that is visible from the street.

The Cathedral of San Gennaro

The wide **Via del Duomo** is a breath of fresh air in this crowded district—exactly what the city intended, when they ploughed it through Old Naples after the cholera epidemic of 1884. The **Duomo** itself is another fine medieval building, though it is hidden behind an awful pseudo-Gothic façade pasted on in 1905. The best things are inside: the Renaissance **Capella Minùtolo**, the tomb of Charles of Anjou and the **Capella San Gennaro**, glittering with the gold and silver of the Cathedral treasure, and with frescoes by Domenichino and Lanfranco, the latter a swirling *Paradiso* in the dome (1643). The **Basilica Santa Restituta**, a sizeable church in its own right, is tacked onto the side of the cathedral. Its columns are thought to be from the temple of Apollo that once occupied the site. Begun in 324, though often rebuilt, this is the oldest building in Naples. The ceiling frescoes are by Luca Giordano. Just off the basilica, the 5th-century **baptistry** contains a good Byzantine-style mosaic by the 14th-century artist Lello di Roma; the baptismal font itself probably comes from an ancient temple of Dionysus. The last and most elaborate of the *guglie*, the **Guglia San Gennaro**, can be seen just outside the south transept.

If the sacristan is around, you can visit the **Crypt of San Gennaro**, patron of Naples, with elaborate marble decoration from the Renaissance, and the tomb of Pope Innocent IV. Whoever is really buried here, San Gennaro (Januarius) is a rather doubtful character; most likely he is a Christian assimilation of the Roman god Janus. The saint's head is kept upstairs in the chapel named after him, along with two phials of his blood that miraculously liquefy and 'boil' three times each year—the first Sunday in May, 19th September, and 16th December—so as to prove that San Gennaro is still looking out for the Napoletani. The only time the miracle has ever failed, during the Napoleonic occupation, the people of the city became enormously excited and seemed ready to revolt. At this the French commander, a true son of the Enlightenment, announced that San Gennaro had 10 minutes to come through—or else he'd shoot the Archbishop. Somehow, just in time, the miracle occurred.

On a small piazza a block north of the Duomo, **Santa Maria Donnaregina** offers more overdone Baroque, but off to the side of this 17th-century work is the smaller, original church, built in 1307 by Queen Mary of Hungary (who was none other than the wife of Charles of Anjou; her title only reflects a claim to the throne). Her elaborate tomb, and some good contemporary frescoes, are the sights of the church. South of the cathedral in the Via del Duomo is the **Filangieri Museum**, housed in the 15th-century Palazzo Cuomo, a small collection of china, armour, and curiosities *(open 9am–2pm Mon–Sat; 9am–1pm Sun; adm)*. Its picture collection includes works by some of Naples' favourite artists, Luca Giordano, Mattia Preti, Ribera and others. Almost all the collection was gathered in the last forty years. Count Filangieri's original collection was much larger, but the Nazis torched it before they left in 1944.

Piazza Garibaldi

In Italian, the word for a market stand is *bancarella*. In Naples they are as much a part of everyday life as they must have been in the Middle Ages; the city probably has as many of them as all the rest of Italy put together. The greatest concentration can be found in the Forcella market district, in the narrow streets east of the Via del Duomo, selling everything from stereos to light bulbs. According to the government's economists, at least one-third of Naples' economy is underground—outright illegal, or at the least not paying taxes or subject to any regulation.

Bootleg cassette tapes are one example; Naples is one of the world leaders in this thriving industry, and you'll have your choice of thousands of titles along these streets, though it might be a good idea to get them to play your tape before you part with any money. Hundreds of tired-looking folks sit in front of little tables, selling contraband American cigarettes. This is one of the easiest means for Naples' poor to make a living, and it is all controlled by the Camorra. As in New York, whenever it rains, shady characters crawl out of the woodwork selling umbrellas. You will see plenty of designer labels on the *bancarelle* —if they're real, don't ask where they came from.

Piazza Mercato, one of the nodes of the Neapolitan bazaar, has been a market square perhaps since Roman times.In the old days this was always the site of major executions, most notably that of 16 year-old Conradin, the rightful heir to the throne, by Charles of Anjou in 1268, an act that shocked all Europe. Charles ordered him buried underneath the Piazza—he couldn't be laid in consecrated ground, since he had just been excommunicated for political reasons by Charles's ally the pope. In 1647, Masaniello's Revolt started here, during the festival of Our Lady of Mount Carmel; Masaniello (Tommaso Aniello), a young fisherman of Amalfi, had been chosen by his fellow conspirators to step up in the middle of the ceremonies and proclaim to the people and the viceroy that the new tax the viceroy had introduced "no longer existed'. As the plotters had hoped, a spontaneous rising followed, and for a week Masaniello ruled Naples while the frightened viceroy locked himself up in Castel Sant'Elmo. In Naples, unfortunately, such risings can burn out as quickly as a match; the viceroy's spies first secretly drugged Masaniello, so that he appeared drunk or mad to the people, and then in an unguarded moment they murdered him and sent his head to the viceroy. That was the end for Naples, but the incident touched off a wave of revolts across the south that it took the Spaniards three years to stamp out.

The incredible **Piazza Garibaldi** is the other main centre of the Forcella area. For rail travellers, it is an unforgettable introduction to Naples; they walk out of the incongruously modern Stazione Centrale into the vast square, paved with asphalt that melts in the hot sun and sticks to their shoes, and enter a world unlike anything else in Italy—bums, addicts and crazies draped picturesquely along the pavement, solid ranks of *bancarelle* wherever there's room, eternal crowds of odd characters from every nation of the world, Italy's worst hotels and its ugliest whores. Most of the piazza is really one gigantic parking lot; traffic whistles through it on lanes marked with yellow paint. Neapolitans don't mind the Piazza Garibaldi; tourists often come to like it. Sailors generally avoid it, as do the police.

The Capua Gate

Northwest of the Piazza Garibaldi, some of Naples' shabbiest streets lead towards the Piazza Enrico di Nicola, once the city's main gate. The **Porta Capuana**, built in 1492, seems a smaller version of the Castel Nuovo's triumphal arch, crowded in by the same squat round towers. The **Castel Capuano**, next to it, began its life as a castle-residence for the Hohenstaufen kings. Since its construction in the 13th century it has been reshaped so many times it doesn't even look like a castle any more; for four centuries it has served as Naples' law courts. If anything makes wandering into this unlikely district worthwhile, though, it is **Santa Caterina a Formiella**, facing the Porta Capuana, a neglected, almost abandoned church by the obscure architect Romolo Balsimelli, that is one of the masterpieces of 16th-century Italian architecture. Completed in 1517, the church's bulky, squarish form was a Renaissance eccentricity, but an important stepping-stone towards the Baroque. Today, Santa Caterina is hardly ever open, and its dome tilts at a more precarious angle with each passing year.

The Archaeological Museum

Back on the western side of the old city, Via Toledo, after passing Spaccanapoli and changing its name to Via Pessina, continues northwards through the **Piazza Dante**, one of the most delightful and animated corners of the city; beyond this, in an area of oversized tenements and busy streets, it opens to display the crumbling red palazzo that contains the **Museo Archeologico Nazionale** *(open 9am–7pm daily; adm)*.

Naples has the most important collection of Roman-era art and antiquities in the world, due partly to Vesuvius, for burying Pompeii and Herculaneum, and partly to the sharp eyes and deep pockets of the Farnese family—many of the best works here come from the collection they built up over 300 years. Unfortunately, the place is run by Neapolitans; at any given time, half of the collections will be closed for 'restorations' that never seem to happen, and what they condescend to let you see may well be the worst-exhibited and worst-labelled major museum in Europe.

On the first floor, room after room is filled with ancient sculpture. Many of the pieces on view are the best existing Roman-era copies of lost Greek statues, including some by Phidias and Praxiteles; some are masterpieces in their own right, such as the huge, dramatic ensemble called the *Farnese Bull*, the *Tyrannicides* (with other statues' heads stuck on them), and the truly heroic *Farnese Hercules* that once decorated the Baths of Caracalla. Several provocative Aphrodites compete for your attention, along with a platoon of formidable Athenas. Also the famous *Doryphorus* (spear-bearer), and enough Greek and Roman busts to populate a Colosseum.

Upstairs, most of the rooms are given over to finds from Pompeii. The collection of **Roman mosaics**, mostly from Pompeii and Herculaneum, is one of the two best anywhere (the other is in Antalya, Turkey); the insight it

Toro Farnese

provides into the life and thought of the ancients is priceless. One feature it betrays clearly is a certain fond silliness—plenty of chickens, ducks and grinning cats, the famous *Cave canem* (beware of the dog) mosaic from the front of a house, comic scenes from the theatre, and especially one wonderful panel of crocodiles and hippopotami along the Nile. Some of the mosaics are very consciously 'art': a detailed scene of the Battle of Issus, where Alexander the Great defeated the Persian king Darius, and a view of the Academy of Athens that includes a portrait of Plato. A recently opened addition is a section devoted entirely to the Temple of Isis at Pompeii. Five rooms display sculptures, frescoes and paintings taken from the temple, which was first dicovered in 1765.

Besides the mosaics, nowhere in the world will you find a larger collection of **Roman mural painting**, and much of it is fascinatingly modern in theme and execution. Many of the walls of Pompeiian villas were decorated with architectural fantasias that seem strangely like those of the Renaissance. Other works show an almost Baroque lack of respect for the gods—see the *Wedding of Zeus and Hera*. Scholars in fact do denote a period of 'Roman Baroque', beginning about the 2nd century. From it come paintings graced by genuine winged *putti*, called *amoretti* in Roman days. Among the most famous pictures are *The Astragal Players*—young girls shooting craps—and the beautiful *Portrait of an Unknown Woman*, a thoughtful lady holding her pen to her lips who has become one of the best-known images from Roman art.

Other attractions of the museum include large collections of jewellery, coins, fancy gladiators' armour, the famous *sezione pornografica* that you may get to see if you ask politely, Greek vases, decorative bronzes and a highly detailed, room-sized **scale model** of the entire city of Pompeii (lovingly restored since the memorable assault on it by the authors' baby boy, back in 1980). The Egyptian collection is not a large one, but it is fun, with a dog-headed Anubis in a Roman toga, some ancient feet under glass, and a mummified crocodile.

Capodimonte

North of the museum, the neighbourhoods along Via Toledo—briefly named Via Santa Teresa degli Scalzi—begin to lose some of their Neapolitan intensity as they climb to the suburban heights. On the way, after changing its name again to Corso Amedeo di Savoia, the street passes an area that was full of cemeteries in Roman times. Three Christian underground burial vaults have been discovered here, with a total area of over 100,000 square metres, only part of which have been completely explored. Two may be visited: the **Catacombe di San Gennaro** *(entrance off the northern end of the Corso; look for the yellow signs. Tours at 9.30, 10.15, 11.00, 11.45am, Fri, Sat, Sun only; adm)* is the more interesting, with extensive early Christian mosaics and carvings, some as early as the 2nd century. The **Catacombe di San Gaudioso** *(tours at 9.45, 11.45am, daily; adm)*, which include the 5th-century tomb of the saint of the same name, a martyred African bishop, were discovered under the Baroque church of **Santa Maria della Sanità**, on Via Sanità.

The **Parco di Capodimonte**, a well-kept and exotically tropical park, began as a hunting preserve of the Bourbons in the 18th century. Charles III built a Royal Palace here in 1738 that now houses Naples' picture gallery, the **Museo Nazionale di Capodimonte** *(open 2–7.30pm Mon; 9am–7.30pm Tues–Sat; 9am–2pm Sun; adm)*. The collection is the best in the south of Italy, and especially rich in works of the late Renaissance. Some of the works you shouldn't miss: an *Annunciation* by Filippino Lippi; a Botticelli *Madonna*; the mystical portrait of the mathematician *Fra Luca Pacioli*, by an unknown quattrocento artist; two wry homilies by the elder Brueghel, *The Misanthrope* and *The Blind*; works by Masaccio and Mantegna, and a hilarious picture of *St Peter Martyr* by Lotto, showing that famous anti-Semitic rabble-rouser conversing nonchalantly with the Virgin Mary—with a hatchet sticking out of his head.

Five big, beautifully restored Caravaggios take up one room; others are devoted to important works by Titian. One entire wing of the museum is filled with delightfully frivolous 18th-century **porcelain figurines**; the Bourbons maintained a royal factory for making such things at Capodimonte, which is still in operation today. In another hall, there are scores of 19th-century watercolour scenes of Naples and the Campanian countryside (the best of them by Giacinto Gigante). Here, for the first time, you will see the Naples that so struck the 18th-century travellers. Not much has changed, really; if only all the traffic could magically disappear, it would still be almost the same spectacular city today.

The museum's collections are mostly up on the second floor; the first, the old *piano nobile* (Royal apartments), is still much the way the Bourbons left it. Persevere through the score of overdecorated chambers; the *Salotto di porcellana*, a little room entirely lined with Capodimonte porcelain, makes the whole thing worthwhile.

The Certosa di San Martino

Up on the highest point overlooking Naples, the 17th-century **Castel Sant'Elmo** *(open 9am–7.30pm Mon–Fri; 9am–2pm Sat; adm)* is an impressive enough Baroque fortification, partly built of the tufa rock on which it stands (the city now uses it to park the cars the police tow away). Next to it, hogging the best view in Naples, the Carthusians built their original, modest, monastery of **San Martino**, some time in the early 14th century. Two centuries later, like most Carthusian branch offices, they were rolling embarrassingly in lucre; building the poshest monastery in all Italy was the only thing to do. The rebuilt **Certosa** (charterhouse) is only marginally smaller than Fort St Elmo. Built on the slope of the mountain, it is supported by a gargantuan platform, visible for miles out to sea and probably containing enough stone to construct a small pyramid.

Nobody knows exactly what is in the **Museo Nazionale di San Martino** *(open 9am–2pm Tues–Sat; 9am–1pm Sun; adm)*, which now occupies the monastery. Intended as a museum specifically of Naples, its history, art and traditions, San Martino suffers from the same mismanagement as the Archaeological Museum; only parts are ever open, and the Grand Cloister, at time of writing, has become a wilderness of weeds and scaffolding. Not that this should discourage you from taking the long ride up the Montesanto Funicular. The views and the architecture are marvellous, and at least they always keep open the collection of *presepi*—what the Neapolitans come here to see (*see* p.72).

Upon entering the complex, the first attraction is the **church**, another of the glories of Neapolitan Baroque, with an excess of lovely coloured inlaid marble to complement the overabundance of painting. The work over the altar, the *Descent from the Cross*, is one of the finest of José Ribera. This tormented artist, often called *Lo Spagnuolo* in Italy, has paintings all over Naples. His popularity does not owe everything to his artistic talent; apparently he formed a little cartel with two local artists, and cornered the market by hiring a gang of thugs to harry all the other painters out of town.

The cloister, the **Chiostro Grande**, even in its present state, is a masterpiece of Baroque, elegantly proportioned and gloriously original in its decoration. Also, thanks to a sculptural scheme by a pious, mad artist named Cosimo Fanzago, it is the creepiest cloister east of Seville. Fanzago (who was also one of the architects of San Martino) gives us eight figures of saints that seem more like vampires in priestly robes and mitres, a perfect background for his little enclosed garden, its wall topped with rows of gleaming marble skulls. Most of the collections are in the halls surrounding the Chiostro Grande—costume, painting, ship models and every sort of curiosity; at the corners are **belvederes** from which to look over Naples (outside the complex, a series of lovely terraced gardens offer a similar view). The *presepi* take up a few large rooms near the entrance.

West of the Piazza del Plebiscito

The hill called Pizzofalcone rises directly behind the Piazza del Plebiscito; around it was the site of Parthenope, the Greek town that antedated Neapolis and was eventually swallowed up by it (though Neapolitans still like to refer to themselves as Parthenopeans). Parthenope had a little harbour, formed by an island that is now almost completely covered by the ancient, strangely-shaped fortress of the **Castel dell'Ovo**—the one Master Virgil is said to have built balanced on an egg, hence the name. Most of it was really built by Frederick II, and expanded by the Angevins.

There isn't much to see today—though the chapel was once covered with murals by Giotto, of which nothing remains—and most of it is closed to the public, but the Egg Castle has been the scene of many unusual events in Italian history. Long before there was a castle, the island may have been part of the original Greek settlement of Parthenope. Later it contained the villa of the Roman general and philosopher Lucullus, victor over Mithradates in the Pontic Wars; Lucullus curried favour with the people by making his sumptuous gardens, and his famous library, open to the public. In the 5th century AD the villa became a home in exile for Romulus Augustulus, last of the western Roman emperors. The Goths spared him only because of his youth and simple-mindedness, and pensioned him off here. Columns from Lucullus' villa are still to be seen among the castle's famous dungeons.

Modern Naples: the Villa Comunale

Once past the Egg Castle, a handsome sweep of coastline opens up the districts of **Chiaia** and **Mergellina**, the most pleasant parts of the new city. Here the long, pretty **Villa Comunale**, central Naples' only park, follows the shore. In it, there is an **Aquarium** *(open 9am–5pm daily; adm)*, built by the German naturalist Dr Anton Dohrn in the 1870s, and perhaps the oldest in the world. All the wide variety of fish, octopuses and other marine delicacies here are from the Bay of Naples; depending on the hour of day, you will find them fascinating, or else overwhelmingly appetizing. When the Allied armies marched into town in 1943, the Neapolitans put on a big party for the officers. There being practically nothing decent to eat anywhere in Naples, they cleaned out the aquarium and managed an all-seafood menu. General Mark Clark, the commander, is said to have got the aquarium's prize specimen, a baby manatee, though how they prepared it is not recorded.

Behind the park, on the Riviera di Chiaia, the **Museo Principe di Aragona Pignatelli Cortes** *(open 9am–2pm Tues–Sat; 9am–1pm Sun; adm)* will show you more of the same kind of decorative porcelain as at Capodimonte, along with a score of 18th- and 19th-century noble carriages, furniture and art.

If you're still not tired of little smiling figurines, you can plunge deeper into Chiaia to see the greatest collection of all at the Museo Nazionale della Ceramica, also known as the Duca di Martina Museum, but familiar to Neapolitans only as the **Villa Floridiana** *(open 9am–2pm Tues–Sat; 9am–1pm Sun; adm)*, after the tasteful 18th-century estate it occupies, with one of the loveliest gardens in Naples and one of Italy's great hoards of bric-a-brac. The museum is on Via Cimarosa, near the Funicolare di Chiaia.

Virgil's Tomb

Beginning a few streets beyond the western end of the Villa Comunale, **Mergellina** is one of the brightest and most popular quarters of Naples, a good place for dinner or a *passeggiata* around the busy Piazza Sannazzaro. Its centre is the **Marina**, where besides small craft there are hydrofoils to Sorrento and the islands in the summer months, and excursion boats which do daily tours of the shore between the Egg Castle and Point Posillipo. From the harbour, Mergellina rises steeply up the surrounding hills; there is a funicular up to the top. On the hillside, between the railway bridge and the tunnel that leads under the hill to Fuorigrotta, there is a Roman funerary monument that tradition has always held to be the **Tomb of Virgil** *(open 9am–1pm daily)*. The poet died in Brindisi in 19 BC, on his way back from a trip to Greece, but Neapolis was a city dear to him—he wrote most of the *Aeneid* here—and the legend may well be true.

Just below it lies the entrance to one of the little-known wonders of the ancient world. The **Crypta Neapolitana**, unfortunately closed at present, is a 606m road tunnel built during the reign of Augustus, to connect Neapolis with Pozzuoli and Baiae, the longest such work the Romans ever attempted.

Shopping

Surprisingly, no one ever thinks of Naples as one of the prime shopping destinations of Italy; this is a mistake, as there are as many pretty and unusual things to be bought here as anywhere else, and usually at lower prices. The back streets around Spaccanapoli and other old sections are still full of artisan workshops of all kinds. The Royal Factory at Capodimonte, founded by the Bourbons, still makes what may be the most beautiful **porcelain and ceramic figures** in Europe, sold at the fancier shops in the city centre. Another old Naples tradition is the making of **cameos** in various materials; you'll see them everywhere, but the shops outside the San Martino monastery have a good selection at relatively low prices.

Via San Biagio dei Librai, the middle of the Spaccanapoli, is as its name implies a street of **booksellers**—some of the best old book dealers in Italy, conveniently near the University—but the street is also full of many more odd surprises for shoppers as well. Many of the religious goods shops have surprisingly good works in terracotta; the **Doll Hospital** at No. 81, ✆ 203067, is one of the most charming shops in Naples.

All around the back streets there are antique and junk shops that won't overcharge you unless you let them. The city has an immense twice-monthly antiques market, the **Fiera dell'Antiquariato**, held on alternate Saturday and Sunday mornings in the gardens of the Villa Comunale. You can buy lovely old prints of Naples and beyond at **Bowinkel**, at Piazza dei Martiri 24, ✆ 7644344, and beautiful candles, including some sculpted to depict well-known Italian political and showbusiness personalities, from the **Antica Cereria** at Via C. Doria 6–8, ✆ 5499745. Finally, for the once-in-a-lifetime souvenir, the 150-year-old **Fonderia Chiurazzi**, Via Ponti Rossi 271, ✆ 7512685, makes artistic bronzes, specializing in reproductions of works in the Museo Archeologico; if you have billions of lire to spare, they'll do them life-size, or even bigger.

Sports and Activities

The best sources of information on forthcoming events of all kinds are the local newspaper *Il Mattino* and the free multi-lingual monthly guide *Qui Napoli.* Many of the city's permanent attractions are concentrated in the Fuorigrotta district, west of Mergellina. **Edenlandia** is the big amusement park there, on Viale Kennedy in the Mostra d'Oltremare, Naples' big trade fair site. There is also a **dog-racing** track and a small but fun **zoo** in the same area.

Nearby on Via Fuorigrotta, just past the tunnel, there's **jai-alai** (Basque Pelota) every night at 8pm. Anything a Neapolitan can bet on flourishes here; the **race-track**, the *Ippodromo di Agnano*, with both Thoroughbred and trotting races throughout most of the year, is out west in Agnano, 10km from the city centre along the *tangenziale*. And of course there's always **football**. With the help of Diego Armando Maradona, Napoli won its first-ever league title in 1987; since his departure the club has fallen on harder times, but every significant victory still calls forth a spontaneous celebration all over town that seems like Carnival in Rio de Janeiro, and any match is likely to prove an unforgettable experience with the Neapolitans to make up the crowd. Matches are played at the **Stadio San Paolo**, Piazzale Vincenzo Tecchio, ✆ 615623. To get there, take the Ferrovia Cumana to Mostra.

However tempting the sea off Naples might look on a scorching summer day, it's worth waiting until you get to one of the islands before taking a plunge. There is a public **swimming pool**, the **Piscina Scandone**, also in the Fuorigrotta area of town, at Via Giochi del Mediterraneo, ✆ 5709154. **Tennis** can be played at the **Tennis Club Napoli**, Viale Dohrn, ✆ 7614656, in the Villa Comunale, the **Tennis Club Vomero**, Via Rossini 8, ✆ 688912, and the **Sporting Club Virgilio**, Via Tito Lucrezio Caro, ✆ 7695261.

Naples does have less than its share of top-quality hotels; the Germans, inexplicably, blew up a few of them before their retreat in 1944. Most of the best are along Via Partenope, near the Castel dell'Ovo, a location where the views over the bay more than compensate for the traffic noise below.

very expensive

Visiting sheiks, kings and rock stars favour the ★★★★★**Excelsior**, Via Partenope 48, ✆ 7640111, fax 411743, Naples' finest, with beautiful suites and a tradition of perfect service ever since 1909, though some of the rooms could do with a bit of sprucing up.

expensive

A dozen or so other expensive hotels cluster in the Excelsior's shadow on Via Partenope. Of these, the nicest is the ★★★★**Santa Lucia**, Via Partenope 46, ✆ 7640666, fax 419044, a beautifully restored 18th-century *palazzo*, with antique paintings and furniture. Next door, the ★★★★**Vesuvio**, Via Partenope 45, ✆ 7640044, fax 407520, is another gracious hotel, with an attractive mix of old and new and a lovely roof garden for dining, with a view over the bay of Naples.

Still on the seafront, the ★★★★**Miramare**, Via N. Sauro, ✆ 427388, fax 416775, is a smaller, more intimate hotel, with 31 pleasantly decorated rooms. The ★★★★**Paradiso**, Via Catullo 11, ✆ 7614161, fax 663527, also has stunning views over the bay—make sure you book a sea-facing room. For a more old-fashioned atmosphere, but further inland, try the ★★★★**Parker**, Corso Vittorio Emanuele 135, ✆ 7612474, fax 663527, which has ample charm, with plenty of polished wood, chandeliers and comfortable furniture.

moderate

One of the most recent arrivals in Naples, the ★★★★**Angioino**, Via De Pretis 123, ✆ 5529500, fax 5529509, owned by the French Mercure hotel chain, offers 86 good-sized rooms in a central location, with efficient service that makes it popular with the business crowd. The ★★★**Rex**, Via Palepoli 12, ✆ 7649227, fax 7649227, is a clean, well-run hotel, also conveniently situated for the centre, with the advantage—essential for drivers—of a garage. In the hotel-packed Piazza Garibaldi area by the station—not the most pleasant place to stay, if you can find somewhere better, such as near the seafront—a reasonable, decent moderate-range hotel is the ★★★**Cavour**, Piazza Garibaldi 32, ✆ 283122, fax 287488. Among the less expensive hotels near the harbour side, the ★★★**Canada**, Via Mergellina 43, ✆ 680952, fax 681595, is a good choice, with 12 rooms, well located in an attractive area near the pretty Mergellina esplanade.

The **★★Ausonia**, Via Caracciolo 11, ✆ 682278, is a clean, comfortable *pensione*, with 20 rooms, all with bath, and an excellent position right on the seafront in Mergellina. Next door is the **★★Bella Napoli**, Via Caracciolo 10, ✆ 680200, a modest walk-up that won't ruin your holiday. Close by, the **★★Fontane al Mare**, Via N. Tommaseo 14, ✆ 7643811, has 21 rooms, some with bath, for similar prices. Still in the Mergellina area, the **★★Muller**, Piazza Mergellina 7, ✆ 669056, is slightly set back from the sea, but still a good deal, with 10 rooms, six of them with baths.

There are thousands of cheap hotel rooms around the Piazza Garibaldi, but most of them are in horrible dives. This is not the best place to make your base, but if you do desire to stay close to the station, one reasonably comfortable but still cheap hotel is the **★★Eden**, Corso Novara 9, ✆ 285344, with decent though not Edenic rooms, a sleepy bar, and a garage. To find it turn right as you leave the station, and it's one block up. Among the very cheap places, the Polish-Italian **★Fiore**, Via Milano 109, ✆ 5538798, rumoured to have Naples' fattest cat, is barely acceptable, but good for the area, and a bit better is the **★Zara**, Via Firenze 81, ✆ 287125, with 10 rooms, six with baths.

Another place to look for cheap accommodation is Via Mezzocannone, south of Spaccanapoli. This street borders the university, and many of the most pleasant cheap lodgings in Naples can be found here—though with so many students it may be hard to find a vacancy. Naples' **youth hostel** is the **Ostello Mergellina**, Salita della Grotta 23, ✆ 7612346, near the Mergellina Metropolitana station. IYHF cards are required.

Naples, ✆ (081–)   ***Eating Out***

'Now, everyone thinks of China as a ponderous, elephantine country; Naples, on the other hand we think of as something exciting, stimulating. Perhaps the Chinese invented slow, pacific fat macaronis, not the spaghetti that moves like the waves of the sea . . .'

Domenico Rea

This local savant, writing in the pages of *Qui Napoli*, is carrying on one of Naples' grand old causes. Forget those old legends about Marco Polo—just imagine anyone brazen enough to say spaghetti doesn't originally come from Naples! This capital of cooking, this citadel of *Italianità*, can already claim pizza, and probably many other Italian specialities as well. Neapolitans spend as much time worrying about what's for dinner as any people in the world, but like most other Italians they have a perfectly healthy attitude towards the subject. Neapolitan cuisine is simple—one of the most celebrated dishes is *spaghetti alle vongole*—and even in some of the more pretentious places you will see favourites of the Neapolitan *cucina povera* sneaking onto the menu, like *pasta e fagioli.* There are very few bad restaurants or tourist restaurants in the city, but an infinity of tiny, family-run trattorie or pizzerie; you will depart from most of them serene and satisfied.

For famous Neapolitan pizza, look for the genuine Neapolitan pizza oven, a built-in, bell-shaped affair made of stone with a broad, clean tile floor; the fire (only certain kinds of wood will do), is at the back, close to the pizza, not hidden underneath. Watch out in restaurants for the house wines; in cheaper places this is likely to be Gragnano from nearby Monte Faito—detestable rough stuff. On the other hand you can find some real surprises from Campania; a dry white called Greco di Tufo, and Taurasi, a distinguished red—as well as Falerno, the descendant of the far-famed ancient *Falernian* that Latin poets never tired of praising. Some restaurants in Naples, you will find, are the cheapest in all Italy—as they cheat on their taxes. Others can be alarmingly expensive, especially if you order fish.

expensive

Restaurants in all price ranges are spread pretty evenly around central Naples. **La Cantinella**, Via Nazario Sauro 23, ✆ 404884, near the Castel dell'Ovo, is believed by many to be Naples' finest—also the place to be seen for the Parthenopeans, with a telephone on each table. Known for its four different kinds of risotto, and a dessert called *Millefoglie con Zuppa Inglese*, it certainly isn't cheap, but you can easily spend more in other establishments nearby. At **Ciro**, Via Santa Brigida 71, ✆ 5524072 (closed Sun), near the Castel Nuovo, go ahead and order *pasta e fagioli* or any other humble pasta dish; that's what the place is famous for, typical Naples cuisine at its best, and they have been a local favourite for decades. **La Sacrestia**, Via Orazio 116, ✆ 6641186 (closed Wed), run for generations by the Ponsiglione family, is another temple of Neapolitan gastronomy, in a superb location overlooking the Bay of Naples. Try the risotto with baby squid (*risotto con neonati di seppietta*).

Giuseppone a Mare, Via Ferdinando Russo 13, ✆ 7696002 (closed Sun), overlooking Cape Posillipo, is one of Naples' institutions, especially popular with wedding parties. The fish is excellent, the setting memorable, and you probably won't forget the bill either. **Don Salvatore**, Via Mergellina 5, ✆ 681817 (closed Wed), similarly, has been around for more than 40 years, during which time it has built up a well-deserved reputation for turning out consistently fine Neapolitan dishes, accompanied by some of the area's best wines. There are set menus for those who want an introduction to Naples' best, and pizza for those who want to keep the bill down. At **Mimi alla Ferrovia**, Via Alfonso d'Aragona 21, ✆ 5538525 (closed Sun), again, you'll find no new-fangled concoctions, just honest-to-goodness dishes based on the freshest ingredients and recipes handed down for generations. For a real blow-out, let the waiters choose for you. You'll be rewarded with a table-groaning succession of antipasti, pasta and *secondi*, all cooked to perfection.

La Cantina di Triunfo, Riviera di Chiaia 64, ✆ 668101 (closed Sun), offers Neapolitan *cucina povera* raised to an art form—wintry soups of chestnuts and lentils, or lighter versions of broad beans and fresh peas in spring, *polpette di baccalà*—small balls of minced salt-cod, fried or served in a fresh tomato sauce— and mouth-watering pasta dishes, all of which change according to the season. The wine list is also exceptional, and the grappas home-made. Be sure to book, as space is very limited. Lively and friendly, **Da Peppino**, Via Palipoli, ✆ 7649582 (closed Sun), offers dining in the Santa Lucia area at a fraction of the price charged by some of the smarter restaurants. Don't expect anything too refined, but the pizza, in all its many forms, is a real treat here.

The **Osteria Canterbury**, Via Ascensione a Chiaia 6, ✆ 413584 (closed Sun), is tastefully decorated, with a warm welcoming atmosphere and a kitchen that turns out consistently good food, especially pasta dishes, including a house speciality, which combines mozzarella, aubergines and *ragù* sauce. At lunchtime, the office crowd comes here for the excellent value set menu. Book for dinner. At the **Taverna e Zi Carmela**, Via Niccolò Tommaseo 112, ✆ 7643581 (closed Sun), Aunt Carmela runs a busy and well-kept ship, with excellent home cooking, much of it done by herself, and other members of the family waiting at table. **O Sole Mio**, Via Tommaso Campanella 7, ✆ 7612323 (closed Tues), is run by a fisherman's family, and though you will find some meat on the menu, you will be better advised to go straight for the seafood, in all its many forms. Try the wonderfully tasty *cassuola di pesce*—fish casserole—but tuck your napkin into your collar, Neapolitan-style, before you start!

Pizza Paradise

Its origins are almost certainly Arab. Some people maintain the word may be derived from *pitta*, the unleavened bread eaten throughout Greece, Turkey and the Middle East. But wherever it hails from, pizza as we know it is an invention of Naples. Neapolitans are fiercely proud of this versatile dish, and haughtily disdainful of imitations and the variations made by others on the formula—the thin-crusted affair served in Roman *pizzerie* is enough to make a Neapolitan cry. And as for the deep-pan version invented in Chicago and served up in many British and American pizza parlours—the less said the better.

For Neapolitans, a real pizza must have an uneven base and be cooked in a real wood-fired oven. Some say the secret is in the flour, others in the water. But all agree the technique for flattening the dough is crucial. Not for the Neapolitans the pedantic practice of stretching out the dough with a rolling pin. In Naples, the *pizzaiolo* is a flamboyant character, flinging the dough up into the air, smashing it down on the marble table and swinging it round his head until it reaches the required shape and thickness. The best *pizzaioli* are much in demand, and take home very respectable salaries. As for the topping, the most authentic is *pomodoro fresco*—fresh tomatoes chopped over a bed of mozzarella, sprinkled with fresh basil and liberally doused with olive oil. Another Neapolitan favourite is the *ripieno*, a gut-buster of a pizza folded in two, and stuffed with fresh ricotta, mozzarella, pieces of salami and cooked ham.

However you order it, pizza should really be eaten with beer rather than wine. Many pizzerias only serve fizzy, bottled wine, which is much more expensive and best left alone. Pizza is usually eaten as a meal in itself, sometimes for lunch but more often in the evening, preceded by an antipasto of *bruschetta*—slices of thick toasted bread soused in olive oil and garlic and topped with tomatoes and basil, or fried bite-sized chunks of mozzarella and vegetables. For anyone on a tight budget— Neapolitans and tourists alike—the pizzeria is a lifeline. The bill for a pizza and a beer comes to about half that of a normal restaurant. In Naples, particularly good pizzerias are rewarded by a *vera pizza* (real pizza) emblem to hang up outside. Some of the best are the **Brandi**, the **Lombardi a Santa Chiara** and the exceptional **Da Pasqualino**, now in its fourth generation (for details *see* below).

inexpensive

Pizza is always the best friend of the budget-minded tourist (*see* above), and you can get two superb pizzas and lots of wine for the price of a plate of pasta in some smarter places at **Da Pasqualino**, Piazza Sannazzaro 78/9, ✆ 681524 (closed Tues), in Mergellina. If you need cigarettes, shout 'Gennaro!' to the balconies above and they will appear. Don't miss the old granny in the corner, whose job it is to make the superb but calorie-laden *crocchette*—potato croquettes spiked with mozzarella cheese, with which the locals invariably start their meal. Nearby, on Via Mergellina, **Tonino il Ragno** is another deservedly popular pizzeria, as is the **Pizzeria Port'Alba**, Via Port'Alba 18, ✆ 459713, where in addition you can get full dinners, including the house speciality, *linguine al cartoccio*—seafood pasta made into a foil parcel and baked in the oven, for a reasonable sum.

Slightly more upmarket, but only slightly, the **Lombardi a Santa Chiara**, Via Benedetto Croce 59, ✆ 5520780 (closed Sun), offers memorable *antipasti* of fried courgettes, baby mozzarella and artichokes, before you ever get to eat your pizza, wonderfully cooked in the classic wood oven. Noisy but friendly, this place fills up quickly, so book ahead or be prepared to wait. At the **Bellini**, Via Santa Maria di Costantinopoli 80, ✆ 459774 (closed Sun), you'll find good pizza and pasta dishes, with a few outdoor tables for summer dining. **Brandi**, Salita Sant'Anna di Palazzo 1/2, ✆ 416928, a pretty, lively pizzeria, claims to have invented the *Margherita*, Naples' most famous pizza, with mozzarella, tomatoes and fresh basil, in honour of the Bourbon queen whose favourite dish it apparently was. Whether or not you believe it, the food is always first-class. At **Da Michele**, Via C. Sersale 1, ✆ 5539204 (closed Sun), you'll probably find yourself sharing a marble-topped table with a noisy Neapolitan family. This is a decidedly no-frills place, with rough and ready service, but the atmosphere is great fun, the pizza sublime and the prices downright miraculous.

Many of the cheapest and homeliest places in Naples can be found on or around Via Speranzella, a block west of Via Toledo in the *Tavoliere*, where few tourists ever penetrate. As for the area around the railway station, restaurants here, more than elsewhere in Naples, have succumbed to opportunity and necessity; Piazza Garibaldi isn't nearly as much fun as it was a few years ago, and its hundreds of restaurants are neither keeping standards up nor prices down. But this area, and also Piazza Mercato, is an open bazaar, and you can get fat and happy just snacking from the bars and stands—slices of pizza, heavy *arancini*, and the flaky pastries called *sfogliatelle*, another Naples speciality.

Finally, we offer you an honest breakfast—bacon and eggs, if you like—at the **Ristorante California**, Via Santa Lucia 101, ℭ 7649752, Italy's greatest rendezvous for homesick Americans and a longtime Naples landmark. For dinner, the menu is split between Italian and Gringo dishes, and the roast turkey isn't bad.

cafés and gelaterie

As well as the inventors of the pizza, Neapolitans are, it is generally recognized, Italy's most dedicated and punctilious coffee consumers, and the city accordingly has its crop of elegant, now often fadedly ornate 19th-century *gran caffè*, mostly not too far from the Galleria and the Piazza del Plebiscito (*see* below). Other fine places to take coffee can be found along the waterfront, particularly out towards Mergellina. Naples also, naturally, produces some great ice cream and pastries. *Gelaterie* can be found all over town, but **Scimmia**, Piazza della Carità 4, just off the Via Toledo not far from Spaccanapoli, has for long been regarded as one of the city's best.

Entertainment and Nightlife

For concerts, shows, and other cultural events—Naples always has plenty— the best information on programmes and times will be found in the newspaper *Il Mattino*, or in the free monthly guide *Qui Napoli*.

opera, classical music and theatre

For opera lovers one of the ultimate experiences is a night at the **San Carlo** (box office ℭ 7972370/7972111), but tickets are extremely hard to come by, and very pricey. Hotels may be able to get them most easily. If you do manage to get a ticket, be sure to dress your best. You may have more luck catching a **concert** at the **Auditorium RAI-TV**, Via Guglielmo Marconi, ℭ 610122, at the **Conservatorio di Musica**, Via San Pietro a Maiella, ℭ 459255, or at the **Associazione Alessandro Scarlatti**, Piazza dei Martiri 58, ℭ 406011. Check with the tourist office or in *Qui Napoli* for programmes, and don't forget also that many, often free concerts are staged in the city's churches. Look out for street bill-boards with details of coming events.

Unless your Italian is fluent, **theatre** will probably be a frustrating experience, and if you go for one of the superbly executed dialect plays, especially by the **Gruppo Repertorio di Eduardo de Filippo**, Piazza Teatro S. Ferdinando, ℂ 444500, you may not understand a word. If that doesn't put you off, the best theatres to try are the **Politeama**, Via Monte di Dio, ℂ 7645016, the **Cilea**, Via S. Domenico, ℂ 646830, the **Bracco**, Via Tarsia, ℂ 5495904 and the **Sannazaro**, Via Chiaia 157, ℂ 411723.

clubs, bars and discos

Neapolitans are night-owls, probably thanks to their Spanish heritage, and many, especially in summer, don't even think about going out to dinner until 10pm. That doesn't leave too much time for partying, once the 2–3 hour eating ritual is over, but there are some reasonable clubs and late-night bars (as well as some terrible ones). The thing to remember is that some areas are best left alone after midnight, most notably the Piazza Garibaldi area near the station, and the so-called *quartieri*, the narrow side streets that run off the Via Toledo. And if the vampish hookers to be seen at every street corner after dark should take your fancy, remember to take a second look—those girls could well be boys. Naples is famous even in drag-obsessed Italy for its transvestites, and some of them are positively remarkable. The genuine female prostitutes tend to be the crones on the other side of the street.

KGB, Salita Scudillo, ℂ 7435206 *(open 11pm–3am Thurs–Sat only)*, is a discotheque which also puts on live bands, some of them quite good. **The Jam Club**, Via G. Martucci 85/7, ℂ 7614864 *(open 8.30pm–4.30am; closed Mon)*, is aimed at a 30-plus age group, which makes it a pleasant place for a late night drink. The barman is a dab hand with cocktails, there is live music every night, and on Fridays pasta is offered on the house. The **Kiss Kiss**, Via Sgambati 47, ℂ 5466566, Naples' biggest disco, is an institution, with different theme nights every night of the week, and an affluent young crowd. **My Way**, Via Cappella Vecchia 30/c, ℂ 7644735 *(open 10pm–4am Fri–Sun only)*, is another popular nightspot, where Neapolitans have been dancing into the small hours for as long as anyone can remember.

At the **Otto Club**, Piazzetta Cariati 24, ℂ 666262 *(closed Mon)*, you'll get **jazz** and plenty of it, including some very talented local musicians. It also serves plates of pasta and light meals, and has a well-stocked bar, but don't take too much cash with you, as this otherwise very pleasant club is in a pretty hard area, and when you leave it's best to get a taxi rather than walk around much outside. The **Virgilio Sporting Club**, Via Tito Lucrezio Caro 6, ℂ 7695261 *(open midnight–4am Fri–Sun only)*, up on Posillipo hill, is a much more tranquil night-club, set in its own parkland, with tables outside in fine weather.

Sorrento

Around the Bay: from Baia to Sorrento

Naples' hinterlands share fully in the peculiarities and sharp contrasts of the big city. Creation left nothing half-done or poorly done; against any other part of the monotonous Italian coastline, the Campanian shore seems almost indecently blessed, possessing the kind of irresistibly distracting beauty that seduces history off the path of duty and virtue. Today, for all the troubles that come seeping out of Naples, this coast is still one of the capitals of Mediterranean languor.

In Roman days, it was nothing less than the California of the ancient world: fantastically prosperous, lined with glittering resort towns full of refugees from the Roman rat-race, as favoured by artists and poets as it was by rich patricians. Like California, though, the perfume was mixed with a little whiff of insecurity. Vesuvius would be enough, but even outside of the regularly scheduled eruptions and earthquakes, the region is Vulcan's own curiosity shop. West of Naples especially, there are eternally rising and sinking landscapes, sulphurous pools, thermal springs and even a baby volcano—altogether, perhaps the most unstable corner of the broad earth's crust.

Getting Around

Naples, of course, is the hub for all transport throughout the area; buses, ferries and local commuter rail lines lead out from the city to all points (*see* pp.60–1).

by rail

Regular FS trains aren't much help here, except for a fast trip between Naples and Salerno. Fortunately, there are the other, local, lines, of which the most important is the refreshingly clean and efficient **Circumvesuviana**, the best way to reach Pompeii, Herculaneum and Sorrento. This line has its own ultramodern station, on Corso Garibaldi just south of the Piazza Garibaldi (© 7792444), but all of its trains also make a stop at the Stazione Centrale itself before proceeding east. At Centrale their station is underground, sharing space with that of the Naples Metropolitana; this can be confusing, since there are no schedules posted and the ticket windows aren't marked—you need to ask someone to make sure you are heading for the right train. The main lines run east through Ercolano (the stop for Herculaneum) and Torre del Greco, and then diverge near Torre Annunziata, one line heading for Sarno, out in the farm country east of Vesuvius, and the other for Sorrento. Both pass Pompeii, though on opposite sides. The Sorrento train leaves you near the main entrance; on the other line the stop at Villa dei Misteri is closest. The Circumvesuviana terminal in Sorrento is two streets east from Piazza Tasso, the town centre. Circumvesuviana trains usually run every half-hour between 5am and 10.45pm. On a *direttissima*, of which there are several daily, the Naples–Sorrento trip takes an hour—locals are considerably slower. An additional Circumvesuviana line has infrequent trains north of Vesuvius to Nola and Baiano.

Bay of Naples

20km
10 miles

91

For the west bay, Naples' own **Metropolitana** goes as far as Pozzuoli-Solfatara. The two other regional lines both have trains about every half-hour from Piazza Montesanto Station, near the Piazza Dante. The **Ferrovia Cumana** (© 5513328) runs along the shore, through Fuorigrotta, Bagnoli, Pozzuoli, and Baia to Torregaveta. The remarkable **Circumflegrea** (also © 5513328) also finishes at Torregaveta, after passing through plenty of places you probably won't want to visit, though it does stop at the archaeological site of Cumae. The Circumflegrea is easily the most macabre railway in the western world; the trip begins by passing a neon shrine to the Virgin Mary in the middle of the Montesanto Tunnel, and then passes through stations that are metal sheds or bombed-out ruins, with smashed and derailed cars lying alongside the tracks to give passengers something to think about. There are no schedules printed or even imagined, but the line usually closes down for a long lunch break. The station at Cumae is gutted and abandoned; head up towards the acropolis, through the thorn bushes and dense, adder-haunted forests, and eventually you'll sneak in the back and get to see the ruins of Cumae for free (there's a bus from Baia to the front gate for sissies).

by bus

Naples city bus No. 152, from Piazza Garibaldi and Via Mergellina, travels to Solfatara and Pozzuoli. Other buses run by the local transport authorities of Baia and Bacoli operate regular services from these towns along the coast road to Naples. All stop frequently along the way. From the bus stop in the centre of Baia, there are connecting buses to Cumae, Bacoli, and Cape Misenum.

The Circumvesuviana makes buses unnecessary for most of the east bay. The express bus from Naples to Salerno, which usually runs every half hour, leaves from the **SITA** office on Via Pisanelli, just off the Piazza Municipio (© 5522176), and arrives in Salerno at the terminal at Corso Garibaldi 117, © (089) 226604. SITA also runs the buses from Salerno for the Amalfi coast, with regular departures for Sorrento (Piazza Tasso), or stopping short at Amalfi, Ravello or other towns along the route; they are usually so frequent that it is easy to see all the main coast towns on a day-trip, hopping from one to the next. Buses are definitely the best way to do it; driving yourself can be a hair-raising experience when it's busy.

by road

Drivers heading for the west bay area and wishing to arrive quite quickly should get onto the *tangenziale* out of Naples and stay on it until past Pozzuoli, before turning off onto the (by then) more tranquil SS7qu, which runs around the Miseno peninsula. Alternately, they can take the SS7qu all the way from the harbourside in Naples, via the Mergellina tunnel, or the pretty but slow coastal road—initially the Via Posillipo—around Cape Posillipo.

If you are heading towards Pompeii and the east bay—where the distances are much greater, and so a car much more useful—then, again, it's advisable to use the A3 *autostrada* to get out of Naples if you don't want to spend a long time on the SS18 coast road through the suburbs. Leave the A3 at the Ercolano exit for Herculaneum; south of here, though still pretty busy, the SS18 gradually becomes more attractive. At Pompeii the SS145 road turns off to the right for the Sorrento peninsula; beyond Sorrento it becomes the famous, or infamous, **Amalfi drive**. This spectacular road—at its most extreme, no more than a winding ledge of hairpins half way up a sheer cliff—is unquestionably worth seeing, but drivers should be aware of what is ahead of them, and avoid it at night or in bad weather. For some idea of the difficulties of the road, consider that it takes the express bus almost three hours to navigate the 66km from Salerno to Sorrento.

West from Naples: Pozzuoli and the Phlegraean Fields

The very pretty coastal road leaving the city, with views of Vesuvius all through the suburb of Posillipo, passes the little island of Nisida; this was a favoured spot in ancient times, and legend has it that Brutus and Cassius planned Caesar's murder here in the villa of one of their fellow conspirators. Naples' suburbs continue through **Agnano**, a town of spas and hot springs set around a mile-wide extinct crater, and stretch as far as **Pozzuoli**.

Pozzuoli today is a modest little city, with only its ruins to remind it of the time when Roman Puteoli, and not Naples, was the metropolis of the bay. In the time of Caesar and Augustus, it was the main port of Italy; at one point the Senate actually considered the bizarre idea of digging a canal from here to Rome to make shipping safer. The city's decline began in the 2nd century with the expansion of the port of Ostia, closer to Rome. During the 5th-century invasions, most of *Puteoli's* citizens took refuge in better-defended Naples.

The **Amphitheatre**, on Via Domiziana, near the railway station, was the third-largest in the Roman world (after those in Rome itself and Capua), with 60 gates for letting the beasts in, and pipes to flood it for mock naval battles. Vespasian built it, in way of thanks to *Puteoli* for its aid in the civil war that made him emperor. Pozzuoli's other important ruin is a little embarrassment to the town; for centuries people here were showing off the ancient **Serapeum**—temple to the popular Egyptian god Serapis—until some killjoy archaeologist proved the thing to be an unusually lavish *macellum*, or market. Only the foundations remain, in a park near Pozzuoli's small harbour, and they are usually underwater, but it was an important tourist sight in the days of the Grand Tour, before the Bourbons stole all the columns for their dreary palace in Caserta.

For all ancient Puteoli's size and wealth, little else remains. There is a reason, and Pozzuoli would like to introduce a new word to your vocabulary to explain it: *bradyseism* is a rare seismic phenomenon that afflicts this town and other spots around the bay. It manifests itself in the form of 'slow' earthquakes; no one notices them, but the level of the land can rise or fall several feet in a few months. Mostly, it has been falling, and all of Puteoli that hasn't been gently shaken to pieces over the centuries is now underwater. Roman moles and docks can still sometimes be made out beneath the surface.

Solfatara

What's troubling Pozzuoli can be seen more clearly just outside the town at **Solfatara**, the storm centre of what the Greeks called the Phlegraean (fiery) Fields, in Italian the *Campi Flegrei*. To the Romans, it was the *Forum Vulcani*, and a major attraction of the Campanian coast. It hasn't changed much since. Solfatara *(open 9am–sunset daily; adm)* is another crater of a collapsed volcano, but one that just can't be still; sulphur gas vents, bubbling mud pits and whistling superheated steam fumaroles decorate the eerie landscape. Guides are around to keep you away from the dangerous spots. Their favourite trick is to hold a flame to one of the gas vents—making a dozen others nearby go off at the same time. Solfatara is perfectly safe, even though the ground underneath feels hot and sounds strangely hollow. It is; scientists keep a close watch on the huge plug of cooled lava that underlies the whole of the area about Pozzuoli, and they say the pressure on it from below is only one-third as much as it was under Vesuvius in AD 79.

We promised you a baby volcano, and you'll see it near the coast west of Pozzuoli. **Monte Nuovo** has been quiet for some time (inexplicably passing up the opportunity to celebrate its 450th birthday, on 29th September 1988). The same earthquake in 1538 that wrecked much of Pozzuoli gave birth to this little cone. It's only about 140m tall, and an easy climb up to the crater (you can have a picnic inside it). Its percolation from the bowels of Campania filled up half of the **Lago di Lucrino**, separated from the sea by a narrow strip of land. Since antiquity, it has been renowned for its oysters. About 90 BC, a sharp Roman named C. Sergius Orata first had the idea of farming oysters here, and selling them to the rich owners of the villas around the bay; from this business he made one of the biggest killings of classical antiquity.

Cape Misenum

Baia, the next town along the coast, was nothing less than the greatest pleasure dome of classical antiquity (see 'Topics', p.47) Anybody who was anybody in the Roman world had a villa here, with a view of the sea, beach access, and a few hundred slaves to dust the statues and clean up after the orgies. You'll find little hint of that today; Goths, malaria and earthquakes have done a thorough job of wrecking the place. Most of ancient Baiae is now underwater, a victim of the same bradyseism that afflicts Pozzuoli. Modern Baia is a pleasant small town, but its lovely bay has been consigned to use as a graveyard for dead freighters. Nevertheless, the extensive but humble remains of the imperial villa can be visited at the **Parco Archeologico** *(open 9am–7pm Tues–Sun; adm)*. Not much is labelled or explained, but the ruins include a part of the famous baths, a thermal spa for wealthy Romans that was probably the largest and poshest such establishment in the ancient world, and an inspiration for the great public baths of Rome and other cities.

At Baia, the coast curves southwards towards Bacoli and **Cape Misenum** (*Capo Miseno*), a beautiful spot that for centuries was the greatest naval base of the Roman Empire, home to 10,000 sailors (mostly Greeks and Syrians). As at Baia, foundations and bits of columns and cornices are everywhere, though nothing of any real interest has survived intact. Nearby Lake Miseno, also called the 'Dead Sea', was once a part of the base, joined to the sea by a canal dug by Augustus's right-hand man Cornelius Agrippa, in 37 BC. A memorable event of antiquity was the time Caligula ordered a double row of boats to be made across the bay, all the way from Bacoli to Pozzuoli. Suentonius wrote that the purpose was to fulfil a prophecy that Caligula would never become emperor until he rode across the bay on his horse (which he proceeded to do); it's more likely, though, that he did it to impress the Persian ambassador with the strength of the Roman Navy.

That same distance was covered by the famous 'boy on a dolphin', a story that inspired many classical works of art. Many reliable witnesses attested to Pliny that they had seen it—a little boy of the peninsula who had befriended a dolphin, which gave him a ride every day to lessons with his tutor in Puteoli. Pliny records that the boy died after an illness, and that the dolphin, after waiting faithfully for his friend for several days, beached himself and died too. The two were burned together.

The pleasant village of **Bacoli**, nearby, has two sights: a covered Roman reservoir called the **Piscina Mirabile**, a vaulted chamber like the famous one in Istanbul; and the vast ruin of a villa that might have belonged to Julius Caesar, called by the locals **Centro Camarelle**, the 'hundred little rooms'.

Two other lakes, both created as a by-product of volcanic action, lie north of Cape Misenum; one, the **Lago di Fusaro**, is a large, shallow oyster farm, cut off from the sea by a sand bar near the woebegone fishing village of Torregaveta, the terminus of the Circumflegrea and Cumana railways. The decaying rococo palace on an island in the centre is the Casino, built in 1782 by the Bourbon kings' favourite architect, Luigi Vanvitelli. **Lago d'Averno**—Lake Avernus—may ring a bell from your school days; it's the mouth of Hell, according to the ancient Greeks, who believed any passing bird would be suffocated by the infernal fumes rising from it. Cornelius Agrippa didn't have much respect for mythology, and he turned the lake into a part of the naval base by cutting another canal. Among the ruins that surround it are the remains of a domed building, perhaps a temple or a sort of spa, originally as big as the Pantheon in Rome. Emperor Nero was fond of this area, and he built a covered canal lined with colonnades from the lake all the way to Pozzuoli; no trace remains of this now.

Cumae

As the story has it, King Tarquin of Rome came here, to the most venerable and respected oracle in all the western Mediterranean, with the intention of purchasing nine prophetic books from the Cumaean Sibyl. Unwisely, he said they were too dear, whereupon the Sibyl threw three of the books into the fire and offered him the remaining six at the same price. Again he complained, and the Sibyl put three more in the flames; finally Tarquin gave up, and took the last three at the original price. It was a good bargain. The Sibylline Books guided Rome's destiny until they too were burned up in the great fire of 82 BC.

Cumae had other distinctions. As one of the first Greek foundations in Italy, the city was the mother colony for Naples and many other cities of Magna Graecia. In 421 BC, Cumae lost its independence to the Samnites, and declined steadily from then on; Arab raiders, who did so much damage everywhere else around Campania, finally wiped the city off the map in the 9th century AD. They did a good job of it, and there is little to see at the site *(open 9am–7pm Tues–Sun; adm)*, only the foundations of a few temples on the high **acropolis**, worth the climb for the views around Cape Misenum. One of the ruins was a famous Temple of Apollo, rebuilt by Augustus in thanks to the god after his victory at Actium.

Just below the summit, you may visit the **Cave of the Cumaean Sibyl** itself, discovered by accident in 1932. This is a place of mystery, a long series of strange, trapezoidal galleries cut out of solid rock—impressive enough, even stripped of the sumptuous decoration they must once have had (all ancient oracles were marvellously profitable). Nobody has a clear idea how old it is; Cumae may well have been a religious centre long before the Greek colonists arrived. By classical times, it took the form of an oracle quite like the one at Delphi. At the far end of the cave, a plain alcove with two benches marks the spot where the Sibyls would inhale fumes over the sacred tripod, chew laurel leaves, and go into their trance.

West of Naples, (© 081–) **Eating Out**

Nobody has made the western side of the bay a base for their holiday since the 4th century AD. But, if you're out looking over the ruins at Pozzuoli, Baia and Cumae, there are a few good places to have lunch.

Pozzuoli

On the harbour in Pozzuoli, the **Martusciello**, Via Emporio 24, © 5261702, is one of the best places for fish you'll find anywhere—*zuppa di pesce, risotto al pescatore* and grilled sea bass are all excellent (moderate). **Del Capitano**, Via Lungomare C. Colombo 10, © 5262283, is another good rendezvous for fish-lovers (moderate). Slightly more expensive, but worth the extra, is **La Lanterna**, Via C. Colombo 20, © 5263081 (closed Mon), a small ristorante on the port, especially attractive in the evening, where chef Giancarlo Schettini produces more refined variations on the usual seafood theme. The menu changes regularly, according to season (moderate/expensive).

At **La Granzeola**, Via Terracciano 1, © 5262777 (closed Sun), owner-chef Carmine Russo turns fish bought directly off the local boats into a dazzling array of unusual and tasty dishes, especially with pasta. Try the *rigatoni con ragù di cozze*—short pasta with a delicious mussel sauce (expensive). **Il Tempio**, Via Serapide 13, © 8665179 (closed Wed), overlooking the ruined temple in Pozzuoli's main square, is justly famous for its antipasti. Leave it to the waiter and he will bring you plate after plate, mostly fish-based, including octopus, fried squid, baby red mullet, clams and giant prawns, until you tell him to stop. Many people call it a day after this, and few ever get beyond the *primi* (moderate).

Baia and Bacoli

At Baia's **L'Altro Cucchiaro**, Via Lucullo 13, ℂ 8687196 (closed Sun evenings, Mon, 3 weeks Aug), you can dine on divine concoctions of seafood and pasta, and superb fish (expensive). Another member of the same family runs the nearby **Franco Cucchiaro**, Via Lucullo 6, ℂ 8687673, where you can feast on a fabulous *linguine alle zucchine*, and not just fish, but also fine lamb, rabbit and veal dishes as well (moderate). At **La Ninfea**, Via Lago Lucrino, ℂ 8661326, you can bask on the lakeside terrace as you dine on fish and grilled meats (expensive).

In Bacoli, two good fish restaurants are the **Giardino degli Aranci**, Via Cuma 75, ℂ 8543120, and the **Villa Chiara**, Via Torre di Cappella 8, ℂ 8687139 (both moderate).

Torregaveta

Restaurants in shabbyish Torregaveta are cheaper than in the towns inside the bay. The **Pizzeria Ristorante Al Pontile**, ℂ 8689180, has pizzas and full dinners for reasonable prices (inexpensive). So too does the **Anfiteatro Cumano**, ℂ 854 3119, with a nice seafront terrace, in nearby Lido Fusaro (open summer only; inexpensive).

East of Naples: Mount Vesuvius and Pompeii

Despite its fearsome reputation, and its formidable appearance looming over Naples, **Mount Vesuvius** is a midget as volcanoes go—only 1281m. No one suspected it even was a volcano, in fact, until it surprised the people of Pompeii, Herculaneum, and Stabiae on 24 August AD 79. That titanic eruption did not include much lava, but it buried Herculaneum under mud and the other two cities under cinders and ash, while coating most of Italy with a thin layer of dust. After that explosion, Roman writers noted that the plume of smoke and ash over the volcano looked exactly like a young pine tree; observers have noted the same sinister tree-shape in many eruptions since.

Over a hundred eruptions since have destroyed various towns and villages, some more than once. But like at Mount Etna in Sicily, people just can't stay away from Vesuvius' slopes. Volcanic soil grows grapes and olives in abundance, though the novelty of it often makes the Italians exaggerate their quality. The AD 79 explosion hasn't been equalled since; it blew the top of the mountain

Il Vesuvio

clean off, leaving two peaks, with the main fissure in between. The lower one is called Monte Somma, or *nasone*—'big nose'—by the Neapolitans; the higher, parallel peak is Vesuvius proper.

Vesuvius was last heard from in 1944. The final eruption left the lava flows you'll see on the upper slopes; it also sealed the main fissure, putting an end to the permanent plume of smoke that once was such a familiar landmark. You can bet the scientists are watching Vesuvius. Despite the long hiatus, they say there is no reason to expect another eruption soon, though if it were to explode now, they warn, it would cause a catastrophe—the area around the volcano has become one of the most densely populated in all Italy. To visit the main crater (between the two peaks), take the Vesuvius bus from the Circumvesuviana stop in Ercolano; then you have a choice of a stiff, one-hour climb over rough stones and ash, or a ride on the cable car *(cars run April–Sept 10am–5.30pm daily; Oct 10am–4pm daily; Dec–Mar 10.30am–3.30pm daily; closed Nov; tickets cost L7600 for round trip, and guide at the top)*.

Tourist Information

There is a well-organized tourist office in Pompei town, at Via Sacra 1, 80045, © (081) 8507255, fax 8632401, which has a branch office near the Porta Marina entrance to the old Pompeii site.

Herculaneum

Naples' discouraging industrial sprawl spreads eastwards as far as Torre del Greco without a break. The drab suburb of **Ercolano** is a part of it, built over the mass of rock that imprisons ancient **Herculaneum**, a smaller and less famous sight than Pompeii but just as much worth visiting *(open 9am–one hour before sunset daily; adm)*. Some people like it even better than its more famous sister site.

Unlike Pompeii, an important commercial centre, Herculaneum seems to have been a wealthy resort, only about one-third the size. Also, Vesuvius destroyed them in different ways. Pompeii was buried under layers of ash, while Herculaneum, much closer to the volcano, drowned under a sea of mud. Over time the mud hardened to a soft stone, preserving the city and nearly everything in it as a sort of fossil—furniture, clothing and even some of the goods in the shops have survived.

Like Pompeii, Herculaneum was discovered by accident. In the early 1700s, a Bourbon officer named Prince Elbeuf had a well dug here; not too far down, the workmen struck a stone pavement—the stage of the city's theatre. The Bourbon government began some old-fashioned destructive excavation, but serious archaeological work began only under Mussolini. Only about eight blocks of shops and villas, some quite fashionable, have been excavated. The rest is covered not only by tens of metres of rock, but also a dense modern neighbourhood; bringing more of Herculaneum to light is a fantastically slow and expensive operation, but new digs are still going on.

At any given time, most of the buildings will be locked, but the guards wandering about have all the keys and will show you almost any of them upon request (they are not supposed to accept tips, though you'll find they often seem to expect them). Many of the most interesting houses can be found along Cardo IV, the street in the centre of the excavated area; on the corner of the Decumanus Inferior, the **House of the Wooden Partition** may be the best example we have of the façade of a Roman house. Next door, the **Trellis House** was a much more modest dwelling, with a built-in workshop; the **House of the Mosaic Atrium**, down the street, is another luxurious villa, built with a mind to the sea view from the bedrooms upstairs. On the other side of the Decumanus, Cardo IV passes the **Samnite House** (so named because of its architectural style), and further up a column with police notices painted on it stands near the **House of the Neptune**, with a lovely mythological mosaic in the atrium.

Other buildings worth a visit are the **House of the Deer**, with its infamous statue of a drunken Hercules relieving himself picturesquely; the well-preserved **Baths**; and the **Palaestra**, or gym, with its unusual serpent fountain and elegant, cross-shaped swimming pool.

Beyond Ercolano, the coastal road passes through three sorry towns. The men of **Torre del Greco** have long been famous for gathering and working coral, a business now threatened by pollution. These days, much of the coral is imported from Asia, though it is still worked locally. Torre del Greco has recently become more famous for organized crime and gangland killings, though the population still turn out en masse to express their devotion to the Madonna in the procession for the Immaculate Conception, on 8 December, when the town gives thanks for having been spared in one the last century's eruptions of Vesuvius (*see* Festivals, p.15). In **Torre Annunziata** they make lots of pasta, and in **Castellammare di Stabia**, beneath a 12th-century Hohenstaufen castle, are the modern shipyards of the Italian Navy. Roman *Stabiae* was the port of Pompeii, and the other big town destroyed by Vesuvius, but it has never been excavated. From Castellammare, you can take a short ride on the funicular railway up to **Monte Faito**, a broad, heavily forested mountain that may well be the last really tranquil spot on the Bay—though a few hotels have already appeared.

Pompeii

Herculaneum may have been better preserved, but to see an entire ancient city come to life, the only place on earth you can go is this magic time capsule, left to us by the good graces of Mount Vesuvius. Pompeii is no mere ruin; walking down the old Roman high street, you can peek into the shops, read the graffiti on the walls, then wander off down the back streets to explore the homes of the inhabitants and appraise their taste in painting—they won't mind a bit if you do. Almost everything we know for sure concerning the daily life of the ancients was learned here, and the huge mass of artefacts and art dug up over 200 years is still helping scholars to re-evaluate the Roman world.

Though a fair-sized city by Roman standards, with a population of some 20,000, Pompeii was probably only the third or fourth city of Campania, a trading and manufacturing centre of no special distinction. Founded perhaps in the 7th century BC, the city came under the Roman sphere of influence around 200; by the fateful year of AD 79, it was still a cosmopolitan place, culturally more Greek than Roman. Vesuvius' rumblings, and the tall, sinister-looking cloud that began to form above it, gave those Pompeiians with any presence of mind a chance to leave. Only about 10 per cent of the population perished.

After the city was buried under the stones and ash of the eruption, the upper floors still stuck out; these were looted, and gradually cleared by farmers, and eventually the city was forgotten altogether. Engineers found it while digging an aqueduct in 1600, and the first excavations began in 1748—a four-star attraction for northern Europeans on the Grand Tour. The early digs were far from scientific; archaeologists today sniff that they did more damage than Vesuvius. Resurrected Pompeii has had other problems: theft of artworks, a good dose of bombs in World War II, and most recently the earthquake of 1980. The damage from that is still being repaired today, though almost all the buildings are once more open to visitors *(site open 9am–one hour before sunset Tues–Sun; adm)*.

There are two ways to see Pompeii; spend two or three hours on the main sights, or devote the day to scrutinizing details, for a total immersion in the ancient world you won't find anywhere else like it (the detailed guidebooks sold in the stands outside will help you with this). The arrangement is the same as at Herculaneum, and you'll need to ask the guards (or follow a tour group) to get into most of the buildings. Guards will discreetly extort large or small sums from you; this is Naples, after all.

Pompeii isn't quite a perfect time capsule; a little background will help to complete the picture. The site today is all too serene, with a small-town air. Remember that almost every building was two or three storeys high, and that most streets of a Roman town were permanent market-places. As long as daylight lasted, Pompeii's would have been crowded with improvised *bancarelle*; any chariot or wagon driver who wished to pass would need all manner of creative cursing. At least the streets are well-paved—better than Rome itself in fact; Campania's cities, the richest in western Europe, could well afford such luxuries. All the pavements were much more smooth and even than you see them now. The purpose of the flat stones laid across the streets should not be hard to guess. They were places to cross when it rained—streets here were also drains—and the slots in them allowed wagon wheels to pass through.

Pompeii

Pompeii

300 metres
300 yards

N

1. Porta Marina/ Antiquarium
2. Temple of Apollo
3. Temple of Jupiter
4. Macellum
5. Basilica
6. Public Offices
7. Temple of Fortune
8. Temple of Fortune
9. House of Pansa
10. House of the Faun
11. House of the Vetii
12. House of Marcus Fronto
13. Theatre
14. Temple of Isis
15. House of Loretus
16. House of the Cryptoporticus
17. Palaestra
18. Amphitheatre
19. Villa of Diomedes
20. Villa dei Misteri

Porta Marina

Porta Ercolano

to Circumvesuviana

to 20

to Circumvesuviana

Porta di Vesuvio

Porta di Nola

Porta Stabiana

Triangular Forum

New Excavations

VICOLO DI MERCURIO

VIA DEGLI AUGUSTALI

VIA DELL' ABBONDANZA

VIA STABIANA

VIA DI NOLA

The shops, open to the street in the day, would be sealed up behind shutters at night, just as they are in the old parts of Mediterranean cities today. Houses, on the other hand, turn a completely blank wall to the street; they got their light and air from skylights in the *atrium*, the roofed court around which the rooms were arranged. Later, fancier villas will have a second, open court directly behind the first, designed after the Greek *peristyle*. As in Rome, no part of town was necessarily the fashionable district; elegant villas will be found anywhere, often between two simple workmen's flats. And don't take the street names too seriously. They were bestowed by the archaeologists, often, as with the Via di Mercurio (Mercury Street), after mythological subjects depicted on the street fountains.

Roman Frescoes

Not surprisingly, Pompeii and Herculaneum have been of prime importance in the study of Roman painting. It is imposible to know how much of this art was borrowed from the Greeks or the Etruscans, although by the time of Augustus it appears that Rome and Campania were in the vanguard.

New fashions set in the palaces of the Palatine Hill were quickly copied in the villas of the Roman California. Or perhaps it was vice versa.

Wealthy Romans tended to regard their homes as domestic shrines rather than a place to kick off their *caligae* and relax after a hard day at the Forum (the public baths served that role—the ancient Italians behaved much like the modern ones, who do everything in groups of ten and can't bear being alone); at home they used as many mosaics and wall paintings as they could afford to lend the place the necessary dignity. In Pompeii and Herculaneum, four styles of painting have been defined by art historians, although as you roam the ruins you'll find that they often overlap. Style I (2nd century BC) was heavily influenced by Hellenistic models, especially from Alexandria: walls are divided into three sections, often by bands of stucco, with a cornice and frieze along the top and square panels (dados) on the bottom, while the middle sections are skilfully painted to resemble rich marble slabs. The prediliction for deep colours, combined with the lack of windows, often makes these small rooms seem claustrophobic to us (see Herculaneum's Samnite House).

Later Romans must have felt the same lack of air and space, for about 90 BC they moved on to the 'architectonic' Style II. Columns and architraves were painted around the edges of the wall, an architectural screen designed to provide an illusion of depth and space on the large central panels. At first the centres were more pseudo-marble, but landscapes and mythological scenes soon became more popular. The Villa of the Mysteries near Pompeii is a prime example; it is also one of the oldest to have portraits of real people, or at least local character types.

Vitruvius, the celebrated writer on architecture, sternly disapproved of Style III, which abandoned the pretence and architectural dissimulation in favour of more playful compositions in perspective, still always done with a strict regard for symmetry. A favourite motif was patterns of foliage, fountains and candelabras, decorated with delicate, imaginative figures; these would be called 'grotesques' in the Renaissance, when Raphael and his friends rediscovered some in a Roman 'grotto' that was really a part of Nero's Golden House. The middle panels are often done in solid colours, with small scenes at the centre to resemble framed paintings. In Pompeii, examples include the Houses of Lucretius Fronto and the Priest Amandus, the latter done by a remarkable artist who comes close to scientific perspective, albeit with several vanishing points.

The last fashion to hit Pompeii before Vesuvius did, Style IV, combines the architectural elements of Style II and the framed picture effects of Style III, but with a greater degree of elaboration and decoration. Additional small scenes are placed on the sides—landscapes, still lifes, genre scenes from everyday life, and architectural *trompe l'oeil* windows done with a much more refined use of perspective (see the House of the Vettii). Sometimes an entire stage would be painted, with the curtain pulled aside to show a scene from a play; borders are decorated with flowers, satyrs, grotesques and frolicking Cupids (Italians call these *amoretti*). Humourous vignettes of the gods and incidents from Virgil's *Aeneid* were popular, along with images of Pompeii's divine patroness, Venus. She also inspired the subject matter of the frescoes you have to bribe the guards to see.

Around the Forum

Past the throng of hawkers and refreshment stands, the main entrance to the site takes you through the walls at the **Porta Marina**. Just inside the gate, the **Antiquarium** displays some of the artworks that haven't been spirited off to the Naples museum, as well as some truly gruesome casts of fossilized victims of the eruption, caught in their death poses. Two blocks beyond the Antiquarium and you're in the **Forum**, oriented towards a view of Vesuvius. Unfortunately this is the worst-preserved part of town. Here you can see the tribune from which orators addressed public meetings, and the pedestals that held statues of heroes and civic benefactors, as well as the once-imposing **Basilica** (the law courts), temples to Apollo and Jupiter, and, among other buildings, a public latrine and a **Macellum**, or market, decorated with frescoes.

Down Mercury Street

Heading for Pompeii's old East End, there are several interesting houses along the Via di Mercurio, including a **Temple of Fortune** on the corner of Via di Nola. The real attractions in this part of town, though, are a few lavish villas off on the side streets: the enormous **House of Pansa**; the **House of the Faun**, with the oldest known welcome mat (set in the pavement, really); and the wonderful **House of the Vetii**, owned by a pair of wealthy brothers who were oil and wine merchants. Here are several rooms of excellent, well-preserved paintings of mythological scenes, but the guards will be whispering in your ear (if you are male) to show you the little niche off the entrance with the picture of Priapus. This over-endowed sport, in legend the son of Venus and Adonis, together with a couple of wall paintings along the lines of the Kamasutra, has managed to make Pompeii something more than a respectable tourist trap. There are quite a few paintings of Priapus showing it off in the houses of Pompeii, besides the phallic images that adorn bakers' ovens, wine shops, and almost every other establishment in town.

The Pompeiians would be terribly embarrassed, however, if they knew what you are thinking. They were a libidinous lot, like anyone else fortunate enough to live on the Campanian coast during recorded history, but the omnipresent phalluses were never meant as decoration. Almost always they are found close to the entrances, where their job was to ward off the evil eye. This use of phallic symbols against evil probably dates from the earliest times in southern Italy; the horn-shaped amulets that millions of people wear around their necks today are their direct descendants. Even so, not so long ago, women visiting Pompeii were not allowed to set eyes on the various erotic images around the site, and were obliged by the guides to wait chastely outside while their spouses or male companions went in for a peek.

The nearby Via di Nola, one of Pompeii's main streets, leads to the north. It passes the **Central Baths**, a new construction that was not yet completed when Vesuvius went off, and the **House of Marcus Fronto**, with more good paintings and a reconstructed roof.

The 'New Excavations'

Beginning in 1911, the archaeologists cleared a vast area of western Pompeii, around what was probably the most important thoroughfare of the city, now called the Via dell'Abbondanza. Three blocks west of the Forum, this street leads to the Via dei Teatri and the **Triangular Forum**, bordering the southern walls. Two **Theatres** here are worth a visit, a large open one seating 5000, and a smaller, covered one that was used for concerts.

The big quadrangle, originally a lobby for the theatres, seems to have been converted at one point into a gladiators' barracks. This is only one of the disconcerting things you will find on the streets of Pompeii. The ruined temple in the Triangular Forum was already long ruined in AD 79, and scholars who study the art of the city find the last (fourth) period to betray a growing lack of skill and coarseness of spirit—altogether, there are plenty of clues that 1st-century Pompeii had its share of urban problems and cultural malaise.

The Via dell'Abbondanza

Next to the theatres, a small **Temple of Isis** testifies to the religious diversity of Pompeii; elsewhere around town there is graffiti satirizing that new and troublesome cult, the Christians. Three blocks north, there is a stretch of Via dell'Abbondanza that is one of the most fascinating corners of Pompeii. Among its shops are a smith's, a grocers, a weaver's, a laundry, and a typical Roman tavern with its modest walk-up brothel. The most common are those with built-in tubs facing the street—shops that sold wine, and oil for cooking and for lamps. Notices painted on the walls announce coming games at the amphitheatre, or recommend candidates for public office.

Some of the best-decorated villas in this neighbourhood are to be found along the side streets: the **House of Loreius**, the **House of Amandus**, and an odd underground chamber called the **Cryptoporticus**. Pompeii's two most impressive structures occupy a corner just within the walls: the **Palaestra**, a big colonnaded exercise yard, and the **Amphitheatre**, the best-preserved in Italy, with seats for two-thirds of Pompeii's population.

Not all of Pompeii's attractions are within the walls. If you have the time, it would be worth visiting the tombs and suburban villas around the **Via delle Tombe**. One, the famous **Villa dei Misteri**, is thought to have been used as a place of initiation in the forbidden Bacchic (or Dionysiac) Mysteries, one of the cults most feared by the Roman Senate, and later by the emperors. Scenes from the myth of Dionysus and of the rituals themselves are painted on the walls.

The town of Pompei (the modern town has one i), an important pilgrimage centre, is also worth a visit, if nothing else for a look at the wonderfully overdone church, dedicated to the **Madonna di Pompei**, who holds a special place in the affections of Neapolitan women. You'll probably see some of them, busily saying their rosaries, asking for the Madonna's intercession to help sort out their problems. If they have bare feet, this is not poverty, but devotion—usually the fulfilment of a personal pledge to the Madonna in thanks for a favour received. Neapolitans who ask for the Madonna's help often promise to walk there barefoot from Naples (26km) if their prayers are answered.

Ercolano/Pompei, ℰ (081–) **Where to Stay**

One, perhaps chancy place for you to base yourself would be the **★★Eremo**, ℰ 7779749, above Ercolano on the very slopes of Vesuvius—an isolated spot, but there is a bar and restaurant on the premises (inexpensive/moderate). Out of reach of possible lava flows, the best resort hotel up on Monte Faito is the **★★★★Grand Hotel Monte Faito**, ℰ 8793134, fax 8793166, with gardens and a pool in a lovely setting close to the funicular; not really Grand, but still a relative bargain (expensive).

As a place of pilgrimage, Pompei is well supplied with hotels, mostly inexpensive pensiones on or around Via Roma. A little fancier is the **★★★Rosario**, also on Via Roma, ℰ 8630624, a serene, older hotel with a garage and pleasant rooms (moderate). Also reasonable is the **★★★Bristol**, Piazza V. Veneto 1/3, ℰ 8503005, fax 8631625 (moderate).

Ercolano/Pompei, ℰ (081–) **Eating Out**

moderate

Restaurants in Pompei have a captive market in visitors to the ruins, and it is true that some of them see the tourists as easy marks. You can choose for yourself among the ubiquitous multilingual menus, or try one of these if you're in the mood for a treat—**Zi Caterina**, Via Roma 16, © 8507447, with live lobsters in the tank and other noteworthy seafood dishes, is also a good place to try Lacrima Cristi wine from the nearby slopes of Vesuvius. At **Al Gamberone**, Via Piave 36, © 8638322 (closed Fri), close to Pompei's main church, you can feast on prawns doused in cognac and other good fish dishes. A little further out is the **Anfiteatro**, Via Roma 125, © 8631245. Here the seafood is more modest—it's one of the few places in Pompei you'll see *baccalà*, salt cod, on the menu, along with truly good *spaghetti alle vongole*.

Sorrento

Tourist Information

There are tourist offices in Sorrento itself, at Via L. de Maio 35, 80067, © (081) 8782104, fax 8773397, and in Vico Equense, at Via S. Ciro 16, 80069, © (081) 8015752.

After Pompeii, the coastline swings outwards to meet Capri. At first, there is little intimation that you are entering one of the most beautiful corners of all Italy. The first clue comes when the coast road begins to climb into a corniche at **Vico Equense**, a pretty village that is becoming a small resort, absorbing some of the overflow from Sorrento; there is a nice beach under the cliffs at the back of the town.

Sorrento began its career as a resort in the early 19th century, when Naples began to grow too piquant for English tastes. The English, especially, have never forsaken it; Sorrento's secret is a certain perfect cosiness, comfortable like old shoes. Visitors get the reassuring sense that nothing distressing is going to happen to them, and sure enough, nothing ever does. It helps that Sorrento is a lovely, civilized old town. Not many resorts can trace their ancestry back to the Etruscans, or claim a native son like the poet Torquato Tasso. (Today, the Sorrentines are more proud of a songwriter named De Curtio, whose *Come Back to Sorrento*, according to a local brochure, ranks with *O Sole Mio* as one of the 'two most familiar songs in the world'. There's a bust of him in front of the Circumvesuviana station).

Sorrento doesn't flagrantly chase after your money, like many places in Italy, and it lacks the high-density garishness of, say, Rimini. If Sorrento has one big drawback, it is its lack of a decent beach—though at some of the fancier hotels you may enjoy taking a lift down to the sea. There are also several *stabilimenti*—piers jutting out into the sea, kitted out with loungers and beach umbrellas, for which you pay a hire charge. Sorrento is built on a long cliff that follows the shore. A narrow ravine cuts the town in half, between a suburban area of quiet, mostly expensive hotels around Via Correale, and the old town itself, which still preserves its grid of narrow Roman streets. There isn't much of artistic or historical interest; Sorrento was never a large town, though in the Middle Ages it was for a while an important trading post. The Sorrentine recall with pride that their fleet once beat Amalfi in a sea battle (897). Even today the population is only 15,000. It's pleasant to walk the old streets; half the shop windows seem to be displaying *intarsia*—surprisingly fine pictures done in inlaid woods, a local craft for centuries. If you are stuck on a rainy day, you can visit the **Correale Museum,** on Via Correale, a grab-bag of Neapolitan bric-a-brac, art and curiosities *(open 9.30–12.30, 3–5, Mon, Wed–Fri; 9.30am–12.30pm Sat, Sun; closed Tues; adm)*.

Around Sorrento, as far as the mountains permit, stretches one of the great garden spots of Campania, a lush plain full of vines and orange groves. Among the excursions that can be made from Sorrento are the visit to the scanty ruins of the Roman **Villa di Pollio**, in a beautiful setting on the cape west of the town, and the short trip to **Massa Lubrense**, an uncrowded fishing village with more fine views as far as Campanella Point, the tip of the peninsula, opposite the rugged outline of Capri. In the old days, a permanent watch was kept on Campanella Point, and it takes its name from the big bell that was hung here and rung to warn the towns around the bay when pirates were sighted.

Sorrento, © (081–)   **Where to Stay**

In Sorrento, some 90 hotels compete for your attention, the best of which are converted villas by the sea—almost indecently elegant, even when they're a bit frayed about the edges. Sorrento isn't the status resort it once was, but it still seems to have more four-star places than anywhere in Italy; most of them are good bargains, too, compared to comparable spots in the north.

expensive

At the top of the list is the ★★★★**Grand Hotel Ambasciatori**, Via Califano 18, © 8782025, fax 8071021, a bit removed from the centre, but with a palatial interior and gardens overlooking the sea. In the same area is the beautifully remodelled ★★★★**Royal**, © 8781920, fax 8772905, with a pool and beach access. In a more central location, set in incredible tropical gardens on Via Vittorio Veneto, the ★★★★**Imperial Tramontana**, © 8782585, fax 8072344, is one of the places long favoured by British travellers, as is evident from the club-like décor. There is an elevator down to the private beach, and also a pool. Another villa-hotel, just around the corner on Via Marina Grande, is the ★★★**Bellevue-Syrene**, © 878 1024, fax 8783963. This one has lush gardens, beautifully restored rooms and a lift to the beach.

moderate

In Vico Equense, the best places are a little outside the town centre, notably the ★★★★**Capo La Gala**, © 8015758, fax 8798747, on the beach at nearby Scrajo (where there are sulphur springs)—a beautiful modern resort hotel where every room has a private terrace overlooking the beach. There's plenty of sea, and a pool too, but note that full board is usually required (moderate).

In Sorrento itself, the ★★★★**President**, Via Nastro Verde, Colle Parise, ✆ 878262, fax 8785411, is slightly out of town, set in its own park, with lovely views and a good-sized pool. At the ★★★**Minerva**, Via Capo 30, ✆ 8781011, fax 8781949 (closed Nov–Mar), you'll find 50 nice rooms, some with stunning views over the sea.

inexpensive

Not all the hotels in Sorrento are luxury villas; one of the charms of the place is that it caters to every budget. A real bargain, in a villa with a private beach and a good restaurant, is the ★★**Pensione La Tonnarella**, Via Capo 31, ✆ 8781153, fax 8782169; it's advisable to make reservations here early. Another clean, well-run *pensione* with lovely sea views is the ★★**Loreley et Londres**, Via Califano 2, ✆ 8781508. There are plenty of simple hotels around the town centre, of which the ★**City**, Corso d'Italia 217, ✆ 877221, is one of the nicest.

Sorrento, ✆ (081–)   ***Eating Out***

expensive

At Nerano, on the road from Vico Equense to Sorrento, **Da Pappone**, ✆ 8081209, specializes in fish fresh out of the sea, and elaborate (but pricey!) antipasto surprises.

Sorrento has every kind of restaurant, including the grand and gloriously decorated **Parrucchiano**, Corso Italia 71, ✆ 8781321, by tradition one of Italy's best, with a choice of anything you could imagine. If you are celebrating a social occasion, though, or just in the mood for a very unusual experience, the place to go nowadays is **Don Alfonso**, Piazza Sant'Agata, ✆ 8780026 (Sept–May closed Sun evenings, Mon), in Sant'Agata sui Due Golfi, a Michelin-starred restaurant that some food critics reckon to be the best in southern Italy. Food here is an art form, beautifully cooked, and presented on fine china with wine served in delicate crystal glasses. The restaurant, run by husband-and-wife team Alfonso and Livia Iaccarino, is actually 9km outside Sorrento, but the trip is well worth it (very expensive).

moderate/inexpensive

Sorrento can also offer restaurants of a completely different variety, like the honestly named **Boozer Pub**, Via P.R. Giuliani 66, ✆ 8783617, with light dinners, English beer and music nightly. **Ristorante Gioiello**, Via Casarlano 19, ✆ 8072200, where the menu changes daily, is very popular with the Sorrentini themselves. For one of the best deals in town, try the **Trattoria da Emilia**, Via Marina Grande 62, ✆ 8781489, a family-run trattoria with tables on a terrace overlooking the sea, and an excellent-value fixed menu based on fresh local ingredients and classic Sorrento recipes.

Capri

The Islands of the Bay of Naples

Without a doubt, the islands in the Bay of Naples—Capri, Ischia, and to a far lesser extent Procida—are the holiday queens of the Italian islands. Every schoolchild has heard of Capri, made so notorious by the antics of Emperor Tiberius and Norman Douglas' 'gentlemanly freaks'.

Ischia, fifty years ago, was the favourite island of jet-setters jaded by Capri. Renowned in ancient times for its mud baths, it has become a home-from-home for the German bourgeoisie. If anyone tries to tell you it's still 'unspoiled', take this into consideration: Ischia is Italy's biggest buyer of spaghetti-flavoured icecream. Still, the smart set can't get there fast enough; both Ischia and Capri are connected to Naples' Capodichino Airport by helicopter.

Procida, on the other hand, has hardly been developed at all, though not through any lack of charm. For many Italians, the very name of the island conjures up the same associations that Alcatraz does for Americans, which has managed to keep the developers away until very recently.

Despite their location, the three islands are of very different geological origins. Ischia and Procida are a part of the enormous submerged volcano of Campano, which stretches from Ventotene in the Pontine Islands down to Strómboli and the Aeolian Islands. In not too ancient times, the two islands were connected to each other and, if the Greek geographer Strabo is to be believed, also to the Phlegraean Fields on the mainland. Phlegraean means 'fiery' in Greek, and Strabo records how, during an eruption of the now dormant volcano Epomeo on Ischia, an earthquake split Ischia–Procida from the mainland, then, in another upheaval, jolted the once united island in twain. In this same geological cataclysm, Capri broke off from the Sorrentine peninsula, a blow that shattered its coasts to form the island's famous cliffs.

Getting There

In summer, there are as many as six ferries and 20 hydrofoils a day from Naples to Capri, and as many to Ischia. There are also regular departures to Procida. In addition, there are a few ferries and hydrofoils daily from Sorrento to Capri, from Pozzuoli to Procida and between the islands of Ischia and Procida. All are very short rides. For more information on long-distance ferry services from Naples, *see* pp.8 and 60.

Local and longer-distance ferries and hydrofoils from Naples leave from three different points along the harbourside—**Molo Beverello** and the **Stazione Marittima**, both in the centre of the port, and **Mergellina**, further to the west. Be sure to check you know the right dock for your ticket and destination. Listed here are the principal ferry and hydrofoil operators; check with them for timetables, or look in the daily newspaper *Il Mattino*.

From **Molo Beverello: Caremar**, © 5513882, for Capri, Ischia and Procida; **Navigazione Libera del Golfo**, © 5527209, for Capri; **Linee Lauro**, © 5522838, for Ischia; and **Alilauro**, © 5522838, for Sorrento.

From the **Stazione Marittima** (used by ferries only): **Tirrenia**, © 7613688, for Palermo, Cagliari, Reggio Calabria and Malta; **Siremar**, © 7613688, for the Aeolian Islands; and **Lauro**, © 5513352, for Corsica.

From **Mergellina** (hydrofoils): **Alilauro**, © 7611004, for Ischia and Sorrento; and **SNAV**, © 7612348, for Capri, Ischia, Procida, and the Aeolian Islands.

In addition, from Salerno there is a boat called the *Faraglione* that offers a different way of seeing the Amalfi coast, a daily ferry that hugs the shore to Capri, stopping at Amalfi and Positano along the way. It leaves Salerno at 7.30pm each day from Molo Manfredi, at the western end of town, and does not run between 15th October and 6th January.

Capri

Capri is pure enchantment, and can lay fair claim to being the most beautiful island in the Mediterranean; it is also the most overrun and exploited to the hilt. With more than 800 species of plant, it is very much a garden perched on a rugged chunk of limestone. Unlike Ischia and other, more recent, tourist haunts, Capri has the relaxed air of having seen it all. No room remains for property speculators. Everything has been built and planted; the tourists come and go every day and night, and they seem to be invisible to the Capriots and other residents who have learned to turn a blind eye to them, since the space they occupy will be filled next day by other anonymous camera-clutching tourists. Between June and September you begin to understand why the word 'trash' is inscribed on the bins in 30 different languages. However, if you don't mind all the trendy shops being closed, try going in November or February, when you may be lucky to arrive for a few brilliant days between the rains, and have this Garden of Eden practically to yourself. It's worth the risk of a soaking or two.

There are various schools of thought on the etymology of the island's name. The belief that it came from the Latin word for goat (*capra*) is now in disfavour; those who think it derived from the Greek *kapros* (boar) have fossils to back them up. Yet another group maintains that it comes from an ancient Tyrrhenian (Etruscan) word meaning 'rocky' (*capr—*) as evidenced by the many other places that begin with this suffix, such as Caprera (an island off Sardinia), Cabrera (off Majorca) and Caprara in the Tremiti Islands, to name just a few. It is the first syllable that is emphasized in the pronunciation of Capri—CAPri, not CapRI, like the Ford.

History

Some time in the Quaternary Period Capri broke away from the Sorrentine peninsula, taking with it elephants and tigers, as we have learnt from the remains discovered by

Ignazio Cerio at the beginning of this century. Other finds have dated the first inhabitants back to the Paleolithic Era. A strong tradition associates the island with the Sirens of The Odyssey, and with the mysterious Teleboeans from the Greek island of Kephalonia, led by their King Telon. Neolithic ceramic-ware decorated with red bands, first found on the island, has since been designated the 'Capri style'.

Little is known of Capri at the time when Augustus arrived, except that it was still very Greek and that a dying ilex (holm oak) suddenly revived and sprouted new leaves. The Emperor thought this was a good portent, and he traded Ischia to Naples for Capri and made the island one of his retreats, reputedly building as many as twelve sumptuous palaces. Life must have been good on Capri; at one point Augustus called it *Apragopolis*, or 'Lubberland', as Robert Graves translates Suetonius' 'land of layabouts'.

Augustus was succeeded by his stepson Tiberius, whose exploits reported by the same Suetonius gave Capri much of its early notoriety. The Roman writer turned the island into a dirty old man's dream come true, with Tiberius hurling his victims off the cliffs to add a touch of reality. Although scholars have now discredited much of Suetonius' yellow journalism, that imaginative writer's images of sexual acrobats dressing up as nymphs and frolicking in Tiberius' gardens, along with the anthropophagous Sirens singing seductive songs on the seashore, have permeated the Capri legends.

In reality, Tiberius made Capri the capital of the Roman Empire between AD 27 and 37. The sheer cliffs made it into a natural citadel, from where the ageing Emperor could conduct (or neglect) the affairs of state as he pleased. Here he nurtured the future Emperor Caligula.

After the death of Tiberius, Capri is occasionally mentioned as a place of exile. Then the Benedictine friars arrived and built chapels on the island, and of course it suffered the usual ravages of Saracens and pirates. In 1371 a Carthusian monastery (La Certosa) was founded on Capri, on land granted by the Angevins, whom the Capriots favoured over the Aragonese until 1442 when they rather capriciously changed sides. A plague in 1656 left the island all but abandoned; only the Carthusians stayed behind, safe inside the walls of La Certosa, picking up the titles to land that had no owners and becoming quite wealthy (and unpopular) in the process.

In 1806, Hudson Lowe was commander of the English garrison on Capri. The life of Napoleon was full of strange coincidences. Lowe, for example, was quartered in Napoleon's house in Ajaccio when the English occupied Corsica, and he later became Napoleon's jailer on St Helena. He took his job on Capri seriously indeed, fortifying the island until it became 'a little Gibraltar', but for all that still managed to lose it to the French in 1808—a 'discreditable Lowe business' according to Norman Douglas, longtime resident and writer on things Capricious.

The last chapter of the island's history began with the 'discovery' of the Blue Grotto by a German artist called Kopisch in 1826; he swam into it 'by accident'. Perhaps it was just a coincidence that Kopisch's discovery followed the landslide that had covered the entrance of another, even lovelier cave. Anyway, the magic of the name, Blue Grotto of Capri, proved irresistible, and the Capriots converted their fishing boats into excursion boats to take tourists to the cave while farmers sold their land and built hotels.

Getting Around

Arriving in Marina Grande, you can ascend to either Capri or Anacapri by **bus**. They run every 15 minutes 8am–10pm, and every half-hour 10pm–midnight, daily. There is also a **funicular** that runs up to Capri town every 15 minutes from 6.35am–10pm, though in April–September only. The **chairlift** from Anacapri to Monte Solaro (a 12-minute ride) runs continuously from 9am to sunset, also in the summer season only. There are also buses from Anacapri to the Blue Grotto, Faro and Marina Piccola. From June until September, there are daily **tours** of Capri by motor launch, which leave from Marina Grande, beginning at 9am.

Tourist Information

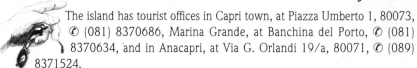

The island has tourist offices in Capri town, at Piazza Umberto 1, 80073, © (081) 8370686, Marina Grande, at Banchina del Porto, © (081) 8370634, and in Anacapri, at Via G. Orlandi 19/a, 80071, © (089) 8371524.

Marina Grande and the Grotta Azzurra

All the ferries and hydrofoils from the mainland call at **Marina Grande** (most pleasure boats anchor in the Marina Piccola on the other side of the island). Here, Capri's dependence on tourism is at its most evident; Marina Grande is little more than a commercialized station platform, but as such does its best to get you off to your destination; the *funivia* (cablecar) will lift you to the town of Capri every 15 minutes, buses will wind you up to Anacapri, glorious old bath-tub convertible taxis hope to trundle you off to your hotel, boats for the Grotta Azzurra and other excursions around the island bob up and down at their landings.

The **Blue Grotto** is well named if nothing else—its shimmering, irridescent blueness is caused by the reflection of light on the water in the morning. Similar caverns are fairly common in the Mediterranean, but Capri's is the yardstick by which they are measured. In summer (1 June–30 Sept), boats for the Blue Grotto leave at 9am—when the sea is calm. The entrance to the cave is quite low, and if there's any swell on the sea at all someone is sure to get a nasty knock on the head.

The **sea excursion around the island** is a rare experience, but again possible only in good weather. Besides visiting other lovely grottoes, such as the **Grotta Bianca** and the **Grotta Verde** (the White Cave and the Green Cave), there are breathtaking views of the cliffs and Capri's uncanny rock formations.

Capri Town

Haunted by the smiling shade of Gracie Fields, the charming white town of Capri is daily worn down by the tread of thousands of her less ectoplasmic followers. The **megalithic walls** supporting some of the houses have seen at least 3000 years of similar comings and goings, although certainly on a much smaller scale than what you'll find here in August. Its architecture complements the island's natural beauty—much of what is typical and 'homemade' in Mediterranean architecture can be seen here in the older quarters: the moulded arches and domes, the narrow streets and stairways crossed by buttresses supporting the buildings, the ubiquitous whitewash, the play of light and shadow, and sudden little squares, just large enough for a few children to improvise a game of football. Most of the island's hotels are scattered throughout the town, generally very tastful and surrounded by gardens. The supreme example is the famous Quisisana, a hotel whose register over the years is like a veritable *Who's Who* of the famous and pampered.

If you go up to Capri by *funivia*, you'll surface right next to the Piazza Umberto and the much photographed **cathedral**, with its joyful campanile and clock. Built in the 17th century in the local Baroque style, the cathedral has a charming buttressed roof. In a little square in the church's shadow, known as **La Piazzetta**, are the outdoor cafés frequented by such a variety of past eccentrics, dilettantes and celebrities that each chair should have a historical plaque on it. The other side of the piazza is a sheer drop down to Marina Grande.

Walks from the Town

For the post office and for buses to Anacapri, take the Via Roma from the piazza; for the exclusive boutiques, head towards the Via Vittoria Emanuele to Via Camarelle and Via Tragara. The latter street eventually leads to the **Faraglioni**, the three enormous sheer-sided limestone pinnacles towering straight up in the ever blue-green sea. These rocks are home to the rare blue lizard (*Lacerta caerulea Faraglionensis*) and a rare species of seagull that supposedly guffaws. From Via Tragara a stairway descends to the point and the **Porto di Tragara**, where you can take a swim from the platforms beneath the vertical rocks.

Nearby is the **Tragara Terrace**, with magnifient views, and the tall skinny rock called **Pizzolungo**. Still following the main track along the coast and up the stairway, you will come upon the **Grotta dii Matromania** (always open). The Romans worshiped the goddess Cybele, or *Mater Magna*, in this cave. Part of Capri's reputation as an island of orgies may derive from this ancient Eastern cult's noisy hypnotic rituals, which culminated rather abruptly with the self-castration of the priest-for-a-day. Only vestiges now remain of the once elaborate decor inside the cave.

From the Grotta di Matromania a stepped path leads down to yet another famous eroded rock: the **Arco Naturale**, where dark pines—as everywhere else on Capri—cling to every tiny ledge they can sink their roots into. On the way back to town you'll pass some of the island's vineyards that produce the rare and famous *Lachrimae Tiberii*, and, in the

Piazza Cerio, the **Centro Caprense Ignazio Cerio**, with fossils and archaeological finds from Capri *(open 10–12, Mon–Fri)*.

The Old Goat of Capri

London has its tabloids, and ancient Rome had Gaius Suetonius Tranquillus, born *c.* 60 AD. All of Suetonius's other books are lost, including such titles as the *Lives of Famous Whores* and the *Physical Defects of Mankind*, but enough copies of his celebrated scandalmongering classic, *The Twelve Caesars*, were written out to ensure that the whole juicy text has survived. Modern historians have always argued over Suetonius's reliability, but the nature of his subjects has been confirmed by enough other sources to suggest that Suetonius couldn't have exaggerated that much. And his book was written with full access to the Imperial archives; the author was chief secretary to Emperor Trajan.

One of the most entertaining chapters deals with the man who put Capri on the map, the Emperor Tiberius, adopted son of Augustus. A good general and, at first, a capable ruler, Tiberius had an unusual habit of declining honours and titles. Suetonius hints that the Emperor knew, or suspected that he would eventually go a bit mad, and wanted no pointless flattery left behind for his enemies to mock later. Mad or not, Tiberius did have a mania for privacy. He left Rome in 26 AD for Capri, which he admired for its beauty and for the fact that it had only one landing port, and he never went back to the capital again. The entire island became his pleasure garden, and while imperial decrees went out prohibiting 'promiscuous kissing' and ordering a clampdown on loose women, the Emperor himself was whooping it up. According to Suetonius:

> *Bevies of young girls and men, whom he had collected from all over the Empire as adepts in unnatural practices, and known as* spintriae, *would perform before him in groups of three, to excite his waning passions. A number of small rooms were furnished with the most indecent pictures and statuary imaginable, also certain erotic manuals from Elephantis in Egypt; the inmates of the establishment would know from these exactly what was expected of them.*

Once aroused, apparently, the Imperial pervert would bore in on anything that caught his fancy, and the smaller the better. Suetonius pictures him rushing through a religious sacrifice to get at the little boy who was carrying the incense casket, and training other little boys, his 'minnows', to 'chase him while he went swimming and get between his legs to lick and and nibble him...such a filthy old man he had become!' Even Suetonius is shocked. Distracted by such pleasures, Tiberius let the Empire go to pot; the Persians invaded from the east, while Germanic bands roamed unchecked in Gaul. The generals and the civil service managed to see that no serious harm was done, but they could not stop the ageing Tiberius, in his island isolation, from turning into a murderous paranoid, torturing and killing anyone who opposed him, or seemed to. All the while the Emperor found time to work on another of his passions—a grammar of the ancient Etruscan language, of all things. Suetonius names all the names and tells all the tales; nobody was ever better at capturing the essential vileness of imperial Rome (and you should read what he has to say about Caligula and Nero).

La Certosa and Gardens of Augustus

A shorter but equally enjoyable walk starting from the Piazza Umberto (take Via Vittorio Emanuele, which becomes Via F. Serena, then Via Matteotti) leads you to **La Certosa**, the Carthusian charterhouse founded in 1371 by Giacomo Arcucci (a member of a famous Capri family) and suppressed in 1808. Built over one of Tiberius' villas, the golden-hued church and cloisters are very pleasing, topped by a Baroque tower added in the 17th century. La Certosa, with its collection of paintings from the 17th to 19th centuries, is open daily from 9 until 2 (closed Mon).

A few minutes away from La Certosa are the **Gardens of Augustus**, founded by Caesar himself. A wide variety of trees and plants grow on the fertile terraces and belvederes over-looking one of the most striking views in the world. A narrow road (Via Krupp, built by the arms manufacturer, who spent his leisure hours studying lamprey larvae off the Salto di Tiberio) takes you down the cliffs in a hundred hairpin turns to the **Marina Piccola**, the charming little port with most of Capri's bathing establishments—Da Maria, La Canzione del Mare, Le Sirene and Internazionale (all but the last connected to restaurants). On one side are the ruins of a Saracen tower; on the other is the **Scoglio delle Sirene** (Sirens' Rock); if you read the books of Norman Douglas and Edwin Cerio, son of Ignazio Cerio the archaeologist, they will convince you that this really was the home of the Sirens. There is a bus, fortunately, that makes the steep climb back up the cliffs to Capri town.

A much longer but equally rewarding walk or drive is to the **Villa Jovis** (Via Botteghe to Via Tiberio) passing the church of **Monte San Michele**, a fine example of local architec-ture, built in the 14th century. The Villa Jovis on Punta Lo Capo (310m) was the most important of the twelve villas on Capri: from here Tiberius governed the Roman Empire for his last ten years. Although much has been sacked through the centuries, the extent of the remaining walls and foundations gives a fair idea of the grandeur of the former Imperial Palace. Near here, the **Faro**, or lighthouse, was believed to have been part of a system of semaphores through which messages were sent to Rome. The great sheer cliff beside the villa, the **Salto di Tiberio**, is always pointed out as the precipice from which the emperor hurled the lovers who bored him, according to Suetonius. The view of the Bays of Salerno and Naples is as spectacular as any.

Towards Anacapri

On the north coast between Capri and Anacapri, the only other town of the island, are the so-called **Baths of Tiberius** and the meagre remains of Augustus' sea palace, the **Palazzo a Mare**. You can swim here at the establishment Bagni di Tiberio. Above here, carved into the escarpment of Anacapri, is the **Scala Fenicia**, in truth Greco-Roman in origin and for thousands of years the only way to reach the upper part of the island. Originally 800 in number, these steps have crumbled over the years and are impassable today. Near here, on the road from Marina Grande to Anacapri, lies the first Christian church on the island, dedicated to patron saint **San Costanzo**. According to legend Costanzo was a bishop of Constantinople whose body, packed in a barrel, floated to Capri during the Iconoclasm in Greece. A church, with a reputation for defending the island from Saracens, was built for him over one of the Roman villas. Four ancient columns support the Byzantine dome of this 11th-century church, designed in the form of a Greek cross.

Anacapri

On top of the green plateau spreads the town of Anacapri (300m), once a fierce rival to Capri below, but since the building of the roads connecting them in 1874, the two towns have learned to reconcile their differences. Although it has its share of hotels, Anacapri retains a rustic air, with its many olive trees and vineyards surrounding it on all sides, and its simple style of architecture, rather Moorish in style with cubic, flat-roofed houses.

In Anacapri's Piazza San Nicola, the 18th-century church of **San Michele** *(open 10–6 April–Oct, 10–2 Sun)* contains a magnificent mosaic floor of majolica tiles, by the Abruzzese artist Leonardo Chiaiese. The design itself, showing Adam and Eve in the Garden of Eden, and their Expulsion, is by D. A. Vaccano. The church of **Santa Sofia** very near it, on the Piazza Diaz, was built in the Middle Ages, but later Baroqued.

From Piazza Vittoria a chairlift travels to the summit of **Monte Solaro**, the highest point on the island at 585m. Also from Piazza Vittoria, take Via Orlandi to Via Capodimonte and the **Villa San Michele** of Axel Munthe (1857–1949), one of the greatest physicians of his day, and a leader in the field of psychiatry. Extremely generous, donating his services to the victims of plagues, earthquakes and World War I, he also found time to establish bird sanctuaries on Capri and elsewhere; in 1929 he wrote his best-selling autobiography *The Story of San Michele* to which his villa owes most of its fame. The house contains Roman artefacts discovered on Capri *(open daily, 9am until sunset; adm)*. Near here is the so-called **Castello di Barbarossa**, after the pirate captain who plagued the Mediterranean for so many years. These ruins date from the 8th and 9th centuries. Via Capodimonte continues through the valley of **Santa Maria a Cetrella**, another white church of local design. From the church the road goes to the top of Monte Solaro.

Another path from Piazza Vittoria (Via Caposcuro to Via Maigliara) skirts Monte Solaro, passing through the vineyards to the **Belvedere della Migliara**, from where you can see the Faraglioni and the entrance of the **Green Grotto**. A bus leaves Anacapri every hour in the summer for Punta Carena and its lighthouse at the southernmost tip of the island. The unusual arched doorways on the left belonged to the **Torre di Materita**; further on, over-looking the **Cala del Tombosiello**, is a ruined watchtower. **Punta Carena** is the most out-of-the-way place on the island for a quiet swim.

Another bus leaves from the piazza for the Grotta Azzurra and the bathing area adjacent to it, passing by way of the old windmill and the **Villa Imperiale**, another of the summer residences built by Augustus, known also as the 'Damecuta', from the tower next to it. After the Villa Jovis, this villa is the best preserved, and has recently been further excavated *(open from 9am until one hour before sunset; closed Mon)*.

Capri, ✆ (081–) **Where to Stay**

As one might expect, hotel prices on Capri are well above average for the surrounding area on-shore, and rooms for the summer months are often booked up months in advance.

very expensive

If money is no object, the ★★★★★**Quisiana e Grand Hotel**, Via Camerelle, ✆ 8370788, fax 8376080, is the place to stay in Capri town, a luxurious palace of a hotel set in its own grounds and equipped with pool, tennis courts and just about everything else needed for a smart holiday on the island.

expensive

Slightly lower down the price-scale, ★★★★**La Palma**, Via V. Emanuele, ✆ 837 0133, fax 8376966, is also in a good central location in Capri town, set in its own gardens, with lovely maiolica-tiled floors in the rooms and a pleasant airy feel. ★★★★**La Scalinatella**, Via Tragara 8, ✆ 8370633, fax 8378291, is a jewel of a hotel, with 30 beautifully decorated rooms and stunning views. Further up on the way to the panoramic Punta Tragara, the ★★★★**Villa Brunella**, Via Tragara 24, ✆ 8370122, fax 8370430, is a pretty hotel looking out over the sea, with a good restaurant and a pool for lazing away hot afternoons.

moderate

Open all year round, the ★★★**Floridiana**, Via Campo di Teste, ✆ 8370166, fax 8370434, in Capri town, also has fine panoramas of the sea. The ★★★**Villa Sarah**, Via Tiberio 3, ✆ 8377817, is a gracious old villa, pleasantly converted into a small, well-run hotel.

inexpensive

Book well ahead if you want to stay at the ★★**Villa Krupp**, Viale Matteotti 12, ✆ 8370362, one of the loveliest, and most historic, lower-priced hotels in Capri. Two budget choices, both no-frills establishments, but clean and well-run, are the centrally located ★**Stella Maris**, Via Roma, ✆ 8370452, and ★**La Tosca**, Via D. Birago, ✆ 8370989, both in Capri town.

Capri, ✆ (081–) **Eating Out**

expensive

Capri's best restaurant has long been **La Capannina**, Via delle Botteghe 14, ✆ 8370732, set in a secluded garden in Capri town, with delicately prepared shellfish, pasta and fish, and good desserts. A close rival is a relative newcomer, **Al Geranio**, Viale Matteotti 8, ✆ 8370616, where the chef has a magic touch with fish, in particular. Tables overlook the classic Capri panorama. **I Faraglioni**, Via Camerelle 75, ✆ 8370320, has delectable house specialities like *crêpes al formaggio*, paper-thin pancakes filled with cheese, and *risotto ai frutti di mare*, risotto with all sorts of shellfish.

moderate

At **Da Paolino**, on Via Palazzo a Mare 11, ✆ 8376102, you'll eat in an arbour of lemon trees, tasting dishes mainly inspired by the fruit—as in the pasta, fish and dessert courses, all heavily lemon-influenced. Further down in Capri town, **Da Gemma**, Via Madre Serafina, ✆ 8370461, is one of the few restaurants that stay open all year round. It's as nice in winter as it is in summer, a welcoming trattoria with walls decked with brass pans and ceramic plates, and superbly cooked local dishes including a delicious mozzarella grilled on a lemon leaf. It also serves very good pizza.

In Anacapri, **Da Gelsomina la Migliara**, on Via La Migliara 6, ✆ 8371499, offers not only home-made wine, but true home-cooked island specialities, including mushrooms collected on Monte Solaro.

Ischia

Ischia is a remarkably lovely island, able to hold its own even with Capri. The sea of vine-yards encircling the island's highest peak, volcanic Monte Epomea (793m), produces the excellent wine named after the mountain, and the villages high on its slopes, like Fontana and Buonapane, remain untouched by the international onslaught of tourists at the resorts of Casamicciola, Forio, Lacco Ameno and Ischia town.

Unlike Capri, Ischia has many long, first-class beaches, on one of which, Maronti, the volcanic nature of the island is very evident. The hot mineral springs that gush all year-round have attracted cure-seekers since Roman times, and are still recommended today for people suffering from rheumatism, arthritis, neuralgia and obesity. Because many of the springs are radioactive, a doctor's permission is often required before you take a soak (there are physicians on the island who specialize in prescribing such treatments, and they charge a pretty penny). The hottest spring on the island is Terme Rita, at Casamicciola, which belches from the earth at around 180°F. For a lark, try the Terme Comunali at the port, or the unique baths at Cavascura above Sant'Angelo.

History

Inhabited by 2000 BC, Ischia became an important stop along one of the earliest trade routes in the Mediterranean, from Mycenean Greece to the Etruscans of northern Italy and the mineral wealth of Elba. The prevailing currents and winds made it natural for the

Greek ships sailing west to circumvent Sicily and land in the Bay of Naples—as did that most famous sailor, Odysseus himself. As an island along the sea lane, Ischia was the perfect place to found an outpost to secure the route and trade, and here in 756 BC Chalcidians and Eretrians from the Greek island of Euboea settled the first Greek colony in western Europe.

They called the island *Pithekoussai*, referring to its abundant pottery clay (*pithos*). However, when Montagnone (a now extinct volcano on Ischia) erupted, the colonists fled to the mainland, establishing themselves at Cumae, where they prospered. Roman writers later refer to the island as *Eneria*, deriving from Aeneas' supposed stop on the island to repair his ships, or *Inarime*, a name of unknown origin. The name Ischia is believed to be a corruption of *insula*, or just plain island.

In the year AD 6, Augustus traded the larger, more fertile island of Ischia for Capri, which then belonged to Naples. For most of its history Ischia and its famous castle remained attached to that great city, sheltering many of its nobles from political adversity; but during one period, in the early 16th century, the island outshone Naples as a cultural centre. This was due to one woman, Vittoria Colonna, who lived much of her childhood in the castle of Ischia, when her father's estates were confiscated by Pope Alexander VI. She was betrothed in the castle at the age of 6 to another leading personage of the era, Francesco Ferrante, nephew of Constanza d'Avolas, the duchess who ruled Ischia for 50 years. On 27 December 1509, Vittoria and Francesco were married at the castle of Ischia in the celebrity wedding of the decade, but two years later Francesco was drawn away by the wars in the north and only once returned to Vittoria and Ischia before he died.

Vittoria was one of the greatest poets of her day, and is particularly known through her spiritual friendship with Michelangelo, who wrote sonnets to her. Few poets of the time were untouched by her graciousness. She was on close terms with the most brilliant men of Rome, her opinions were sought after, and her behaviour was always perfectly proper amidst the intrigues that surrounded her belligerent family. The contrast between the elegant court that surrounded her during her years on Ischia and the ravages and slave-taking wrought on the island by the corsairs Barbarossa and Dragut, a few years after her departure for Rome, illustrate the extremities of the period.

Another writer of far-reaching influence to find inspiration on Ischia was Giambattista Vico. In the mid-17th century he was offered an easy tutoring job on the island, giving him the leisure to formulate his murky and celebrated *New Science*, a work that had a profound influence on James Joyce. George Bishop Berkeley, the Irish philosopher, visited the island at the beginning of the 18th century and wrote of it extensively in his Journals; Henrik Ibsen spent the summer of 1867 at Casamicciola and wrote much of the play *Peer Gynt* during his stay.

In the 19th century, Ischia, like so many islands, was a political prison. During the Napoleonic Wars it suffered in the battles between French and English, and for a brief period was Nelson's base.

Getting Around

Ischia is considerably larger than Capri, with several self-contained communities. Buses to the various towns on the island depart from the square next to Santa Maria di Portosalvo in Ischia Porto, near the beginning of the SS270, which circles the island. An entire circuit of the island takes about 2½hours. Buses marked CD run clockwise, while those marked CS run anti-clockwise. Cars can be hired relatively cheaply here, from **Davidauto**, Via G. Mazzella 84, ℂ (081) 998043, or **Rentcar Ischia**, Via Alfredo de Luca 59, ℂ (081) 992444. Bikes can be rented from **Autonoleggio-Moto**, Via dello Stadio 16, ℂ (081) 980055.

Tourist Information

There are two offices, both in Ischia Porto, at Corso Vittoria Colonna 116, 80077, ℂ (081) 991464, and Via Iasolino, 80077, ℂ (081) 991146, near the ferry landing.

Ischia Porto

The first hint you receive of Ischia's volcanic origins comes when you enter the almost perfectly round harbour of Ischia Porto, formed by a sister crater of Monte Epomeo. Only in 1854 was it connected to the sea, the narrow strip of land carved out by the engineers of Ferdinand II. Full of yachts, lined with restaurants, and a step away from the tourist information office, it is everything a Mediterranean port should be. Note that while ships to Naples and Capri dock at one side, by the neoclassical church of **Santa Maria di Portosalvo**, and the hydrofoils near the newly modernized **Terme Comunali** (built in 1845), ships to Procida and Pozzuoli call at the other side of the lighthouse.

Via Roma, the main shopping street of Porto, with cafés and boutiques, passes the **Chiesa dell'Assunta**, built in 1300 and since

Ischia

remodelled in the Baroque style. Further on, when Via Roma becomes the more fashionable Corso Vittoria Colonna, turn down Via V. F. d'Avalos for the numerous seaside hotels and *pensioni*, or in the other direction, Via V. E. Cortese for the **Pineta** (pinewood), and lovely shady divider between Ischia Porto and Ischia Ponte.

Ischia Ponte

Ischia Ponte, once a separate fishing village, is slowly being gobbled up by tourist sprawl. 'Ponte' refers to the causeway built by Alfonso (il Magnifico) of Aragon in 1438 to the **Castello d'Ischia** on its offshore rock. With the large dome of its abandoned church in the centre, the fortress where Vittoria Colonna spent so many years looks like a fairytale illustration from the distance. As King Alfonso also financed most of the walls around the islet, which can be visited, it is sometimes called the Castello Aragonese, and can be visited. Not only are the narrow streets and 500-year-old houses interesting; the views from the walls are superb. During the festival of Sant' Anna (end July), near the castle, you can see the island's traditional dance, the *'ndrezzata*, a ritualistic dagger dance dating from the time of Vittoria Colonna, accompanied by clarinets and tambours.

Even better views can be had from the summit of the extinct volcano, **Montagnone** (255m); a cablecar goes from Via Baldassarre Cossa at Ischia Porto (only 5 minutes from the station). Views from the top take in the Phlegraean Fields on the mainland, Ischia's little sister island Procida, and the rest of Ischia as well.

Popular beaches line much of the town's shore. Some are organized, like Ciro, Medusa, Lauro and Starace; others, like the Spiaggia degli Inglesi (named after the English occupation at the beginning of the 18th century) and Dei Pini, are free. The public tennis courts are on the Lido C. Colombo (© (081) 991 013).

Around Ischia: Casamicciola

Besides the state highway (SS270) there are many scenic secondary roads zigzagging across the island that you will be able to enjoy if you have a car or a sturdy constitution and a good pair of shoes. A few miles west of Ischia Porto (bus every half-hour) is the popular resort of **Casamicciola Terme**,the oldest spa on the island and the probable location of a Greek settlement. All remains of this, however, were obliterated in the 1883 earthquake in which 7000 people were killed. Henrik Ibsen spent a summer in a nearby villa (a medallion minted in his honour can be seen in the Piazza). The mineral springs of Casamicciola are particularly potent—Rita and Gurgitello rate as the hottest—and contain large quantities of iodine.

Casamicciola, spread out under its pines, is more a conglomeration of hotels than a proper town, although there is a centre at the **Piazza Marina** with shops, car-hire firms, banks and the AVET tourist information office (© (081) 994 441). Besides the Lido, there are beaches at Suorangela and Castagna. The heliport lies just west of the town. From Piazza Marina, an hour's walk will take you to the **Geophysical Observatory**, built in 1891.

Lacco Ameno

A half-hour's walk along the coast from Casamicciola leads you to the more fashionable **Lacco Ameno**, another large resort, where the local landmark is the **Fungho**, a mushroom-shaped rock that dominates the beach. In the centre of town you can pay your respects at the bright pink **Sanctuary of Santa Restituta**, patron saint of Ischia. Martyred in the 3rd century, her body was thrown into the sea, then floated ashore at Lacco Ameno. The oldest part of the Sanctuary dates from 1036, and was constructed on the site of an early Christian basilica. Excavations in the church crypt have produced evidence of Roman baths. Greek and Roman tools and vases have also been discovered west of Lacco Ameno at Monte Vico and behind the town on Fundera plain. Some of these may be seen in the local **Museum** *(open mornings only)* near the church and the neo-Pompeian **Terme Regina Isabella**, connected to the luxury hotel in Piazza Santa Restituta.

For the hardy, there is a charming country path, the **Calata Sant'Antonio**, leading from Lacco Ameno (off Via Roma) to the Chiesa dell'Immacolata in Casamicciola; the local milkmen, after delivering their wares udder-fresh from door to door, would herd their goats home along this path every evening.

Forio

Forio, the wine-producing centre of Ischia and a growing resort, is one of the prettiest towns on the island and supports a small art colony. Forio has three outstanding landmarks, the first of which is the huge tower known as the **Torrione**, built by King Ferrante in 1480 on the site of an even older tower. It did little, however, to defend the island from pirate raids and was later converted to a prison and, nowadays, a gallery of local art. Near it rises the dome of **Santa Maria di Loreto**, a fine Baroque church built in the 14th century; the two towers are decorated with majolica tiles. On the point furthest west stands the white **Church of the Soccorso**, to whom the local fishermen pray for help, as can be seen from the numerous votive offerings inside.

Behind Forio there are several paths leading up into the hills, towards Monterone, Sant'Antuono and Santa Maria del Monte, below Monte Epomeo. There are beaches on either side of Forio, along with the very popular Citara and Cava dell'Isola to the south, and at Ghiaia and San Francesco to the north. Near Citara are the **Gardens of Poseidon**, a recently-built complex of swimming pools set in a Mediterranean formal garden.

Sant'Angelo

From Forio, still heading counterclockwise, the SS270 passes through the hill village of **Oanza** and on to **Serrara Fontana**, both of which have roads leading down to **Sant'Angelo**. The buses to this lovely fishing port stop at the top of the hill because there isn't enough room for them to turn around in Sant'Angelo itself. The walk down at the edge of the cliff is quite lovely, with numerous views of the **Punta Sant'Angelo**, a small islet connected to Ischia by a narrow isthmus of sand. Only a stump remains of the **Torre Sant'Angelo** which once stood on top.

East of the village stretches the lovely beach of **Maronti**, which you can reach either by taking the path or by hiring a boat. The path runs past numerous fumaroles, hissing and steaming, and the beach itself has patches of scalding hot sand where you can wrap your picnic lunch in foil and cook it, if you so wish. Above the beach are the hot springs of **Cavascura**, at the mouth of an old river canyon; the sheer sides of the canyon, the little wooden bridges and the individual baths carved in the rock—each named after a mythological deity—make it an unusual place indeed.

Monte Epomeo

From Serrara Fontana the road towards Barano is most picturesque, winding its way around the inner valleys of Monte Epomeo (790m). If you're going by bus, stop off at Fontana, where you can start your climb up to the old volcano itself—it hasn't erupted since 1302. Mules may be hired if you're not up to the climb yourself, and there's a hermitage where you can spend the night, located in the very crater itself. Watching the sun rise or set from such vantage points is always memorable, but with the entire Bay of Naples spread out below you, it is sublime.

The next village along the route is **Buonopane** (the name means 'good bread'), followed by **Barano**, an oasis of tranquillity on exuberant Ischia. In the Piazza San Rocco, in the centre of town, the church of the same name has a characteristic campanile. The road from here to Ischia Ponte passes scattered homes and summer villas, half-hidden in the lush vegetation and pine trees.

Ischia, © (081–)   ***Where to Stay***

very expensive

The swankiest hotel on Ischia is the ★★★★★**Regina Isabella**, Piazza Santa Restituta, Lacco Ameno, © (081) 994322, fax 986043, right on the waterfront in Lacco Ameno, with a private beach and every kind of spa and gym facility imaginable. Another pricey beauty, but with a very different style, is Forio's ★★★★★**Grand Albergo Mezza Torre**, Via Mezza Torre, Forio, © 986111, fax 987892. This 60-room hotel is housed in a small castle that used to belong to the film director Visconti. Set in its own grounds, it lacks the facilities of the Regina Isabella, but for good old-fashioned luxury it can't be beaten.

expensive

The finest hotel in Ischia Porto is the ★★★★**Excelsior Belvedere** at Via Gianturco 19, © 991522, fax 984100 (closed Nov–Mar). Not only is it quieter than most, but guests can enjoy the fine pool and garden. You can also indulge in luxury at the ★★★★**Mare Blu**, Via Pontano 40, © 982555, fax 982938, which sits in a charming position on the waterfront with a view of the Aragonese Castle, and is open all year.

For those who want to try Ischia's famous thermal treatments, without spending the kind of sums charged in the smarter hotels, the ★★★**Parco Verde**, Via Mazzella 29, Ischia Porto, ✆ 992282, fax 992773, is a good bet. Set in an attractive park, close to the main drag in Ischia Porto, this hotel offers full thermal facilities and trained staff. If you prefer to do without mudbaths, this pleasant hotel also has a pool, and is close to the beach.

In pretty Sant'Angelo, on the south side of the island, the ★★★★**Miramare**, Via Comandante Maddalena 29, ✆ 999219, fax 999325, is a lovely hotel, with panoramic views over the small harbour. Further west at Forio is the ★★★**Punta del Sole**, Piazza Maltese, ✆ 998208, fax 998209, another hotel that has its own thermal facilities, as well as a pool and garden. In Lacco Ameno, the ★★★**San Montano**, Via Monte Vico, ✆ 994033, fax 980242, offers a pool, tennis courts and many other comforts, in addition to thermal baths. Prices tend to be a bit lower in Casamicciola. One pleasant hotel there is the ★★★**Ibsen** at Corso V. Emanuele 10, ✆ 994919, fax 994253, which has special facilities for wheelchair users.

Also in Casamicciola, the ★★**Delle Rose**, Via Casa Mennella 9, ✆ 994082, fax 995855, is a very good-value hotel with charm, a swimming pool and 24 nice rooms, all with bath. In Ischia Porto, one of the least expensive places to stay is near the Castello Aragonese, and open all year, ★**Il Monastero**, Via Castello Aragonese, ✆ 992435, which has 14 clean rooms, all with bath. Also a bargain by Ischia standards is the ★★**Bristol**, Via Fundera 72, Lacco Ameno, ✆ 994566, with a small garden and swimming pool.

Ischia, ✆ *(081–)* **Eating Out**

In Ischia, fish features prominently on the menu, but you will also find meat here, and specifically, rabbit. For some reason, Ischia is fairly hopping with rabbits, and the locals have dreamed up endless ways of eating them, in stews, roast, or even with pasta.

At Ischia Ponte the loveliest place to eat is **Da Ugo Giardini Eden**, Via Nuova Cartaromana 50, ✆ 993909, set right on the sea. You couldn't find fresher fish or lobster anywhere, as they pluck it right out of the water in front of you. Along the port, **Gennaro**, Via Porto 66, ✆ 992917, serves superb giant prawns and much more. Still in Ischia Porto, **Il Damiano**, on the SS270, Ischia Porto, ✆ 983032 (open evenings only), offers diners superb views over the sea, plus beautifully cooked seafood and fish dishes, most of all the *linguine all'aragosta*, long pasta with a lobster sauce.

On the seafront at Ischia Porto, **Zi Nannina a Mare**, Lungomare Cristoforo Colombo, © 991350, is a delightful family-run trattoria with an outdoor terrace offering well-cooked Ischian specialities, based on either fish or meat. Near Forio, in the open countryside, the **Cavé Gran Diavolo**, Via Bocca 88, Forio, © 989 282, serves more meat than fish, with pride of place going to the famous Ischian dish *bucatini con sugo di coniglio*—fat spaghetti served in rabbit sauce. The rustic feel and good local wine make this a very pleasant place for lunch or dinner. Right on the water's edge at Forio, the **Cava dell'Isola**, Via G. Mazzella, Forio, © 997452, is especially enjoyable at lunchtime, perhaps after a morning spent on the nearby beach. Good local specialities are the mainstay.

At Sant'Angelo the **Conchiglia**, Via Sant'Angelo, © 999270, offers al fresco dining on a tiny but charming terrace, overlooking the harbour. There are also a handful of nice, inexpensive rooms to let above the restaurant.

Procida

Lovely, uncomplicated and tiny, Procida is in many ways the archetypal image of all that an 'Italian island' evokes in any holiday dreamer's mind. Scented by lemon groves, said to produce the finest lemons in Italy, embellished with colourful houses as original as they are beautiful, a setting for two famous love stories, Procida is an island where most people still earn a living from the sea, as fishermen or sailors, and also from carving exquisite models of historic ships. Its very proximity to the glamour, chaos and more celebrated charms of Naples, Capri and Ischia has saved it from the worst ravages of touristic excess. The pace of life is delightfully slow, and when there's talk of closing the penitentiary and converting it into a Grand Hotel, the locals shudder—they prefer the cons to any Capri-like transformation of their idyllic life. Connected to Procida by a modern bridge is the minute islet of Vivara—officially, though it sounds bizarre, a natural park of Naples. It teems with wild rabbits, an important ingredient in Procida's cuisine, along with the more obvious fruits of the sea.

History

Only a few miles from the mainland and Monte Procida itself, Procida the island was near enough to Naples to have a minor, or at least a spectator's role in many of the turbulent events that transpired there, but far enough away to stay out of trouble. Like Ischia, to which it was once connected, Procida (ancient *Prochyo*, or 'deep', in some way connected with Aeneas' wet-nurse) was inhabited in the Neolithic period. The Romans used the island as a hunting reserve, and there was at least an agricultural settlement there in the Dark Ages—Pope Gregory the Great wrote a letter in the 6th century praising the wine of Procida. Shortly thereafter the first chapel of San Michele Arcangelo was erected on Punta Lingua, on the site where a statue of the saint stood; according to legend, during a pirate attack the people prayed fervently to the statue for deliverance, and the saint responded and saved his beloved Procida at least this once.

In the 11th century a Benedictine abbey was founded by the chapel, and the fortifications of the Terra Murata ('the walled land') were begun. These proved insufficient against the ravages of first Barbarossa (1544), then Dragut (1562) and Bolla (1572). After Barbarossa burned the church, the fishermen had to donate a third of their income to reconstruct it—Pope Julius III generously decreed they could fish on Sundays and holidays as well for ten years to make ends meet, permission which was extended for fifteen more years after Dragut. By then, however, the Benedictines had long abandoned Procida.

The Bourbon kings, like the Romans before them, often came to Procida to hunt; Fernando IV made the island and its town a royal domain, but turned its fortress into a prison. Procida prefers to recall another event of the period: the visit in 1811–12 by the wandering French poet Alphonse Lamartine. A beautiful daughter of a fisherman fell in love with him and gave up an advantageous marriage for his sake, only to be jilted by the fickle Frenchman. Inconsolate, she died two months later, and at least received the dubious compensation of immortaility in his novel *Graziella*, a spectacular bestseller in its day. Procida, for its part, pays hommage to her memory with an annual end-of-summer Miss Graziella beauty pageant.

Another famous personage connected with the island was so fond of it that he incorporated it in his name, becoming Giovanni da Procida. Born in 1210 in Salerno, this nobleman, a good friend of Emperor Frederick 'Stupor Mundi' and his son Manfred, had a castle on the island which he visited often on tours of his domains. When Charles of Anjou, a Guelph, took Naples, he confiscated all the property of Ghibelines like Giovanni da Procida, and the latter was forced to flee to Spain. Here Constance, the last of the Swabians and wife of King Peter of Aragon, received him well and made him Baron of Valencia.

But Giovanni got his revenge on Charles of Anjou. When the proud Sicilians began to chafe under the harsh rule of the French, Giovanni acted as a middleman to assure them that should they rise up in arms, Peter of Aragon would support their cause and be their king. The Sicilian Vespers resulted, and some 8000 Frenchmen died in that island's spontaneous combustion. The French were at least symbolically revenged on Giovanni da Procida. When they occupied Procida in 1806 during the Napoleonic Wars—about 650 years after the Sicilian Vespers—they destroyed his marble coat-of-arms, the last reminder of his presence on the island.

Readers of Boccaccio may recognize Giovanni's nephew, Gianni da Procida, from the Sixth Tale of the Fifth Day of the *Decameron*. Gianni so loved a girl of Ischia named Restituta that he sailed over daily, to look at the walls of her house if nothing else. One foul day a band of Sicilians pounced upon her and carried her off to Palermo, determined to give such a lovely prize to their king, Frederick of Aragon, who stowed Restituta in his garden villa, La Cuba, for future pleasures. Meanwhile Gianni in despair went in search of his sweetheart and finally discovered her whereabouts; he contrived to enter La Cuba with the aid of Restituta to plot an escape and make love; the king caught them *in flagrante* and was about to burn them publicly at the stake when a courtier recognized Gianni, and informed the king he was about to execute the nephew of the man who gave him the throne of Sicily, and there's a happy ending. A good story—and according to scholars, a true one.

Getting Around

There are frequent ferry and hydrofoil services from both Naples and Ischia to the smallest of the islands, **Procida**. The harbour itself is tiny, and if you want to explore further afield, jump on one of the colourful diesel-powered buggies that serve as taxis. Alternately, there is a bus service about every half hour between the harbour and the other end of the island at Chiaiolella, stopping more or less at every point in between.

Tourist Information

The tourist office is at Via Rodia, 80079, © (081) 8969624, in the Marina Grande (the only substantial town), near the ferry departure point.

The Port and Corricella

Ships and hydrofoils call at the port, the **Marina Grande**, also called Sancio Cattolico, or known locally as Sent'Co. The church near the landing, **Santa Maria della Pietà** (1760), immediately gives you a taste of Procida's delightful architecture—wide arches in random rhythms and exterior rampant stairs crisscrossing the façades, all in softly moulded lines and colour either faded pastel or more racy deep pinks, blues and yellows. The style reaches its epiphany over the hill at **Corricella** the oldest village on the island, built on a protected cove by fishermen, under the citadel of the Terra Murata. Steep stone stairways cascade down amongst the rounded arches; from the little port they're like a hundred watchful eyes, scanning the sea for the return. Some have been so remodelled over the centuries according to the needs of its inhabitants as to give immediate proof of an old island saying, that 'a house isn't only a house. A house is a story.' The same could be said of Corricella's simple church, **San Rocco**, restored numerous times throughout the centuries. From here Via San Rocco leads to the Piazza dei Martiri where twelve Procidanese were executed in 1799 by the Bourbons for plotting a revolt. Near the Piazza is the domed **Madonna delle Grazie** (1700), containing a much-loved statue of the Virgin.

The Terra Murata

Via Madonna delle Grazie leads to the Terra Murata (91m, Procida's highest point), passing on the right the romantic if roofless ruins of **Santa Margherita Nuova**, built in 1586 at the edge of the Punta dei Monaci. The fortifications of the citadel belong to different dates, the latest portions from 1521; the oldest section of the medieval walls can be seen near the Porta Mezz'Olmo, at the beginning of the Via San Michele. Rising above the walls, houses and prison of Terra Murata are the three domes of **San Michele Arcangelo**, which, despite its exotic, almost Saracen appearance from a distance, wears a simple unadorned façade, rebuilt after the various pirates' depredations. The domes are untiled—Procida receives so little rain that tiles aren't strictly necessary, or at least worth the cost. Of the original pre-16th-century structure, only part of the ceiling in the Sala del Capitolo remains. Many rich works of art in the three-naved church itself attest to the former splendour of the monastery; the ceiling frescoes date from the 17th century, as do the apse paintings by Nicola Rosso, the most interesting of which shows the God's aide-de-camp Michael and his troop of *putti* swooping down to save Procida from the Turks. Pride of place goes to a splashy canvas by Neapolitan Luca Giordano.

In the Piazza d'Armi is the Cardinal of Aragon's 1563 **Castello d'Aragona**, a fancy name for the clink (pop. 90, who wish they could catch the next boat to Naples); here, too, you can see parts of the walls, in which are crammed tortuous alleyways and steep narrow houses. Other old palaces may be seen along the escarpment over **Chiaia beach**— including the **Palazzo Minichini**, on Via Marcello Scotti, adjacent to the fine old church of **San Tommaso d'Aquino**. Over the south side of the beach is the so-called 'Casa di Graziella'.

Across Procida

North of Marina Grande is the quarter known as Annunziata, after the old **Chiesa dell'Annunziata**, reconstructed in 1600 and containing a miraculous Madonna, to whom are the many, varied votive offerings that adorn the interior of the church. There are pretty views from here of Punta Pioppeto and the **faro**, or lighthouse, where people often come for a swim. Nearby stands the only remaining watchtower of the original three constructed in the 16th century. From Punta Cottimo you can see the island of Ventotene, geologically related to Procida.

The rest of the island has many rural beauty spots, shaded walkways and narrow roads, old farmhouses and crumbling small palazzi, such as that of Giovanni da Procida on Via Giovanni da Procida. The areas around **Centane**, especially Punta Solchiaro, is most typical, and has the most striking belvedere, with views over the entire east coast of the island.

On the west end of the island, the long stretch of sand between Punta Serra and the peninsula of Santa Margherita Vecchia has been divided into three beaches—**Spiaggia Ciraccio**, where two Roman tombs were discovered; **Spiaggia Ciraciello**, on the other side of the pyramid-shaped rock, Il Faraglione di Procida; and towards the peninsula, the **Lido**. The hillock on the peninsula is capped by the tower-like ruin of the church of **Santa Margherita Vecchia**, once a Benedictine abbey abandoned in 1586; on the other side of it lies the small fishing port and beach **Marina di Chiaiolella**, on a rounded cove that long ago was a volcanic crater.

From here you can cross the new pedestrian-only bridge to the islet of **Vivara**, where the birds are protected these days but the rabbits are fair game. Here were discovered the Neolithic implements (at Capitello and Punta de Mezzodi) now in Ischia's museum. A narrow road leads towards the summit of Vivara, through the crumbling arch of an old hunting lodge, to the Belvedere, with fine panoramas of Procida and Pozzuoli on the mainland.

Procida, ☎ (081–)   **Where to Stay and Eating Out**

moderate

Right on the main harbour front, the ★★★**Crescenzo**, Via Marina Chiaiolella, ☎ 8967255, fax 8101260, is a landmark in Procida. Its rooms are simply but pleasantly furnished, and the restaurant, which serves local specialities and pizza in the evening, is worth a try even if you are not staying here.

There are several good restaurants along the port at Marina Grande, like **La Medusa**, ☎ 896 7481, serving seafood and meats at reasonable prices. **Il Cantino**, Via Nitrodi 6, ☎ 99071, serves a very good *fritto misto di pesce* (fresh fried fish), with decent local wine.

inexpensive

The only hotel open all year round on the island is the ★★**Oasi** at Via Elleri 16, ☎ 8967499, a villa with a restaurant and garden. Another good inexpensive hotel, on the beach at Chiaia, is the ★★**Riviera**, Via Giovanni da Procida 36, ☎ 896 7197, with 23 rooms, most with bath.

Amalfi Coast

The Amalfi Coast

> *...the only delectable part of Italy, which the inhabitants there dwelling do call the coast of Malfie, full of towns, gardens, springs and wealthy men.*
>
> Bocaccio

When confronted with something generally acclaimed to be the most beautiful stretch of scenery in the entire Mediterranean, the honest writer is at a loss. Few who have been there would argue the point, but describing it properly is another matter. Along this coast, where one mountain after another plunges sheer into the sea, there is a string of towns that not long ago were accessible only by boat. Today, a spectacular corniche road of 'a thousand bends' covers the route, climbing in places to a thousand feet above the sea; necessity makes it so narrow that every oncoming vehicle is an adventure, but everyone except the driver will have the treat of a lifetime. Nature here has created an amazing vertical landscape, a mix of sharp crags and deep green forests; in doing so she inspired the Italians to add three of their most beautiful towns.

This coast has always attracted foreigners, but only relatively recently has it become a major resort area. Places like Positano have become reserves for the wealthy, and swarms of day trippers are likely to descend at any moment. They'll never spoil it, though; all the engineers in Italy couldn't widen the Amalfi road, and the impossible terrain leaves no room at all for new development. For a map, *see* p.91.

Tourist Information

There are tourist offices along the peninsula in **Positano**, at Via Saracino 4, 84017, © (089) 875067, fax 875766; **Amalfi**, at Corso Roma 19, 84011, © (089) 871107, fax 872619; **Ravello**, Piazza Vescovado, 84010, © (089) 857096, fax 857977; and **Maiori**, at Corso Regina, 84010, © (089) 877452. In **Salerno** the helpful EPT is at Via Velia 15, 84109, © (089) 224322, fax 251844. Their excellent *Annuario Alberghi* has, besides a list of hotels throughout the province (which includes the Amalfi coast), a map and just about everything else you may need to know.

Getting Around

Buses are the only form of public transport on the Amalfi coast. SITA services travel between Sorrento and Salerno about every 50min (*see* p.9).

Positano

To complement the vertical landscape, here is Italy's most nearly vertical town. Positano spills down from the corniche like a waterfall of pink, cream and yellow villas. The day trippers may walk down to the sea; only the alpinists among them make it back up (fortunately, there is a regular bus service along the one main street). After World War II Positano became a well-known hideaway for artists and writers—many of them American, following the lead given by John Steinbeck —and fashion was not slow to follow. Now, even though infested with boutiques, Positano reverts to the Positanesi in the off-season, and quiets down considerably. When you get to the bottom, there is a soft, grey beach and the town's church, decorated with a pretty tiled dome like so many others along this coast. A highlight of the town's year is its spectacular *festa* on the Feast of the Assumption, 15 August—the main holiday of the summer throughout Italy— when the local people take their town back in order to stage a performance recreating the Amalfi coast's centuries-long battles with the Saracens (*see* Festivals, p.15).

If you have time, take a trip further up to **Montepertuso**, a village perched three kilometres above Positano, and which takes its name (meaning 'hole in the mountain') from an old legend—the devil challenged the Virgin Mary to blow a hole in the mountain, saying the winner could have control of the village. The devil tried, but failed miserably, while the Virgin coolly walked through the mountainside, leaving a hole still visible today. The locals re-enact the scene each 2 July, with much merriment and fireworks. On the last Saturday in August, the village stages another of the best festas in all Italy, the *sagra del fagiolo*—the feast of the bean. The streets are decked out with stalls selling beans cooked in every possible way, plus a great many other home-cooked dishes, washed down with local wine served from oak barrels by waiters dressed in traditional costume.

The next town east along the drive from Positano, **Praiano**, could be Positano's little sister: with a similar beach and church, but not quite as scenic and perpendicular, and not quite as beleaguered by tourism. The last part, at least, is changing fast. After Praiano, keep an eye out for the most impressive natural feature along the drive, the steep, impenetrable **Furore Gorge**. On either side are tiny isolated villages along the shore, with beaches—if only you have a way to get to them. Further down the road you'll notice the lift leading down to the **Grotta Smeralda** *(open April–Oct 9.30am–5pm daily; Nov–Mar 10am–6pm daily; adm)*. The strange green light that is diffused throughout this sea-level cavern gives it its name. Beyond this, **Conca dei Marini** is another vertical village, with a beach and a Norman lookout tower to climb.

luxury

With Positano's new-found status has come some of the highest hotel prices in Italy. If you're feeling self-indulgent—and very rich— you may care to stay at a place many believe to be the finest resort hotel in the country. The ★★★★★**San Pietro**, ✆ 875455, fax 811449, 1½km from Positano on the Amalfi drive, is an intimate paradise, 60 rooms with individual terraces, strung down the cliffs next to Positano and connected to the coast road on top by a long elevator. The entrance is hidden behind an old chapel; there are no signs, which is all part of the management's plan to maintain the privacy and tranquillity of its celebrity clientele. It also offers a private beach, tennis courts, and its own excursion boat.

very expensive

★★★★★**Le Sirenuse**, Via Cristoforo Colombo 30, ✆ 875066, fax 811798, is the former home of a noble Neapolitan family. It became a hotel in 1951, and has since established itself as one of Positano's best. Everything is done with style, from the beautifully decorated drawing room to the swimming pool with its mosaic tiles.

expensive

The ★★★★**Palazzo Murat**, Via dei Mulini 23, ✆ 875177, fax 811419, in Positano, an 18th-century palazzo which once belonged to Napoleon's brother-in-law Joachim Murat, briefly King of Naples, also has plenty of old-world charm, with antiques in many rooms and a beautiful courtyard where classical concerts are sometimes staged in summer.

moderate

On a more modest level, the ★★★**Casa Albertina**, Via Favolozza 4, ✆ 811149, fax 875540, is done in a lovely, understated manner, the better to accentuate the views over Positano and the sea. It's a family-run place, with a nice restaurant on the rooftop terrace, a few minutes from the beach, and in the busy season its quietness can be an advantage. A little closer to the water is the ★★★**Ancora**, on Via Columbo, ✆ 875318, fax 811784, a peaceful and professionally run place, though it too is family-owned. A good bargain is the ★★**California**, Via Colombo 141, ✆ 875382, with 10 very pleasant rooms, all with bath, and a lovely terrace for breakfast and other meals.

If you have a car, you can expand your horizons to include some of the more secluded spots along the coast. In Praiano, new hotels seem to be opening at least once a month; for the time being, the better choices are just outside the village at Vettica Maggiore, a little way back towards Positano along the Amalfi drive. One exceptional bargain here is the ★★★**Tramonto d'Oro**, ✆ 874008, fax 874670, which offers tennis courts, a pool, beach access, and great views; the restaurant isn't exceptional, but will do. Further towards Amalfi at Conca dei Marini, the ★★★**Belvedere**, ✆ (089) 831282, fax 831439, is an airy and modern resort hotel in a delightful setting, with a nice beach and an old Norman tower in the grounds.

inexpensive

In Positano the ★**Maria Luisa**, Via Fornillo 40, ✆ 875023, also has 10 rooms, all with baths, and a friendly family atmosphere. A few very inexpensive *pensioni* can also be found along Via Fornillo and on the other streets leading down to the beach. In Praiano, similarly, there are some cheaper old pensions by the port, but they are usually full to bursting in the summer.

Positano, ✆ (081–)　　　　　　　　　　　　　　　　　　　　　**Eating Out**

In the high season at least, most of the resort hotels along the coast will coerce you into dining with them. Not that that's always bad—some of the better hotels have well-known gourmet restaurants—but there are also some equally good places elsewhere to enjoy if you can escape. Like many of the restaurants on the *Costiera*, a good number of Positano's eateries close from November till Easter.

expensive

La Cambusa, Spiaggia Grande, ✆ 875432, in a lovely position with a terrace looking out onto the beach, is a Positano favourite. The chef serves excellently cooked fresh fish and seafood in as many ways as you can think of, and more, and a house speciality is *penne con gamberetti, rugola e pomodoro*—penne with prawns, rocket and fresh tomatoes. Across the road, the **Buca di Bacco**, Via Rampa Teglia 8, ✆ 875699, is another Positano institution, *the* place to stop off for a drink on the way back from the beach. The fish is always well cooked here, and you'd be crazy to go for anything else.

moderate

Down on Positano's beach, the centre of the action in the summer is **Chez Black**, Via Brigantino, ✆ 875036, a slick and sophisticated spot that fortunately turns out to be a good deal cosier—and less expensive—than it looks. Good Neapolitan favourites like *spaghetti alle vongole*—with clams—are done well here, leading up to a vast choice of seafood, and maybe a banana split with *liquore Strega* for dessert. **O'Caporale**, near the water on Via Regina Giovanna, ✆ 811188, offers much of the same (and who needs anything fancier?)—the swordfish and *zuppa di pesce* are particularly good.

Lo Guarracino, Via Positanesi d'America 12, ✆ 875794, is situated in one of Positano's most lovely spots, on a terrace perched over the sea, reached by a half-kilometre walk along a cliff path. Its informal atmosphere and well-cooked local dishes make this a favourite with the Positanesi. Further uptown, the **Grottino Azzurro**, Via Chiesa Nuova, ✆ 875466, is a family-run trattoria, where the *signora* comes to the table to advise you on the catch of the day, and how best you should sample it.

In summer, for a memorable experience, watch out for boats marked **Da Laurito** leaving the jetty at Positano beach. This is a free ferry service to a delightful trattoria around the next bay, set on a small beach, with makeshift tables under a straw canopy. The speciality here is good old-fashioned recipes such as *totani con patate*—squid cooked with potatoes in a wonderful sauce of oil and garlic, all washed down with white wine spiked with fresh peaches. At the end of your meal, they'll ferry you back again as part of the service (✆ 875022).

Just east of Praiano, tucked away in a tiny bay at the foot of Il Furore, is the **Petit Ristorante**, Via Praia 15, ✆ 874706 (closed Oct–Easter). Diners eat at tables outside, surrounded by gaily painted fishing boats, choosing from a menu that features mainly simple dishes such as fresh grilled fish and salad.

inexpensive

Given Positano's fashionable standing genuinely cheap places to eat are hard to find, though there are some pizzerias around Via Fornillo, and some of the restaurants listed above, such as Chez Black, also provide pizzas at less than their main-menu prices. At Montepertuso, above Positano, **Il Ritrovo**, Via Monte 53, ✆ 811336, is a pretty trattoria, with tomatoes strung from its beams and good local dishes including, a rarity for these parts, grilled meats. Also, just outside Praiano, in a dramatic setting in a cave reached by a cliff path, is the prime-spot nightclub for the Amalfi coast, the **Africana**, Via Torre a Mare, Praiano, ✆ 874 042). Open 10pm–3.30am during the season, it also offers light meals.

Amalfi

Sometimes history seems to be kidding us. Can it be true, can this miniscule village once have had a population of 80,000? There is no room among these jagged rocks for even a fraction of that—but then we remember that in Campania anything is possible, and we read how most of the old town simply slid into the sea during a storm and earthquake in 1343. The history is a glorious one. Amalfi was the first Italian city to regain its balance after the Dark Ages, the first to recreate its civic pride and its mercantile daring. As such, she showed the way to Venice, Pisa and Genoa, though she would get to keep few of the prizes for herself.

History

It is only natural that the Amalfitani would try to embroider their history a bit to match such an exquisite setting. Legends tell of a nymph named Amalphi who haunted this shore and became the lover of Hercules. As for their city's founding, they'll tell you about a party of Roman noblemen, fleeing the barbarians after the fall of the Empire, who found the site a safe haven to carry on the old Roman spirit and culture. Amalfi first appears in the 6th century; by the 9th it had achieved its independence from the dukes of Naples, and was probably the most important trading port of southern Italy, with a large colony of merchants at Constantinople and connections with all the Muslim lands. In 849, the chroniclers record the Amalfitano fleet chasing off an Arab raid on Rome. At the beginning, the Amalfitano Republic was ruled by officers called *giudici*, or judges; the year 958 brought a change in constitutions, and Amalfi elected its first doge, in imitation of Venice. At about the same time, the city's merchants developed the famous *Tavola Amalfitana*, a book of maritime laws that was widely adopted around the Mediterranean.

All of this came at a time for which historical records are scarce, but Amalfi's merchant adventurers must have had as romantically exciting a time as those of Venice. Their luck turned sour in the 11th century. The first disaster was a sacking by Robert Guiscard in 1073. Amalfi regained its freedom with a revolt in 1096, but the Normans of the new Kingdom of Sicily came back to stay in 1131. These, unfortunately, proved unable to protect it against two more terrible sackings at the hands of its arch-enemy Pisa, in 1135 and 1137. Today, Amalfi only gets a chance to recapture its glory days once every four years, when it hosts the Pisans, Genoese and Venetians in the antique boat race of the Four Maritime Republics.

The Cathedral and the Cloister of Paradise

The disaster of 1343 ensured that Amalfi's decline would be complete, but what's left of the place today—with its 5000 or so people—is beautiful almost to excess. Over the little square around the harbour, a conspicuous inscription brags: 'The Judgement Day, when the Amalfitani go to heaven, will be a day like any other day'. The square is called **Piazza Flavio Gioia**, after Amalfi's most famous merchant adventurer; he's probably another fictitious character—more Amalfitano embroidery—but they claim he invented the compass in the 12th century.

From here, an arch under the buildings leads to the centre of the town, the **Piazza del Duomo**, with a long flight of steps up to what may be the loveliest **cathedral** in all the south of Italy (9th–12th centuries). Not even in Sicily was the Arab-Norman style ever carried to such a flight of fancy as in this delicate façade, with four levels of interlaced arches in stripes of different-coloured stone (much restored a century ago). The lace-like open arches on the porch are unique in Italy, though common enough in Muslim Spain, one of the countries with which Amalfi had regular trade relations. The cathedral's greatest treasure is its set of bronze doors, cast with portraits of Christ, Mary, St Peter and Amalfi's patron St Andrew; the first of such bronze doors in Italy, they were made in Constantinople in 1066 by an artist named Simon of Syria (he signed them), commissioned by the leader of the Amalfitan colony there. The cathedral's interior, unfortunately, was restored in the 18th-century Baroque à la Napoletana, with plenty of frills in inlaid coloured marble. The red porphyry baptismal font, in the first chapel on the left, is believed to have come from the ruins of Paestum. Down in the crypt you can see more coloured marble work and frescoes, a gift of Philip II of Spain, and also the head of St Andrew; this relic was a part of Amalfi's share of the loot in the sack of Constantinople in 1204.

One of the oldest parts of the cathedral to survive is the **Chiostro del Paradiso**, a whitewashed quadrangle of interlaced arches with a decidedly African air. Many of the bits and pieces of old Amalfi that have survived its calamities have been assembled here: there are classical sarcophagi, medieval sculptures and coats-of-arms. Best of all are the fragments of Cosmatesque work, brightly-coloured geometric mosaics that once were parts of pulpits and pillars, a speciality of this part of Campania.

Duomo di Amalfi

From the centre of Amalfi, you can walk in a few minutes out to the northern edge of the city, the narrow 'Valley of the Mills', set along a stream bed between steep cliffs; some of the mills that made medieval Amalfi famous for paper-making are still in operation, and there is a small **Paper Museum** *(open 9–1, 3–6, Tues–Sun; adm)* in the town. You can also watch paper being made and buy paper products at **Armatruda**, Via Fiume, ✆ (089) 871315, in central Amalfi, near the museum. If you'll be staying some time in this area, one of the best ways to spend it is walking the many lovely paths that navigate the steep hills into the interior of the peninsula, passing through groves of chestnut and ash; these, such as they are, were the main roads in the days of the Republic. One particularly nice one is the Amalfi–Pontone path, passing the ruins of the old monastery of Sant'Eustacchio, and there are many others around Ravello and Scala; ask the locals to point them out.

Amalfi, ✆ (089–)　　　　　　　　　　　　　　　　**Where to Stay**

Unlike Positano, Amalfi has been a resort for a long time, and some of its older establishments are among the most distinctive on the Mediterranean.

very expensive

The ★★★★★**Santa Caterina**, ✆ 871102, fax 871351, with perhaps the loveliest gardens of all, is a converted villa with wonderful sea views from most rooms.

St Francis himself is said to have founded the ★★★★**Luna**, ✆ 871102, fax 871333, though the lifts and Hollywood-style pool are a little more recent. This former monastery, above the drive on Amalfi's eastern edge, was already a hotel in the waning days of the Grand Tour—Wagner stayed here while searching for his Garden of Klingsor, and they can show you the room where Ibsen wrote *A Doll's House*. Among other famous guests, the owners claim the Luna to have been a favourite of both Mussolini and Otto von Bismarck; modern-day authoritarians will enjoy the comfortable rooms and attentive service. If Franciscan accommodation isn't to your taste, see what the 12th-century Capuchins could come up with at the ★★★★**Cappuccini Convento**, Via Annunziatella, ✆ 871877, fax 871886, built by Emperor Frederick II on a mountainside over the town, with a lift running down through the cliffs to the beach. The monks would have enjoyed seeing the Persian rugs and elegant furnishings in their old digs, though perhaps they might have been dismayed to see their cloister converted into a conference centre. The restaurant is also one of the town's best.

moderate

Not all of Amalfi's accommodation offers such heights of luxury. Two pleasant hotels that stand out, and which are both conveniently placed for the town and the beach are the ★★★**Miramalfi**, ✆ and fax 871588, and the well kept ★★★**Amalfi** on Via dei Pastai, ✆ 872440, fax 872250.

inexpensive

★★**La Conchiglia**, ✆ 871856, at the end of the Lungomare by Amalfi's little harbour, has 11 nice rooms, all with bath. There is also a fair collection of inexpensive places around the Cathedral. Three particularly good ones are the ★★**Sole** on Largo della Zecca, ✆ 871147, the prettily furnished ★★**Sant'Andrea**, Via Santolo Camera 1, ✆ 871145, and the ★★**Fontana**, Piazza Duomo 7, ✆ 871530.

Amalfi, ✆ (089–)　　　　　　　　　　　　　　　　　　**Eating Out**

Amalfi has several fine restaurants, including those in the luxury hotels mentioned above.

expensive

Da Gemma, Via Fra Gerardo Sasso 9, ✆ 871345, is one of Amalfi's oldest restaurants, with an attractive terrace for outdoor dining and an excellent fish-based menu. Their *zuppa di pesce* (fish soup) is a wonderfully rich mixture of all sorts of different fish and seafood. Almost directly under the Cathedral, the **Taverna degli Apostoli**, Via Sant'Anna 5, ✆ 872991, also has a fine *risotto marinaio* and other fish dishes.

At **Lo Smeraldino**, Piazzale dei Protontini 1, ✆ 871071, at the far end of the port, you'll be offered the house speciality, *scialatiello*, fresh pasta with mixed seafood, and a range of good *secondi*, most notably an excellent *fritto misto*—mixed fried fish. You can also order pizza here. **La Caravella**, Via Matteo Camera 12, ✆ 871029, serves a delicious ravioli stuffed with seafood, and a good range of home-made desserts.

There's a pretty old-fashioned trattoria-wine shop a little way north of the Cathedral on Via Pietro Capuana, called **La Vinicola**, and though the choice is limited the cooking is good. Close by, the **Tarì**, Via P. Capuana, ✆ 871832, is another pretty, welcoming trattoria with friendly service, and no unpleasant surprises when it's time for the bill.

At the **San Giuseppe**, Via Ruggiero II 4, ✆ 872640, a family-run hostelry, the pizza is sublime—it should be, as the owner is a baker. Good local pasta and fish dishes are also available at reasonable prices. In the centre of town, **Da Maria**, Via Lorenzo d'Amalfi 14, ✆ 871880, is a lively trattoria and pizzeria where the waiters are cheerful and helpful, and the food a cut above some of the other less expensive places.

Villages Inland: Ravello and Scala

As important as it was in its day, the Amalfitan Republic never grew very big. At its greatest extent, it could only claim a small part of this coast, including these two towns up in the mountains; like Amalfi they were once much larger and more prosperous than you see them today. **Ravello** is another beauty, a balcony overlooking the Amalfi coast and a treasurehouse of exotic medieval art. Ravello seems to have been a resort even in Roman times; numerous remains of villas have been found. As the second city of the Amalfitan Republic, medieval Ravello had a population of 30,000 (at least that's what they claim); now it provides an example of that typically Italian phenomenon—a village of 2000 with a first-rate cathedral.

Ravello's chief glories are two wonderful gardens: that of the **Villa Cimbrone** *(open 9am–one hour before sunset daily; adm)*, laid out by an Englishman in the 1900s, with a priceless view over the Amalfi coast, and that of the **Villa Rùfolo** *(open 9.30am–1pm, 3–7pm daily; adm)*—which, as fans of Wagner will be interested to know, is none other than Klingsor's magic garden. Wagner says so himself, in a note scribbled in the villa's guest book. He really had come here looking for it, for the proper setting in which to imagine the worldly, Faustian enchanter of *Parsifal*. The villa itself is a remarkable 11th-century pleasure palace, a temporary abode of Charles of Anjou, various Norman kings, and Adrian IV, the only English pope (1154–59), who came here fleeing a rebellion in Rome. Even in its present, half-ruined state, it is worth a visit; inside there is a small collection of architectural fragments. The garden, with more fine views, is a small semi-tropical paradise, full of fountains and flowers in every imaginable colour.

The **cathedral** is named after Ravello's patron San Pantaleone, an obscure early martyr; they have a phial of his blood in one of the side chapels, and it 'boils' like the blood of San Gennaro in Naples whenever the saint is in the mood. Lately he hasn't been, which makes the Ravellans worry. The cathedral has two particular treasures: a pair of bronze doors by Barisano of Trani (1179), inspired by the Greek ones at Amalfi, and an exquisite pair of marble *ambones*, or pulpits, that rank among the outstanding examples of 12th–13th-century sculptural and mosaic work; the more elaborate one, its columns resting on six curious lions, dates from 1272. The sacristy contains two paintings by the southern Renaissance artist Andrea da Salerno, including an unusual subject, the *Assumption of the Magdalen*. In this Cathedral in 1149, the English pope, Adrian IV, crowned William the Bad King of Sicily. Two other Ravello churches where you can see decorative work similar to the cathedral's are **Santa Maria a Gradello** and **San Giovanni del Toro**.

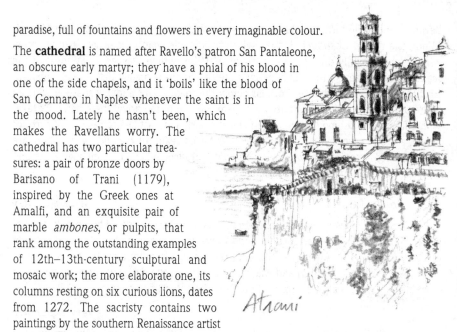

Atrani

From Ravello, it is only a lovely 1½km walk to **Scala**, smallest and oldest of the three Amalfitan towns; along the way you'll pass an ancient bridge and a small waterfall. Scala has another interesting old cathedral, **San Lorenzo**; inside, over the main altar is a 13th-century wooden crucifix. Gerardo da Sasso, a citizen of Scala, started out running a small hostel for pilgrims in Jerusalem and ended up founding the Knights Hospitallers, or Knights of St John (1118); his family's ruined palace can be seen near the village. Above Scala, the chapel of **San Pietro in Campoleone** has medieval carvings of St Michael and St Catherine inside, if you can find someone with the key.

Between Amalfi and Ravello, before reaching the turn off inland, the Amalfi drive passes through **Atrani**, an old village whose church of San Salvatore has another tiled dome, and yet another set of bronze doors from Constantinople; inside it, note the lovely Byzantine relief of a pair of peacocks (peacock flesh was believed to be incorruptible back then, and therefore a symbol of immortality; but why the birds are standing, respectively, on a man and a rabbit is anybody's guess). In the days of the Republic this church was called San Salvatore della Biretta; the Amalfitan doges wore cloth caps like those of Venice, and they would come here for their ceremonies of investiture. Atrani and Amalfi don't much care for each other. Such Lilliputian rivalries are common on this coast (it's the same with Ravello and Scala); in Amalfi they'll tell you how Atrani was ruined after the Pisan raids, and how Emperor Manfred repopulated it with Muslims from Sicily. Such neighbours!

Beyond the Ravello turn, next along the way towards Salerno come **Minori** and **Maiori**. Minori is a typical *Costiera* hill-town, with considerable charm. Its bigger sister is somewhat less so, mainly due to a major flood in 1954, which washed away most of the seafront; today, most of the buildings and hotels along the shore are depressingly modern. **Erchie**, a tiny hamlet on the shore far below the road, seems a lovely spot—if you can figure out a way to get down to it. Then, near the end of the drive, there come **Cetara**, with a fine beach behind the mole of the fishing port, and, just before Salerno, **Vietri sul Mare**, a pretty town famous throughout Italy for its beautiful *maiolica* ware. There are ceramics shops everywhere, where you can watch craftsmen hand-painting jugs, vases and tiles, and pick up souvenirs at surprisingly good prices.

Around Ravello, © (089–) **Where to Stay**

Ravello also has its share of dream hotels: offering no beaches, but unforgettable gardens and views down over the coast. In the shadow of Amalfi and Ravello, the two thoroughly pleasant beach lidos of Minori and Maiori may seem a little dull, but they can be useful bases, especially if hotels in the better known resorts are full.

very expensive

Ravello's finest, with an incredible guest book full of the names of the famous over the last 120 years, is the ★★★★★**Palumbo**, Via S. Giovanni del Toro 28, © 857 244, fax 857347. The service is perfect, the 12 rooms are individually decorated with antiques, the restaurant is equally renowned for seafood, local and international dishes, and the excellent house wine really is house wine—made on the premises. Still, lovely as it it, there are no sports facilities, and the room prices may seem a bit hard to justify. There is also a simpler *dipendenza*, with 7 rooms for slightly lower prices.

expensive

In Ravello the ★★★★**Caruso Belvedere**, Via S. Giovanni del Toro, © 857111, fax 857372, once popular with the Bloomsbury set and with Greta Garbo (she had room 21), has the quiet elegance of the old patrician villa it was before its present owner's grandfather, a cousin of the famous Neapolitan tenor Enrico Caruso, opened it as a hotel 100 years ago. In the beautifully laid out gardens, there is a belvedere over the sea and mountains, and the well-tended vegetable garden and vineyard on another level provide fresh produce and the hotel's own wine. Guests are encouraged to take half-board, which is no real hardship since the food is superb, and meals are taken on one of the loveliest terraces in Ravello.

With the lushest gardens on the coast, the ★★★**Villa Cimbrone**, Via Santa Chiara 26, © 857459, fax 858072, is a lovely place to stay: another elegant old villa, once the property of an English duke, set in its own parkland perched dizzyingly high on the cliffs. The rooms are beautifully decorated, and the only drawbacks are the lack of a restaurant and the ten-minute walk needed to get there; cars have to be parked further down in the villlage. It does, though, have a swimming pool.

In Maiori the ★★★★**San Pietro**, ℂ 877220, fax 877025, with a pool and tennis courts, is typical of the modern, middle-range resort hotels you'll find in Minori and Maiori. Further along the coast at Vietri sul Mare is the ★★★★★**Raito**, ℂ 210033, fax 211434, a luxurious hotel, recently restored from top to bottom, with views over the whole coast stretching as far as Paestum.

moderate

Further down from the Villa Cimbrone is one of the prettiest hotels in Ravello, the delightful ★★★**Villa Maria**, Via Santa Chiara 2, ℂ 857255, fax 857071, a gracious and tastefully converted villa made all the more attractive by the helpful and friendly owner, Vincenzo Palumbo, known to everyone as *Il Professore*. The vast suite (more expensive than the normal rooms) has one of the most breathtaking terraces in Ravello. Even if you don't stay here, it's worth coming to eat at the very fine-quality but reasonably priced restaurant in the lovely gardens, with a view over the hills. Under the same ownership, a few minutes' walk away, is the ★★★**Hotel Giordano** (same address and phone numbers as the Villa Maria), which is slightly more modern, but still comfortable and well-run, with the added advantage of a solarium and a heated outdoor pool. Villa Maria guests have equal access to these facilities.

Below Ravello and along the coast in Minori, the ★★★★**Villa Romana**, ℂ 877237, fax 877302, is a stylish, comfortable modern hotel. On the way to Salerno at Cetara is the ★★★★**Cetus**, ℂ and fax 261388, another lovely, newer hotel, built into the cliffs and with steps down to a secluded beach.

inexpensive

A very enjoyable budget choice in Ravello is the ★★**Villa Amore**, with 12 clean simple rooms, and a lovely terrace which has the same breathtaking views as the more expensive hotels.

In Maiori, there are several simple hotels near the beaches, such as the ★★**Baia Verde**, ℂ 877276, and the ★**Vittoria**, ℂ 877652, that offer some of the most convenient budget accommodation on the Amalfi coast. In neighbouring Minori the ★★★**Santa Lucia**, ℂ and fax 877142, is the best in the lower price range.

Around Ravello, ℂ (089–)   **Eating Out**

Unusually, most of the best dining in Ravello is in the hotels, most notably at **Villa Maria** and at the **Caruso** (*see* above); non-residents are welcome at all of them for lunch or dinner. By comparison the rest of the restaurants pale into insignificance, but one exception is **Cumpà Cosimo**, Via Roma 44–46, ℂ 857156, where owner-cook Signora Netta is always happy to advise diners on her latest concoctions and try out her school English on visitors. Her tour de force is the *piatto misto di primi*, a gargantuan helping of six or seven different pasta dishes, served on the same ceramic plate (moderate). If you make the trip up to Scala, alongside Ravello, try the wide range of delicious antipasto dishes and desserts at **La Margherita**, Via Torricella, © 857106, in the village centre (moderate). **Zi'Ntonio**, © 857118, further along the same road, serves out well-cooked local dishes on a beautiful covered terrace (moderate).

At Maiori, you'll get good fresh fish at **Mammato**, Via Arsenale 6, © 877036 (moderate), and in Minori try **Il Giardinello**, Corso V. Emanuele, © 877050, where the house speciality is *risotto al nero di seppia*—risotto with squid ink. There are also good pasta dishes, and pizza (inexpensive/moderate).

Salerno

Anywhere else in the south of Italy, a city like Salerno would be an attraction in itself; here it gets lost among the wonders of the Campanian coast—just the big town at the end of the Amalfi drive—and few people ever stop for more than a very brief visit. Nevertheless, Salerno has its modest charms, not least of which is that it is a clean and orderly place; that should endear it to people who hate Naples. Its setting under a backdrop of mountains is memorable. The Italian highway engineers, showing off as usual, have brought a highway to the city on a chain of viaducts, one lofty span after another, an unusual and pleasing ornament for the city; at night the road lights hang on the mountain slopes like strings of fairy lights on a Christmas tree.

Salerno's ancient distinction was its medical school, the oldest and finest of medieval Europe. Traditionally founded by the legendary 'Four Doctors'—an Italian, a Greek, a Jew and an Arab—the school was of the greatest importance in the transmission of Greek and Muslim science into Europe. Most of us, however, may recognize Salerno better as the site of the Allied invasion in September 1943, one of the biggest and most successful such operations of World War II.

Salerno's port is on the outskirts of town, and the shore all through the city centre is graced with a pretty park, the Lungomare Trieste. Parallel with it, and two streets back, the Corso Vittorio Emanuele leads into the old town. Here it changes its name to Via dei Mercanti, most colourful of Salerno's old streets. The **cathedral**, a block to the north on Via del Duomo, is set with its façade behind a courtyard, or *quadroporticos*, with a fountain at the centre, and a detached campanile—as if it were not a church at all, but a mosque. The Corinthian columns around it come from the ancient city of Paestum, not far down the coast. The cathedral's treasures are of the same order as those of the Amalfi coast: another pair of bronze doors from Constantinople, and another beautiful pair of Cosmatesque pulpits. The building itself has been much restored, and many of the best original details have been preserved in the adjacent **Museo del Duomo** *(open 9–1, 4–7, daily)*.

Robert the Cunning and his Blushing Bride

On the inscription across the cathedral façade, you can read how the cathedral was built by 'Duke Robert, greatest of conquerors, with his own money'. This was Robert Guiscard, 'the Cunning', one of the first and greatest of the Norman warriors who came to plunder southern Italy in the 11th century. Robert de Hauteville came to Italy in 1046, one of the younger brothers of that remarkable Norman family that would one day found a dynasty in Sicily. His elder brother Drogo, chief of the clan, had no lands to give him, so Robert was on his own, hiring his sword out first to the Lombard Count Pandulf of Capua, later to his brothers or anyone else who could pay for it.

Contemporary accounts describe Robert as a fair-haired, blue-eyed giant. The Byzantine Anna Comnena wrote of him as, 'in temper tyrannical, in mind most clever, brave in action, very clever in attacking the wealth and substance of magnates...' He earned his sobriquet Guiscard for tricks like the taking of Malvita, a fortified monastery in Calabria. One day a party of unarmed Normans came up to the gate with a coffin, and asked to have a funeral mass said for one of their comrades. The monks let them in, and once inside, the coffin burst open to reveal a very live knight laying on a pile of swords. Combined with cleverness like this, Robert's formidable strength and skill in battle soon earned him an important position in the south. In 1058 he found a fitting bride, Princess Sichelgaita of the ruling Lombard house of Salerno. Nearly as tall and as strong as Robert himself, she loved nothing better than accompanying him into battle, her long blond hair pouring out from her helmet. The pair went from success to success, and capped it with Robert's papal investiture as Duke of Apulia and Calabria.

But Robert's greatest exploit would not come until 1084, a year before his death. That year there were two popes in Rome, a common occurrence, one supported by the German emperor Henry and the other, Gregory VII, by Robert. When the Normans brought up a big army to force the issue, Rome resisted, and Robert's men (along with Saracen mercenaries from Sicily) took the city and treated it to the worst sacking in its history, far more destructive than anything the 5th-century barbarians ever dared. Gregory, the great reformer Hildebrand before becoming pope, had worked unceasingly for decades to build the power of the papacy; now he had his victory, but the Romans hated him so thoroughly he could not stay in the city. He was forced to accompany Robert to Salerno, where he died soon after. Robert buried him in this cathedral, which he had begun, perhaps in expiation, the same year.

From Salerno you can make an easy excursion up into the mountains to the town of **Cava de' Tirreni**. Near it, perched precariously on the slopes of the Val di Bonea, is a little-visited Benedictine monastery called **La Trinità di Cava**—rebuilt, as usual, in tiresome Baroque, but preserving a wealth of 12th–14th-century frescoes, stone-carving and Cosmati work.

expensive

Salerno's hotels are fairly modest and utilitarian. The ★★★★★**Jolly Hotel delle Palme**, Lungomare Trieste 1, ℭ 225222, fax 237571, is pleasant and reliable, and right on the seafront.

moderate

More than acceptable for an overnight stay is the ★★★**Plaza**, Piazza Ferrovia, ℭ 224477, fax 237311, right across from the station. Close by, in the pedestrian area, is the recently refurbished ★★★**Montestella**, Corso Vittorio Emanuele, ℭ 225122. Convenient for the beach is the ★★★**Fiorenza**, Via Trento 145, ℭ 338 800, fax 337722, a clean, well-run hotel with 30 bedrooms.

inexpensive

Several cheaper hotels are to be found on or around the Corso Vittorio Emanuele. Try the ★★**Salerno**, Via G. Vicinanza 42, ℭ 224211—simple but comfortable.

expensive

Nicola dei Principati, Corso Garibaldi 201, ℭ 225435, in the old centre of Salerno, serves mainly fish dishes, including an excellent *linguine con astice*, long pasta with lobster. At **Il Timone**, Via Generale Clark 29, ℭ 335111, the speciality is *tubetti alla pescatrice*, short pasta served with a delicious fish sauce. The second courses, almost all fish, are equally good.

moderate

One of the liveliest restaurants in town, right in the *centro storico*, is the **Vicolo della Neve**, Vicolo della Neve 24, ℭ 225705, an attractive place decorated with wall paintings by some of the many artists who have established it as their local. The chef turns out good Campanian favourites such as *melanzane alla parmigiana*, aubergines cooked in layers with mozzarella, parmesan, tomato and basil, and the classic *pasta e fagioli*. You can also order excellent pizza. At **La Lampara**, Lungomare Colombo 333, ℭ 337750, you'll also find pizza on the menu, together with a host of other dishes, mainly fish, including octopus and squid served in a variety of unusual ways. At **Alla Brace**, Lungomare Trieste 13, ℭ (089) 225159, as well as the usual fish dishes, you will be offered a host of delicious local specialities such as stuffed peppers, ravioli filled with ricotta, and a remarkable potato soufflé. There is also a wide range of home-made desserts.

inexpensive

Da Sasa at Via Diaz 42, ℭ 225696, is a good inexpensive trattoria, with traditional home-cooking and especially tasty pasta courses at very accessible prices.

Reggia di Caserta

Campania Inland

There's more to the region than just the Bay of Naples. However, the coast and its endless attractions draw off most of the tourists, and it's a rare soul indeed who ever makes it up to old Capua, or the excellent little city of Benevento.

Getting Around

The interior of Campania makes up a rather large piece of territory—the three main towns are all provincial capitals. None are on the main **railway** lines, however, and you will have to scrutinize the schedules in Naples carefully to find your way around. Some Rome–Naples trains pass through Caserta and Capua. **Buses** for Caserta, Capua, Avellino, and Benevento leave Naples from Piazza Garibaldi, in front of the Stazione Centrale. The **ACTP**, ✆ (081) 7005091, runs regular buses to Caserta (one hour).

By far the fastest way to get to the interior of Campania is **by car**, along the A2, which passes between Caserta and Capua, or the A16 Bari *autostrada*, which runs past Avellino. A slower but slightly quieter route to Caserta is along the old SS87 road. To get to it, take the Viale Maddalena to the left of Capodichino airport, and then follow the signs for Caserta.

Tourist Information

The provincial EPT tourist office is at Caserta, right in the Royal Palace, 81100, ✆ (0823) 322170.

Capua

This is a double city, consisting of the modern town, founded in the 9th century, and the ancient one, once the second city of Italy, but deserted in the Dark Ages and now modestly reborn as **Santa Maria Capua Vetere**.

Capua can trace its founding to the Oscans, blithe folk of ancient Italy who introduced farce to the theatre, and who probably give us the word *obscene*. It is believed that the Oscan farces, banned by all decent Roman emperors, created the prototypes of the *commedia dell'arte* stock characters, including Naples' favourite Pulcinello—Punch. All that should give you some idea of the spirit of old Capua, a city best known for beautiful women and the manufacture of perfume, and as renowned for loose morals in its day as Sybaris. Everyone but the jealous Roman historians liked to give Capua credit for defeating the great Hannibal. The Capuans had always hated those dreary dour Romans, and they eagerly took the Carthaginians' part. Hannibal's men enjoyed Capuan hospitality in the winter of 216 BC; they came out in the spring so dreamy-eyed and dissipated that they never beat the Romans again.

Of course there was hell to pay when the Romans came back, but Capua survived, and even flourished for several centuries more as the greatest city of the region. Finally though, some even worse drudges than the Romans arrived—the Arabs, who utterly destroyed the city in about 830. The survivors then refounded Capua on a new site, a few kilometres to the north. Of old Capua, at Santa Maria Capua Vetere, you can see the remains of the second-largest **amphitheatre** in Italy—largest of all before Rome built its Colosseum. Here Spartacus began his gladiators' revolt in 73 BC. Few sections of the stands are still intact, but there is an underground network of tunnels and trap doors much like that in Rome.

While there, ask the attendant to show you something much more interesting—a short walk away is perhaps the best example of a **Mithraeum** discovered anywhere in the Mediterranean. The cult of the god Mithras, imported from Persia by the legionaries, was for a while the most widespread of the cults that tried to fill the religious vacuum of the Imperial centuries. Some scholars see in it much in common with Christianity. The resemblance isn't readily apparent; Mithraism was an archaic, gut-level cult, with mystery initiations and lots of bull's blood splashing about. Though it originally took hold in the army, and always remained a men-only affair, as late as the 3rd century AD it could probably claim more adherents than Christianity. The upper classes were never too impressed with it; that is why it lost out to the Christians, and why such well-executed frescoes as these are rare. The *mithraeum* is an underground hall, used in the initiations, and dominated by a large scene of Mithras, a typical Mediterranean solar hero, slaying a white bull with a serpent under its feet; the complementary fresco representing the moon on the opposite wall is less well-preserved.

Also around Santa Maria, there is a crumbling triumphal arch, and some elaborate Roman tombs, off the road to Caserta. The new Capua has all the most interesting finds from the old one at the **Museo Provinciale Campano** *(open 9–1, 2–5, Tues–Sun; adm)*. Just north of the town, on the slopes of Mount Tifata, a site once occupied by a temple of Diana now contains the 11th-century basilica of **Sant'Angelo in Formis**. The 12th-century frescoes here are some of the best in the south, oddly archaic figures that would seem much more at home in Constantinople than in Italy. And, more than mere artistry, there is an intense spiritual vision about these paintings—note especially the unearthly, unforgettable face of the enthroned St Michael above the portal.

North of Capua, near the border with Lazio, the last town in Campania along the Via Appia is **Sessa Aurunca**, with a Roman bridge and some other scanty ruins, as well as a 12th-century cathedral, interesting for its surviving ancient and medieval sections.

Caserta

In one shot, you can see the biggest palace in Italy, and also the most wearisome; both distinctions belong uncontestably to the **Reggia**, or Royal Palace, built here by the Bourbon King of Naples, Charles III *(open 9am–1.30pm Mon–Sat; 9am–12.30pm Sun; adm)*. His architect, Luigi Vanvitelli (really a Dutchman named Van Wittel) spared no expense; like the Spanish Bourbons, those of Naples were greenly jealous of Versailles, and wanted to show the big Louies back home that they, too, deserved a little respect. The

Reggia, begun in 1752, has some 1200 rooms, not much compared to the 2800 of the Bourbon palace in Madrid, but larger than its Spanish cousin just the same (it's also larger than Versailles); the façade is 245m across. Inside, as in Madrid, everything is tasteful, ornate and soberingly expensive; the only good touches from Vanvitelli's heavy hand are the elegant grand staircases. Only the gardens make the trip worthwhile, an amazingly long axis of pools and cascades climbing up to the famous **Diana fountain**, with a lifelike sculptural group of the goddess and her attendants catching Actaeon in the act. There is also an **English garden**, of the sort fashionable in the 18th century. The Reggia was commandeered for use as Allied military headquarters in Italy in 1943, and it was here that the final surrender of the German armies in Italy was accepted two years later.

The village of **San Leucio**, nearly three kilometres north of Caserta, was founded by the Bourbon kings as a paternalistic utopian experiment, and also an establishment for the manufacture of silk. Ferdinand IV, for most of his life, personally saw to every detail of its operation, even christening the children of the workers. The successor of his *Real Fabbrica* is still a centre for silk. Some 9km to the east there is the half-deserted town of **Caserta Vecchia**. The building of the Reggia drew most of the population down to modern Caserta, but the old town still has the 12th-century **Cathedral**, with a great octagonal *ciborium* (a cylindrical or prismatic dome) that is one of the glories of Arab-Norman architecture.

Caserta, ✆ (0832–) **Eating Out**

Neither of these towns makes a very attractive base for an overnight stay. Caserta, though, does have some good restaurants.

moderate/expensive

At **La Castellana**, Via Torre 5, ✆ 371230, in the centre of Caserta Vecchia, you can feast on wild boar or venison, when available, as well as a wonderfully innovative selection of soup and pasta openers.

Outside the town, at the **Ritrovo dei Patriarchi**, Via Conte Landulfo, Località Sommana, ✆ 371510, you'll find game in abundance, including pheasant, venison, partridge and wild boar, depending on the time of year. There are also good hearty soups and vegetable dishes.

moderate

Near La Castellana, the **Rocca di Sant'Andrea**, Via Torre 8, ✆ 371232, offers delicious pasta dishes and a variety of *secondi*, many of which are based on meat grilled on the open fire in front of you. There is also a good selection of home-made desserts. **La Massa**, on Via Mazzini 55, ✆ 321268, is a simple and convenient place for lunch near the Reggia.

Getting Around

Remote Benevento is not well connected with any of Italy's main transport systems. It is on the Naples–Foggia **railway** line, but be careful about Naples–Benevento trains, as some but not all of them are operated by a private railway, and you will need to find out which—ask at the information booth in Naples' Stazione Centrale—to buy the right ticket.

The most frequent public transport connections are by **bus**. The **Consorzio Trasporti Irpini**, © (081) 5534677, has regular services to Avellino (50min) and Benevento (1½ hours) from Piazza Garibaldi in Naples. In Benevento, buses to Naples and a surprising variety of other places (including one daily to Rome) leave from Piazza Pacca, on Corso Dante just west of the Cathedral. There are several companies; check at the Benevento EPT for schedules.

To get to Benevento **by road** from Naples take the A2 north and then south of Caserta look for the SS265 eastwards, which joins up with the SS7, the Via Appia, for Benevento. This road is quite slow. An alternative is to take the A16 *autostrada* to Avellino, and then the SS88 north from there to Benevento.

Tourist Information

Benevento's EPT is east of the city centre at Via Nicola Sala 31, 82100, © (0824) 21960. Its information office is at Via Giustiniani 34, 82100, © (0824) 25424, fax 312309.

The Duchy of Benevento

Ever since the Middle Ages, the land around Caserta and Capua has been called the *Terra del Lavoro*—cultivated land—a broad garden plain that is one of the most fertile corners of Italy. Today its lush landscapes have suffered a bit from creeping industrialism, though it's in the stretch to the south, between Caserta and Naples, where the worst modern depredations can be seen. Nowadays, the Napoletani call the towns around Afragola, Acerra and Secondigliano the 'Triangle of Death', an industrial wasteland of shanties and power lines ruled by the Camorra that has Italy's worst unemployment, and some of its worst social problems.

Go east instead, up into the foothills of the Apennines towards **Benevento**, yet another smallish city that has often played a big role in Italian history. On an old tower in the centre of town, the city fathers have put up maps of southern Italy, showing the boundaries of the two important states of which Benevento was the capital.

At first, as *Malies* or *Maloenton*, it was the leading town of the Samnites, the warlike mountain people who resisted Roman imperialism for so long. The Romans were later to make a big city of it, an important stop along the Appian Way. They Latinized the name to

Maleventum—ill wind—but after a lucky defeat of Pyrrhus of Epirus here in 275 BC, they thought it might just be a *Beneventum* after all. In 571, the city was captured by the bloodthirsty Lombards, becoming their southern capital. After the Lombards of the north fell to Charlemagne, the Duchy of Benevento carried on as an independent state; at its greatest extent, under relatively enlightened princes like Arechi II (*c.* 800), it ruled almost all of southern Italy. The Normans put an end to it in the 1060s.

Coming to Benevento in the winter, you're bound to think the Romans were crazy to change the name. When people in Salerno are ready to hit the beaches, you'll find the Beneventani shivering on street corners like Muscovites in their fur caps, victims of traditionally the worst weather in southern Italy. It is often claimed this makes them more serious and introspective than people on the coast—certainly coming here from Naples seems metaphorically like a trip of a thousand miles. Benevento has often been the scene of earthquakes, and the city took plenty of hard shots during the battles of 1943, but there are still enough attractions around to make a stop worthwhile.

Benevento's **cathedral** is in the lower town, the part that suffered the most in the bombings. The cathedral itself was almost a total loss; only the odd 13th-century façade remains, built of miscellaneous bits of Roman buildings—inscriptions, reliefs, friezes and pillars—arranged every which way. In the old streets behind the cathedral, you can see a well-preserved **Roman Theatre** *(open daily, 9am–sunset)*—not an amphitheatre, but a place for classical drama, something rare this far north. By the time the Romans conquered them, the culture of the Samnites was almost completely Hellenized. This theatre, built under Hadrian, originally seated 20,000. All through this quarter, called the **Triggio**, you will see bits of Roman brick and medieval masonry—something ancient built into the walls of every house. There is half a Roman bridge over the Sabato (one of Benevento's two rivers), ruins of the baths, remains of a triumphal arch, and plenty of gates and stretches of wall from the fortifications built by the Lombards. On Via Posillipo, a Baroque monument houses the **Bue Apis**, a sacred Egyptian bull sculpture found in Benevento's Temple of Isis.

Trajan's Arch

Some people claim Benevento's triumphal arch to be better than those of Rome itself; built in AD 117, it is a serious piece of work—over 15m of expensive Parian marble from Greece—and certainly better preserved than the ones in the capital. It marks the spot where the Appian Way entered Beneventum, (now Via Traiana on the northern edge of the old town) and the skilfully carved reliefs on both faces record significant events in the career of the emperor.

Trajan (AD 98–117), the conqueror of Dacia (modern-day Romania) and Mesopotamia, ranks among the greatest of the emperors, and a little commemoration would not seem out of hand; nevertheless cynics will enjoy the transparent and sometimes heavy-handed political propaganda of ornaments like this. In one of the panels, Trajan (the handsome fellow with the curly beard) is shown distributing gifts to children; in another he presides over the *institutio alimentaria*—the dole. Most of the scenes are about victories: Trajan announcing military reforms, Trajan celebrating a triumph, Jove handing Trajan one of his thunderbolts, and finally the Apotheosis, where the late emperor is received among the gods while the goddess Roma escorts Hadrian to coronation as his divinely ordained successor.

The Museo Sannio

Corso Garibaldi is Benevento's main street, just south of Trajan's Arch. Near its eastern end stands the city's oldest church, **Santa Sofia**, built in the late 8th century. It is unusual for its plan, an irregular six-pointed star, and was built for the Lombard Duke Gisulfo by an architect thoroughly grounded in the mystic geometry of the early Middle Ages. The vaulting is supported by recycled Roman columns, and other columns have been hollowed out for use as holy water fonts.

The church cloister contains one of the south's more interesting provincial museums, the **Museo Sannio** *(open 9–1, 3–6, Tues–Sun). Sannio* refers to Samnium, as Benevento's province is still officially called. The 12th-century cloister is itself well worth a look, with a variety of strange twisted columns under pulvins carved with even stranger scenes: monster-hunting, dancing, fantastical animals, bunnies, and a camel or two. The best things in the museum are in the archaeological section. Almost all the classic vases are Campanian copies of Greek ware—the production of ceramics was the engine that drove *Campania Felix*'s economy in its glory days.

Some Samnite Curiosities

Two rooms in the museum are filled with objects from the Temple of Isis. Anyone who has read Apuleius' *The Golden Ass* will remember just how important the cult of the transcendent goddess Isis was throughout the Roman world. This Egyptian import certainly seems to have found a home in Beneventum; nowhere in Europe has so much fine Egyptian statuary been retrieved. The temple had imperial backing. One of the statues is of the founder, Emperor Domitian himself, in Egyptian dress. Other works portray priestesses, sacred boats and sphinxes, another Apis bull, and a porphyry 'cista mistica', carved with a snake. The image of Isis is also there, formidably impressive, even without a head.

Somehow this leads naturally to Benevento's more famous piece of exotica—the witches. In the days of the Lombards, women by the hundreds would dance around a sacred walnut tree on the banks of the River Sabato ('sabbath'). Even after the official conversion to Christianity in 663, the older religion persisted, and Benevento is full of every sort of 'witch' story as a result. The best piece of modern sculpture in the Museo Sannio is a representation of the witches' dance. Of course the city has found ways to put the legend to use. In any bar in Italy, you can pick up a bottle of 'liquore Strega' (*strega* means witch) and read on the label the proud device: 'Made next to the train station in Benevento, Italy'.

Just a few streets west of the museum on Corso Garibaldi, the dedicatory **obelisk** from the Isis temple stands in front of the town hall. East of the museum, the Corso takes you to the **Rocca de' Rettori**, a fortress built by the popes in the 14th century; for centuries Benevento was a papal enclave surrounded by the Kingdom of Naples. The fortress is now a part of the Museo Sannio. Behind it is a lovely park, the Villa Comunale.

Benevento, ✆ (0824–) **Where to Stay**

In spite of what it has to offer, Benevento sees few tourists, and accommodation is limited.

moderate

The ★★★★**Gran Hotel Italiano**, Viale Principe di Napoli 137, ✆ 24923, fax 21758, is a pleasant, simple place a block from the train station—hardly grand, now or ever, but it will do fine.

inexpensive

At the cheap end of the scale, ★**Genova**, down the same street at No.130, ✆ 42926, has rooms without baths.

Benevento, ✆ (0824–) **Eating Out**

Dining in Benevento can be interesting; it's another world from the Campanian coast, with seafood replaced on the menu by rabbit, duck, lamb and veal. Samnium makes some good but little-known wines; you might ask for a bottle of stout-hearted Solopaca red with your Samnite repast.

moderate

Benevento's favourite restaurant is probably the **Antica Taverna**, at Via Annunziata 41, ✆ 21212, not far from the Museo Sannio, where roast kid is one of the more unusual items on the menu. A good traditional restaurant where you can dine for a reasonable price can be found in the back streets around Trajan's Arch, the **Ristorante Palmieri**, at the end of Via Manciotti, ✆ 24947. Some of the best food, however, and most of the Beneventani, can be found in the stand-up *tavola calda* on the corner of Corso Dante and Corso Vittorio Emanuele, a block west of the Cathedral, which provides really fine pizza.

Samnium

Samnium is one of Italy's smallest provinces, but there are a few towns and villages of interest; the countryside, full of oak and walnut forests, is often reminiscent of some corner of Umbria. **Morcone**, to the north, has a memorable setting, draped on the curving slope of a hill like a Roman theatre. **Telese**, to the west on the road towards Lazio, lies near a small but pretty lake of the same name, with a popular spa establishment. The nearby ruins of the Samnite-Roman town of *Telesia* are remarkable for their perfectly octagonal walls, with gates at the cardinal points.

Best of all, perhaps, is the town of **Sant'Agata dei Goti**, some kilometres north of the Via Appia between Benevento and Caserta, with its long line of buildings like a man-made cliff overhanging a little ravine. Sant'Agata takes its name from the Goths who founded it in the 6th century; it was badly damaged in the 1980 earthquake, and its modest monuments, the **Castello** and the 12th-century **Church of Santa Menna**, are still undergoing restoration.

South of Benevento

Tourist Information

Avellino's tourist office is at Via Due Principati 5, 83100, © (0825) 35169.
Continuing this broad arc around Naples, south and east of Benevento there are few attractions, but some attractive mountain scenery in a region called **Irpinia**, consisting of most of the province of Avellino. In places, the mountains bear fine forests of oaks and chestnuts, as well as plantations of hazelnut trees; other parts are grim and bare, an introduction to the 19th-century deforestation that ruined so much of southern Italy. Irpinia was the region worst affected by the 1980 earthquake.

The main highway south from Caserta, around the back side of Vesuvius, isn't that much more promising. **Nola**, the biggest town on the route, began as another Oscan foundation. It had a famous early bishop, St Paulinus, a friend of St Augustine and also, it is claimed, the inventor of the bell (bells are *campane* in Italian, from their Campanian origin). To celebrate the anniversary of St Paulinus' return from imprisonment at the hands of the Vandals, every 27 June the people of Nola put on one of the more spectacular festivals of the south, the 'Dance of the Lilies', a procession of 15m wooden steeples, elaborately decorated and carried by the men of the town (*see* Festivals, p.15). Further south, in the hills above the city of **Nocera Inferiore**, an ancient hamlet called **Nocera Superiore** has somehow kept intact its 4th-century church, an unusual round building with a cupola that may have been converted from a pagan sanctuary.

The road into the mountains of Irpinia begins at Nola, leading towards **Avellino**. This little provincial capital, important in Norman times, has been wrecked so many times by invaders and earthquakes that little remains to be seen. In the centre, the 17th-century Palazzo della Dogana has a façade of ancient statues and a big clock tower; nearby stands a Baroque fountain with Bellerophon dispatching the Chimaera. Archaeological finds, ancient and medieval, from around Irpinia are kept in the modern Museo Irpino on Corso Europa.

Northwest of Avellino, **Montevergine** has been the most important pilgrimage site of this region since the arrival of a miraculous 'Black Madonna' in 1310—a Byzantine icon of the Virgin, stolen from Constantinople by the Crusaders in the sack of 1204; like the others across Europe, the oxidation of its yellow paint has turned it black over the centuries. Montevergine can be reached either by a long and tortuous road, or by a cable railway from the village of Mercogliano. The 12the-century church, built over a sanctuary of Ceres and many times reconstructed, has two fine tombs of the 1300s.

North of Avellino, separate roads lead to Taurasi, the centre of a wine region, and **Prata di Principato Ultra**, a tiny village with one of the oldest Christian monuments in the south. The Basilica dell'Annunziata was probably begun in the 3rd century; there are fragments of paintings and two small catacombs. Eastern Irpinia is a wild and mountainous area where villages are few and far between. **Monte Terminio**, lately become a modest skiing area, has extensive woods and rushing mountain streams, along with plenty of pheasants, stags and boars, wild mushrooms and chestnuts—and a few truffles, perhaps the southernmost truffles found anywhere. **Sant'Angelo dei Lombardi**, further east, was an important medieval monastic centre; the earthquakes have spared bits of two simple churches (12th and 13th centuries).

Paestum

Southern Campania

After the Bay and the Amalfi coast—two heavy courses for a holiday banquet—we can offer the Cilento peninsula, as a light, refreshing dessert. The Cilento is a squarish low massif jutting out from the coast between the Gulf of Salerno and the Gulf of Policastro. Its mountain scenery may not be quite as breathtaking as the Amalfi drive, but the Cilento makes up for it by being delightfully wild and unspoilt, and altogether one of the most beguiling out-of-the-way places to spend your time in southern Italy. The interior of the Cilento is not traversed by any easy roads, and the traveller heading south from Salerno will have a choice of two routes: a long, leisurely drive along the coast, past the remarkable ruins of ancient Paestum and a number of small, very casual resorts, or along the present main road, the A3 *Autostrada del Sole*, over the mountains and skirting the eastern edge of the Cilento, a route of often beautiful, wild scenery down the valley of the Tanagro River.

Paestum and the Cilento

Getting Around

Paestum has a station on the main **railway** line between Naples and Reggio Calabria, but only local trains stop there. More conveniently, there are frequent **buses** from the Piazza Concordia in Salerno (on the shore, by the Porto Turistico). They are run by several companies; some follow the coast route, while others go through Battipaglia. Some of these continue on to various resort towns on the Cilento coast.

All the Cilento towns are connected by **bus** to Salerno's Piazza Concordia; there is a bewildering list of companies, towns and schedules, but fortunately the EPT in Salerno publishes a full list of them in the front of their annual hotel book. The **railway** line only touches the Cilento coast at two points—Ascea and Pisciotta—and, as at Paestum, not too many trains stop.

As we have mentioned, there are only two main **road** routes, the SS18 coast road and the A3 and parallel SS19 further inland. At Agropoli the SS267 leaves the SS18 and runs round the Cilento coast. North of Paestum there is also another turn off the SS18, the SS166 to the east, a long and winding road across the Cilento interior that eventually connects up with the A3.

Tourist Information

The Salerno EPT at Via Velia 15, 84100, © (089) 224322, fax 251844, has the most complete information on transport and accommodation in Paestum and the Cilento. There is also the AAST, in the central Piazza Amendola, 84100, © (089) 224744, fax 752839.

There are information offices in Paestum, Via Aquilia, ℭ (0828) 811016, fax 722322, and Palinuro, in Piazza Virgilio, ℭ (0974) 931147.

Paestum: A Lost City

Along the coast, the route begins in a fertile plain that meets the Cilento near the ruins of **Paestum**, site of the only well-preserved Greek temples north of Sicily *(site open 9am–two hours before sunset Tues–Sun; museum open 9am–2pm only, Tues–Sun; joint adm for both)*. And there is another important player on the Mediterranean stage who needs to be introduced. The anopheles mosquito, as fate would have it, gets the credit for preserving Paestum's ruins so well. By the 9th century or so, this once-great city was breathing its last, a victim of economic decline and Arab raiders. As its people gradually abandoned it for safer settlements in the hills, Paestum was swallowed up by the thick forests of this subtropical corner of Italy.

As usual on a Mediterranean coastal plain, when the people leave the malaria mosquitoes take over. By the Middle Ages, the site of Paestum became utterly uninhabitable—it meant certain death to stay there overnight—and after a while the city's very existence was forgotten. After being hidden away, like the Mayan temples in the Mexican jungle, for almost a thousand years, the city was re-discovered in the 18th century; a crew of Charles III's road builders stumbled onto the huge temples in the midst of the forest.

Originally *Poseidonia*, the city was founded in the 6th century BC by the Sybarites, as a station on the all-important trade route up Italy's west coast. The Romans took over in 273 BC, and the name became Latinized to Paestum. As a steadfast supporter of the Roman cause throughout the Punic Wars, Paestum was a favoured city. Famous around the Mediterranean for its flowers, especially roses, it prospered until the end of the Roman era. Today the forests have been cleared, and the ruins of the city stand in the open on the green and quiet plain. Not only the celebrated temples have survived; much of the 4km circuit of **walls** still stands to some height, along with some of the towers and gates.

Most of Paestum's important buildings were grouped along an axis between the Porta Aurea and the Porta Giustizia, with the forum at its centre. The two grand temples that everyone comes to see are at the southern end: the **Basilica** and the **Temple of Neptune**, two Doric edifices in the finest classical style. The names were just guesses on the part of the early archaeologists; both temples in fact were dedicated to Hera, the tutelary goddess of the city. The 'Neptune' temple, the best preserved, was built about 450 BC. It is about 60m long, and all of the structure survives except the roof and the internal walls. The second temple, the 'Basilica', is a century older, and a little smaller.

The aesthetic may not be quite what you expected—dimensions squat and strong rather than graceful and tall. Still, this is the classic austerity of Greek architecture at its best. There is more to it than meets the eye. If you look closely along the rows of columns, or the lines of the base, you may notice that nothing in either of them is perfectly straight. The edges bulge outwards, as they do in the Parthenon and every other Greek building;

this is an architectural trick called *entasis*; it creates an optical illusion, making the lines seem straight at a distance. Greek temples like this are the most sober and serious buildings in western architecture, based on a simple system of perfect proportion. The form may seem austere and academic, but with some imagination you can picture them in their original beauty—covered in a sort of enamel made of gleaming ground marble, setting off the brilliant colours of the polychromed sculptural reliefs on the pediments and frieze.

To the west, some of the streets of the city have been excavated, though very little is left to see. To the north, around the broad Forum—really a simple rectangular space in the manner of a Greek *agora*—are the remains of a theatre, a round *bouleterion*, or council house, and other buildings. Still further north is the third and smallest of the surviving temples, the **Temple of Ceres**.

Paestum's **Museum** holds most of the sculptural fragments and finds from the town. Some of the best reliefs are not from Paestum at all, but from the recently discovered sanctuary of Hera, a few kilometres north at the mouth of the river Sele. This temple, mentioned by many ancient writers, is said to have been founded by Jason and the Argonauts during their wanderings. From tombs excavated just outside the city come some examples of Greek fresco painting—nothing special in themselves, but probably the only ones in existence. Look out for the most famous fresco, *The Diver*, which you have probably seen reproduced innumerable times elsewhere. Even though the Greeks took painting as seriously as they did sculpture, you will not find any similar surviving examples in Greece, or anywhere else.

While you are exploring Paestum, keep an eye out too for the wild flowers. More than one 19th-century traveller claimed to have found descendents of Paestum's famous roses (*bifera rosaria Paestum*) growing wild, and some may still be around.

The Cilento Coast

For many, one of the best attractions of Paestum will be the fine, long beaches that line this part of the coast. South of the ruins, the shore becomes jagged and mountainous, passing groves of pines alternating with rugged cliffs and pocket-sized beaches. Most of the villages along it have become quiet, cosy resorts that cater mostly to Italians. One is usually close to the next, and if you care to stay over, you can keep going until you find one that suits your fancy.

Agropoli comes first, then **Santa Maria di Castellabate**, **San Marco**, and **Punta Licosa**, on the westernmost point of the Cilento. From here, you can take a small boat out to an uninhabited islet, also called Licosa, where there are some unidentified ancient ruins. Further down the coast, **Acciaroli** and **Pioppi** are among the nicer resort towns of the Cilento. South of the latter, and just inland from the village of Ascea Marina, you can visit the ruins of another Greek city, **Velia**.

Don't expect any spectacular ruins on the order of Paestum. Velia disappeared gradually, and most of its buildings were carried off for building stone long ago. *Elea*, as it was

Sta. Maria Castellabate

known back then, was a colony of the Ionian city of Phocaea, and a sister city of another important Phocaean foundation—Marseilles, in France. Elea was never large or important, but its name lives on gloriously in philosophy; the Elean school of philosophers produced some of the most brilliant minds of the ancient world: logical grinds like Parmenides, who proposed the first theory of atoms, and wiseacres like Zeno with his pesky paradoxes. Some of the fortifications survive, including one well-preserved gate, and just enough of the *agora*, baths, and streets are left to enable us to guess at how the city may have looked.

Both **Ascea Marina** and its neighbouring locality of **Casalvelino** have pretty beaches, but the best ones of all, perhaps, can be found in the rugged terrain around **Palinuro**. This town, which has a small museum of archaeological finds, takes its name from Aeneas' pilot Palinurus, who is supposedly buried here—Virgil made the whole story up for the *Aeneid*, but that hasn't stopped it from sticking fast in local legend. Beyond Palinuro, the coast curves back north into the Gulf of Policastro; here two more pleasant beach villages, **Scario** and **Sapri**, mark the southern boundary of Campania.

The Inland Route: Around the Cilento

South from Salerno, the *autostrada* skirts the back edge of the Cilento on its way to Calabria. Christ may have stopped at **Eboli**, as a local saying goes, but there's no reason why you should—and that goes for **Battipaglia** and **Polla** too. The true delights of this region are subterranean, two first-rate caves on opposite slopes of the Monti Alburni. **Pertosa** *(open 9am–5.30pm Tues–Sun; adm)*, near the highway, is the easier and probably the better choice; the pot-holers (spelunkers) suspect it is connected to the other one, at **Castelcivita**, near the village of Controne.

At **Teggiano**, there is a 13th-century castle and cathedral, as well as a little museum. **Padula**, just off the highway, is the unlikely location of the **Certosa di San Lorenzo**, after San Martino in Naples probably the biggest and richest monastery in the south. The Certosa has been closed for over a century, but in its heyday it would have held hundreds of Carthusians, in a complex laid out in the form of a gridiron (recalling the martyrdom of St Lawrence, the same plan used in El Escorial in Spain, also dedicated to the saint). Though it was continuously expanded and rebuilt over 400 years, the best parts are Baroque: an enormous, elegant cloister, some wonderfully garish frescoes and stucco figures in and around the chapel, and eccentric but well-executed decorative details throughout. A small archaeological museum is part of the complex.

Where to Stay

Most people think of Paestum as a day trip, but there are enough hotels around the site, and on the nearby beaches, to make an overnight stay possible—and very convenient, if you have a car. Some of the best accommodation is at Laura beach, about 5km north of Paestum.

Hotels on the Cilento are on the whole modern and unremarkable, though there are some exceptions. For a stay of three days or more, an alternative to a hotel may be a *villaggio turistico*, of which there are dozens (look out for signs along the coast, or consult the rear section of the hotel guide-book distributed free by the Salerno tourist office). These are Italian-style holiday camps, but are much nicer than they sound, often with small bungalows set in well-landscaped grounds overlooking the sea, and with excellent sports and recreation facilities usually included in the all-in price.

expensive

The ★★★★★**Ariston**, ℂ (0828) 851333, fax 851596 is a large hotel that's one of Paestum's best; on the beach, and very well-run.

In Castellabate, at San Marco, there is one special resort hotel, the attractive ★★★★**Castelsandra**, ℂ and fax (0974) 966021, with a pretty setting, pool and tennis courts, a fine restaurant, and TV in many rooms to help your insomnia.

Towards the southern end of the Cilento coast, Ascea has a small collection of hotels around its marina, but Palinuro has developed into a fully-fledged holiday town. Try the ★★★★**Gabbiano**, ℂ (0974) 931155, fax 931948, which has a pool and private beach.

Near Paestum, ★★★★**Le Palme**, ✆ (0828) 851025, fax 851507, is a modern place with plenty of facilities for sports and recreation as well as its own stretch of beach. The ★★★★**Schumann**, ✆ (0828) 851151, fax 851183, is set in its own gardens, close to the beach, and the ★★★**Clorinda**, ✆ (0828) 851091, fax 851588, is a recently-built hotel that's well-equipped with sports facilities.

A less expensive choice in San Marco is the ★★★★**Approdo**, ✆ (0974) 966001, fax 966500, right on the harbour front.

Most hotels in Acciaroli are similarly modest, and good bargains too; the best is ★★★**Il Faro**, ✆ (0974) 904389.

Outside Palinuro, the ★★★★**King's Residence**, ✆ (0974) 931324, fax 931418, is in a stunning setting, perched in a crow's nest position high on the cliffs. A pathway runs down to the pretty little private beach, kitted out with a small bar for drinks and light meals. The hotel's own boat takes guests to visit the five grottoes along the coast. ★★★**La Torre**, ✆ (0974) 931264, is another attractive hotel, covered with bougainvillea and close to the beach. In the town of Palinuro, the ★★★**Conchiglia**, ✆ (0974) 931018, has 25 pleasant rooms, all with baths.

Camerota, near the southeastern point of the Cilento, has a fairly uninspiring bunch of hotels. The ★★★**America**, ✆ (0974) 932131, fax 932522, is acceptable, though without any particular charm.

Just north of Paestum, the ★★**Laura**, ✆ (0828) 851068, is a good budget choice, with its own private beach and 13 rooms, all with baths. Near the ruins, close to the Porta Giustizia entrance, the ★★★**Martini**, ✆ (0828) 811451, fax 823717, is a set of small bungalows set in a wooded area close to the beaches.

Most of the less expensive hotels around the Castellabate area of the Cilento are found in Santa Maria and Ogliastro—★★**Da Carmine** at the Ogliastro Marina, ✆ (0974) 963023, has pleasant doubles, all with bath.

In Acciaroli, ★★★**La Vela**, ✆ (0974) 905025, fax 905140, right on the beach, is a pleasant family-run hotel with prices that won't break the bank.

In Palinuro the ★**Carminella**, ✆ (0974) 931237, close to the King's Residence, is a small *pensione* with eight clean, comfortable rooms, all with baths.

Further south in Camerota, the ★**Pinguino**, ✆ (0974) 932115, is typical of the no-fuss, no-frills accommodation in the region, as is the ★**San Giorgio**, ✆ (0974) 932468, on the road going up to Camerota Alta, a small, family-run pension with 13 rooms, all with bath.

In the Cilento, most of the restaurants are in the hotels, and in summer the chances are you'll be stuck on full or at least half-board. There is some consolation to be had from the fact that such arrangements are often an excellent deal. Nevertheless, there are some good restaurants to look out for.

moderate

At Paestum there are two good and typical restaurants specializing in seafood in the archaeological zone itself: the excellent **Nettuno**, near Porta Giustizia, © (0828) 811028, and the **Museo**, © (0828) 811135, at the centre of the site. Both are well worth their moderate-range prices.

In Palinuro, **Da Carmelo**, © (0974) 931138, 1km along the road towards Camerota, is a lively trattoria where guests dine well on dishes prepared according to old traditional recipes, often to the strains of Neapolitan songs belted out by a strolling minstrel with a guitar.

Camerota has one first-class restaurant, **Da Valentone** on Piazza San Domenico, © (0974) 932004, which specializes in freshly caught seafood, and first courses including such local specialities as spaghetti with anchovies.

moderate/inexpensive

Two good places to eat near the beach in Palinuro (no phones, no reservations needed) are the **Taverna del Porto**, with tables a stone's throw from the water's edge, and **O' Guarracino**, a pretty trattoria with tables under a pleasantly shady canopy.

inexpensive

If you don't mind the wait, the tiny **Reganata e Vasulara**, località S. Vito (no phone), in Camerota Alta, is a delightful spot, one of a kind fast disappearing in Italy. Guests eat cheek by jowl, choosing from a limited but excellent menu based on Neapolitan *cucina povera*—home-made *pizzette*, stuffed tomatoes, aubergines and all sorts of pasta. There is often a queue outside, and once all the food has been eaten, the kitchen closes up.

Acroterion: decorative protrusion on the rooftop of an Etruscan, Greek or Roman temple. At the corners of the roof they are called *antefixes*.

Ambones: twin pulpits in some southern churches (singular: *ambo*), often elaborately decorated.

Atrium: entrance court of a Roman house or early church.

Badia: *abbazia*, an abbey or abbey church.

Baldacchino: baldachin, a columned stone canopy above the altar of a church.

Basilica: a rectangular building, usually divided into three aisles by rows of columns. In Rome this was the common form for law courts and other public buildings, and Roman Christians adapted it for their early churches.

Borgo: from the Saxon *burh* of San Spirito in Rome: a suburb.

Bucchero ware: black, delicately thin Etruscan ceramics, usually incised or painted.

Calvary chapels: a series of outdoor chapels, usually on a hillside, that commemorate the stages of the Passion of Christ.

Campanile: a bell-tower.

Campanilismo: local patriotism; the Italians' own word for their historic tendency to be more faithful to their home towns than to the abstract idea of 'Italy'.

Camposanto: a cemetery.

Cardo: transverse street of a Roman *castrum*-shaped city.

Carroccio: a wagon carrying the banners of a medieval city and an altar; it served as the rallying point in battles.

Cartoon: the preliminary sketch for a fresco or tapestry.

Caryatid: supporting pillar or column carved into a standing female form; male versions are called *telamones*.

Architectural, Artistic and Historical Terms

Castrum: a Roman military camp, always neatly rectangular, with straight streets and gates at the cardinal points. Later the Romans founded or refounded cities in this form, hundreds of which survive today.

Cavea: the semicircle of seats in a classical theatre.

Cenacolo: fresco of the Last Supper, often on the wall of a monastery refectory.

Ciborium: a tabernacle; the word is often used for large freestanding tabernacles, or in the sense of a *baldacchino* (q.v.).

Comune: commune, or commonwealth, referring to the governments of the free cities of the Middle Ages. Today it denotes any local government, from the Comune di Roma down to the smallest village.

Condottiere: the leader of a band of mercenaries in late medieval and Renaissance times.

Confraternity: a religious lay brotherhood, often serving as a neighbourhood mutual-aid and burial society, or following some specific charitable work (Michelangelo, for example, belonged to one that cared for condemned prisoners in Rome).

Cosmati work: or *Cosmatesque*: referring to a distinctive style of inlaid marble or enamel chips used in architectural decoration (pavements, pulpits, paschal candle-sticks, etc.) in medieval southern Italy. The Cosmati family of Rome were its greatest practitioners.

Cupola: a dome.

Cyclopean walls: fortifications built of enormous, irregularly polygonal blocks, as in the pre-Roman cities of Latium.

Decumanus: street of a Roman *castrum*-shaped city parallel to the longer axis, the central, main avenue called the Decumanus Major.

Duomo: cathedral.

Forum: the central square of a Roman town, with its most important temples and public buildings. The word means 'outside', as the original Roman Forum was outside the first city walls.

Fresco: wall painting, the most important Italian medium of art since Etruscan times. It isn't easy; first the artist draws the *sinopia* (q.v.) on the wall. This is covered with plaster, but only a little at a time, as the paint must be on the plaster before it dries. Leonardo da Vinci's endless attempts to find clever short-cuts ensured that little of his work would survive.

Ghibellines: one of the two great medieval parties, the supporters of the Holy Roman Emperors.

Gonfalon: the banner of a medieval free city; the *gonfaloniere*, or flag bearer, was often the most important public official.

Grotesques: carved or painted faces used in Etruscan and later Roman decoration.

Guelphs: (see *Ghibellines*). The other great political faction of medieval Italy, supporters of the Pope.

Hypogeum: underground burial caverns, usually of pre-Christian religions.

Intarsia: work in inlaid wood or marble.

Narthex: the enclosed porch of a church.

Naumachia: mock naval battles, like those staged in the Colosseum.

Opus Reticulatum: Roman masonry consisting of diamond-shaped blocks.

Palazzo: not just a palace, but any large, important building (though the word comes from the Imperial *palatium* on Rome's Palatine Hill).

Palio: a banner, and the horse race in which city neighbourhoods contend for it in their annual festivals. The most famous is at Siena.

Pantocrator: Christ 'ruler of all', a common subject for apse paintings and mosaics in areas influenced by Byzantine art.

Pietra Dura: rich inlay work using semi-precious stones, perfected in post-Renaissance Florence.

Pieve: a parish church, especially in the north.

Predella: smaller paintings on panels below the main subject of a painted altarpiece.

Presepio: a Christmas crib.

Pulvin: stone, often trapezoidal, that supports or replaces the capital of a column; decoratively carved examples can be seen in many medieval southern cloisters.

Putti: flocks of plaster cherubs with rosy cheeks and bums that infested much of Italy in the Baroque era.

Quadriga: chariot pulled by four horses.

Quattrocento: the 1400s—the Italian way of referring to centuries (*duecento, trecento, quattrocento, cinquecento*, etc.).

Sinopia: the layout of a fresco (q.v.), etched by the artist on the wall before the plaster is applied. Often these are works of art in their own right.

Stigmata: a miraculous simulation of the bleeding wounds of Christ, appearing in holy men like St Francis in the 12th century, and Padre Pio of Apulia in our own time.

Telamon: see *Caryatid.*

Thermae: Roman baths.

Tondo: round relief, painting or terracotta.

Transenna: marble screen separating the altar area from the rest of an early Christian church.

Travertine: hard, light-coloured stone, sometimes flecked or pitted with black, sometimes perfect. The most widely used material in ancient and modern Rome.

Triclinium: the main hall of a Roman house, used for dining and entertaining.

Triptych: a painting, especially an altarpiece, in three sections.

Trompe l'oeil: art that uses perspective effects to deceive the eye—for example, to create the illusion of depth on a flat surface, or to make columns and arches painted on a wall seem real.

Tympanum: the semicircular space, often bearing a painting or relief, above the portal of a church.

Language

The fathers of modern Italian were Dante, Manzoni, and television. Each had a part in creating a national language from an infinity of regional and local dialects; the Florentine Dante, the first to write in the vernacular, did much to put the Tuscan dialect in the foreground of Italian literature. Manzoni's revolutionary novel, *I Promessi Sposi*, heightened national consciousness by using an everyday language all could understand in the 19th century. Television in the last few decades is performing an even more spectacular linguistic unification; although the majority of Italians still speak a dialect at home, school, and work, their TV idols insist on proper Italian.

Perhaps because they are so busy learning their own beautiful but grammatically complex language, Italians are not especially apt at learning others. English lessons, however, have been the rage for years, and at most hotels and restaurants there will be someone who speaks some English. In small towns and out of the way places, finding an Anglophone may prove more difficult. The words and phrases below should help you out in most situations, but the ideal way to come to Italy is with some Italian under your belt; your visit will be richer, and you're much more likely to make some Italian friends.

Italian words are pronounced phonetically. Every vowel and consonant is sounded. Consonants are the same as in English, except the *c* which, when followed by an 'e' or 'i', is pronounced like the English 'ch' (*cinque* thus becomes cheenquay). Italian *g* is also soft before 'i' or 'e' as in *gira*, or jee-ra. *H* is never sounded; *z* is pronounced like 'ts'. The consonants *sc* before the vowels 'i' or 'e' becomes like the English 'sh' as in *sci*, pronounced shee; *ch* is pronouced like a 'k' as in *Chianti*, kee-an-tee; *gn* as 'ny' in English (*bagno*, pronounced ban-yo; while *gli* is pronounced like the middle of the word million (*Castiglione*, pronounced Ca-stee-lyon-ay).

Vowel pronunciation is: *a* as in English father; *e* when unstressed is pronounced like 'a' in fate as in *mele*, when stressed can be the same or like the 'e' in pet (*bello*); *i* is like the 'i' in machine; *o*, like 'e', has two sounds, 'o' as in hope when unstressed (*tacchino*), and usually 'o' as in rock when stressed (*morte*); *u* is pronounced like the 'u' in June.

The accent usually (but not always!) falls on the penultimate syllable. Also note that in the big northern cities, the informal way of addressing someone as you, *tu*, is widely used; the more formal *lei* or *voi* is commonly used in provincial districts.

Useful Words and Phrases

yes/no/maybe	*si/no/forse*
I don't know	*Non lo so*
I don't understand	*Non capisco*
Does someone here speak English?	*C'è qualcuno qui che parla inglese?*
Speak slowly	*Parla lentamente*
Please	*Per favore*
Thank you (very much)	*(Molte) grazie*
You're welcome	*Prego*
It doesn't matter	*Non importa*
All right	*Va bene*
Excuse me	*Scusi*
Nothing	*Niente*
How are you?	*Come sta?*
What is your name?	*Come si chiama?*
Hello	*Salve* or *ciao* (both informal)
Good morning	*Buongiorno* (formal hello)
Good afternoon/evening	*Buona sera* (also formal hello)
Goodnight	*Buona notte*
Goodbye	*Arrivederla* (formal), *arrivederci, ciao* (informal)
What?	*Che?*
Who?	*Chi?*
Where?	*Dove?*
When?	*Quando?*
Why?	*Perché?*

How?	*Come?*
How much?	*Quanto?*
I am hungry, thirsty	*Ho fame, sete*
I am sorry	*Mi dispiace*
I am tired	*Sono stanco*
I am ill	*Mi sento male*
Leave me alone	*Lasciami in pace*
good	*buono/bravo*
bad	*male/cattivo*
It's all the same	*Fa lo stesso*
slow, fast	*piano, rapido*
big, small	*grande, piccolo*
hot, cold	*caldo, freddo*
up, down	*su, giù*
here, there	*qui, lì*

Shopping, Service, Sightseeing

I would like...	*Vorrei...*
Where is/are...?	*Dov'è/Dove sono...?*
How much is it?	*Quanto viene questo?*
open, closed	*aperto, chiuso*
cheap/expensive	*a buon prezzo/caro*
bank	*banca*
church	*chiesa*
entrance, exit	*entrata, uscita*
hospital	*ospedale*
money	*soldi*
museum	*museo*
newspaper (foreign)	*giornale (straniero)*
pharmacy	*farmacia*
police station	*commissariato*
post office	*ufficio postale*
shop	*negozio*
telephone	*telefono*
tobacconist	*tabaccaio*
WC	*toilette/bagno*
men	*Signori/Uomini*
women	*Signore/Donne*

Time

What time is it?	*Che ore sono?*

month	*mese*
week	*settimana*
day	*giorno*
morning	*mattina*
afternoon	*pomeriggio*
evening	*sera*
today	*oggi*
yesterday	*ieri*
tomorrow	*domani*

Days

Monday	*lunedì*
Tuesday	*martedì*
Wednesday	*mercoledì*
Thursday	*giovedì*
Friday	*venerdì*
Saturday	*sabato*
Sunday	*domenica*

Numbers

one	*uno/una*
two	*due*
three	*tre*
four	*quattri*
five	*cinque*
six	*sei*
seven	*sette*
eight	*otto*
nine	*nove*
ten	*dieci*
twenty	*venti*
thirty	*trenta*
forty	*quaranta*
fifty	*cinquanta*
sixty	*sessanta*
seventy	*settanta*
eighty	*ottanta*
ninety	*novanta*
hundred	*cento*
thousand	*mille*
million	*milione*

Transport

airport	*aeroporto*
bus stop	*fermata*
railway station	*stazione ferroviaria*
train	*treno*
port station	*stazione marittima*
ship	*nave*
automobile	*macchina*
taxi	*tassì*
ticket	*biglietto*

Travel Directions

I want to go to...	*Desidero andare a...*
How can I get to... ?	*Come posso andare a... ?*
Where is... ?	*Dov'è... ?*
When does the... leave?	*A che ora parte ... ?*
How much is the fare?	*Quant'è il biglietto?*
near, far	*vicino, lontano*
left, right	*sinistra, destra*
straight ahead	*sempre diritto*
forward, backward	*avanti, indietro*
north	*nord/settentrione*
south	*sud/mezzogiorno*
east	*est/oriente*
west	*ovest/occidente*
street/road	*strada*
square	*piazza*

Driving

car hire	*noleggio macchina*
motorbike/scooter	*motocicletta/Vespa*
bicycle	*bicicletta*
petrol/diesel	*benzina/gasolio*
garage	*garage*
This doesn't work	*Questo non funziona*
map/town plan	*carta/pianta*
breakdown	*guasto* or *panne*
driver's licence	*patente di guida*
danger	*pericolo*
parking	*parcheggio*
no parking	*sosta vietato*

Italian Menu Vocabulary

Antipasti

These before-meal treats can include almost anything; among the most common are:

antipasto misto	mixed antipasto
carciofi (sott'olio)	artichokes (in oil)
frutti di mare	seafood
funghi (trifolati)	mushrooms (with anchovies, garlic, and lemon)
gamberi al fagiolino	shrimp with white beans
mozzarella (in carrozza)	buffalo cheese (fried with bread in batter)
prosciutto (con melone)	raw ham (with melon)
salsiccia	dry sausage

Minestre e Pasta

A selection of first courses (primi) served throughout Italy (excluding obvious dishes like spaghetti).

agnolotti	ravioli with meat
cannelloni	meat and cheese rolled in pasta tubes
cappelletti	small ravioli, often in broth
crespelle	crêpes
frittata	omelette
gnocchi	potato dumplings
orecchiette	ear-shaped pasta, usually served with turnip greens
panzerotti	ravioli filled with mozzarella, anchovies and egg
pappardelle alla lepre	flat pasta ribbons with hare sauce
pasta e fagioli	soup with beans, bacon, and tomatoes
pastina in brodo	tiny pasta in broth
penne all'arrabbiata	quill shaped pasta in hot spicy tomato sauce
polenta	cake or pudding of corn semolina, prepared with meat or tomato sauce
stracciatella	broth with eggs and cheese
tortellini al pomodoro/panna/in brodo	pasta caps filled with meat and cheese, served with tomato sauce/cream, or in broth
vermicelli	very thin spaghetti

Second Courses–Carne (Meat)

agnello	lamb
arista	pork loin
arrosto misto	mixed roat meats
bocconcini	veal mixed with ham and cheese and fried
bollito misto	stew of boiled meats
brasato di manzo	braised meat with vegetables

bresaola	dried raw meat similar to ham served with lemon, olive oil and parsley
carne di castrato/suino	mutton/pork
carpaccio	thin slices of raw beef in piquant sauce
cassoeula	winter stew with pork and cabbage
cotoletta (alla milanese/alla bolognese)	veal cutlet (fried in breadcrumbs/with ham and cheese)
fegato alla veneziana	liver and onions
involtini	rolled slices of veal with filling
maiale (al latte)	pork (cooked in milk)
manzo	beef
ossobuco	braised veal knuckle with herbs
petto di pollo	boned chicken breast
pizzaiola	beef steak with tomato and oregano sauce
pollo (alla cacciatora/alla diavola/alla Marengo)	chicken (with tomatoes and mushrooms cooked in wine/grilled/ fried with tomatoes, garlic and wine)
rognoni	kidneys
saltimbocca	veal scallop with prosciutto and sage, cooked in wine and butter
scaloppine	thin slices of veal sautéed in butter
spiedino	meat on a skewer or stick
tacchino	turkey
vitello	veal

Pesce (Fish)

aragosta	lobster
aringa	herring
branzino	sea bass
calamari	squid
cozze	mussels
fritto misto	mixed fish fry, with squid and shrimp
gamberetto	shrimp
granchio	crab
insalata di mare	seafood salad
merluzzo	cod
ostriche	oysters
pescespada	swordfish
polipo	octopus
pesce San Pietro	John Dory
rombo	turbot
sgombro	mackerel

sogliola	sole
tonno	tuna
triglia	red mullet (rouget)
trota	trout
trota salmonata	salmon trout
vongole	small clams
zuppa di pesce	mixed fish in sauce or stew

Contorni (Side Dishes, Vegetables)

asparagi (alla fiorentina)	asparagus (with fried eggs)
broccoli (calabrese, romana)	broccoli (green, spiral)
carciofi (alla giudia)	artichokes (deep fried)
carote	carrots
cavolfiore	cauliflower
cavolo	cabbage
fagioli	white beans
fagiolini	French (green) beans
funghi (porcini)	mushrooms (boletus)
insalata (mista, verde)	salad (mixed, green)
melanzana (al forno)	aubergine/eggplant (filled and baked)
patate (fritte)	potatoes (fried)
peperoni	sweet peppers
piselli (al prosciutto)	peas (with ham)
pomodoro	tomato
spinaci	spinach
zucchini	zucchini (courgettes)

Formaggio (Cheese)

bel paese	a soft white cow's cheese
cacio/caciocavallo	pale yellow, often sharp cheese
fontina	rich cow's milk cheese
groviera	mild cheese
gorgonzola	soft blue cheese
pecorino	sharp sheep's cheese
provolone	sharp, tangy cheese; *dolce* is more mild
stracchino	soft white cheese

Frutta (Fruit, Nuts)

albicocche	apricots
ananas	pineapple
arance	oranges
banane	bananas

cocomero	watermelon
fragole (con panna)	strawberries (with cream)
lamponi	raspberries
macedonia di frutta	fruit salad
mele	apples
melone	melon
nocciole	hazelnuts
noci	walnuts
pera	pear
pesca	peach
pignoli/pinoli	pine nuts
pompelmo	grapefruit
prugna/susina	plum
uva	grapes

Dolci (Desserts)

coppa gelato	assorted ice cream
crema caramella	caramel-topped custard
crostata	fruit flan
gelato (produzione propria)	ice cream (homemade)
granita	flavoured ice, usually lemon or coffee
panettone	sponge cake with candied fruit and raisins
semifreddo	refrigerated cake
spumone	a soft ice cream
tiramisù	mascarpone, coffee, chocolate and sponge fingers
torta	tart
zabaglione	whipped eggs, sugar and Marsala wine, served hot
zuppa inglese	trifle

Bevande (Beverages)

acqua minerale con/senza gas	mineral water with/without fizz
aranciata	orange soda
birra (alla spina)	beer (draught)
caffè (freddo)	coffee (iced)
cioccolata (con panna)	chocolate (with cream)
gassosa	lemon-flavoured soda
latte	milk
limonata	lemon soda
succo di frutta	fruit juice
tè	tea
vino (rosso, bianco, rosato)	wine (red, white, rosé)

Note: Page numbers in *italics* indicate maps. **Bold** references indicate chapter headings.

Index